EIGHT HUNDRED HEROES

EIGHT HUNDRED HEROES

China's Lost Battalion and the Fall of Shanghai

STEPHEN ROBINSON

EXISLE
PUBLISHING

First published 2022

Exisle Publishing Pty Ltd
PO Box 864, Chatswood, NSW 2057, Australia
226 High Street, Dunedin, 9016, New Zealand
www.exislepublishing.com

A CiP record for this book is available from the National Library of Australia.

ISBN: 978-1-922539-20-5

Designed by Nick Turzynski, redinc. Book Design, www.redinc.co.nz
Typeset in Baskerville Regular 11/15
Printed in Singapore by KHL Printing Co Pte Ltd

This book uses paper sourced under ISO 14001 guidelines from well-managed forests and other controlled sources.

10 9 8 7 6 5 4 3 2 1

While every effort has been made to ensure that the information in this book was correct at time of going to press, in a comprehensive history such as this, errors and omissions may occur. The author and publisher welcome any correspondence on such matters, but do not assume and hereby disclaim any liability to any party for any loss, damage, or disruption caused by such errors or omissions.

Dedicated to Emeritus Professor Edmund S.K. Fung FAHA,
an inspirational teacher of Chinese history

German-equipped Chinese soldiers run past Sihang Warehouse.
(Author's Collection)

CONTENTS

INTRODUCTION

Go tell the Spartans, stranger passing by, that here, obedient to their laws, we lie.
Epitaph for the 300 Spartans

China will not die, China will not die,
Look at our national hero Lieutenant Colonel Xie.
China will not die, China will not die,
Watch the eight hundred heroes of the lone battalion fight for every inch of land,
From four sides come the gunfire, from the four sides come the wolves,
They would rather die than retreat, they would rather die than surrender.
Amidst the sea of chaos our nation's flag flies proudly, flies proudly, flies proudly, flies proudly.
Eight hundred heroic hearts all beat as one, unstoppable to the thousands of enemies,
Our actions are mighty, our integrity heroic
Comrades, arise! Comrades, arise!
Let's answer the call to arms, and follow the example of the eight hundred heroes
China will not die, China will not die![1]
Song of the 800 Heroes

AN EPIC LAST STAND

In October 1937 a battalion of around 420 Chinese soldiers led by the stoic 32-year-old Lieutenant Colonel Xie Jinyuan defended Sihang Warehouse in Shanghai against an overwhelming force of invading Japanese troops. The lone battalion, comprised of soldiers from the elite 88th Division, were loyal to the Republic of China, ruled by Chiang Kai-shek's *Kuomintang* (Nationalist) Government. As these determined men fought the Japanese with intense bravery, the rest of the Chinese Army withdrew from the city. However, as the isolated Chinese detachment was only a small force, they informed the outside world that 800 soldiers were defending the warehouse in order to deceive the Japanese into not realizing their true number. This successful ruse created the legend of the 'Eight Hundred Heroes' and their demonstration of valour raised Chinese morale during the first year of the long Sino-Japanese War (1937–45).

The Eight Hundred Heroes performed an incredible feat of heroism that quickly gained international fame and sympathy. Even before the fighting ended, *The New York Times* declared: 'The stand of the battalion stirred Shanghai Chinese to patriotic frenzy.'[2] The story of Sihang Warehouse created its own mythology that helped define the modern Chinese nation. The actions of the Eight Hundred, as the journalists Chen Yu-fu and Jonathan Chin explained in 2017, is 'considered one of the most heroic and symbolic events in the Republic of China Army's history'.[3]

The defence of Sihang Warehouse in military terms was a minor incident during a titanic conflict that claimed the lives of between fifteen and twenty million Chinese people — a scale of human suffering beyond comprehension. The action took place during the Battle of Shanghai, a brutal urban conflict which lasted almost three months, resulting in over 187,000 Chinese and 32,000 Japanese casualties. Although Japan emerged victorious, their triumph was a pyrrhic victory as the Japanese Empire became overextended in a war it could not win without a workable strategy to end the conflict on favourable terms, fighting an enemy that refused to capitulate. Chinese soldiers in Shanghai demonstrated that they could successfully resist Japanese troops, which surprised many observers. 'Japan announced that she would finish her campaign in China in three months', an American journalist reported during the war. 'Some American experts

Lieutenant Colonel Xie Jinyuan, commander of the Eight Hundred Heroes.
(Author's Collection)

believed Japan. They watched the Shanghai battle during that summer of 1937 and waited for Shanghai to fall like a house of cards. But it didn't fall so easily.' The Eight Hundred formed a core part of this narrative as the reporter continued: 'The story of the "lone battalion" which held out in a warehouse against the rest of a captured city was blazoned across the newspapers of the world.'[4]

The defence of Sihang Warehouse more than any other event symbolized Chinese defiance during the long years of war as Lu Pan explained:

> Although the Chinese eventually lost the battle, the warehouse became the symbol of the tenacious spirit of national resistance in the enemy-occupied Shanghai. Later, it emerged as a highly mythologized narrative in the whole Sino-Japanese War propaganda effort.[5]

The Eight Hundred personified the David versus Goliath nature of the conflict with a clear underdog standing up against a powerful aggressor, a narrative that naturally generates sympathy, and this was no accident as

Sihang Warehouse on the bank of Suzhou Creek seen from Shanghai's International Settlement. (Contributor: Imaginechina Limited/Alamy Stock Photo)

their last stand occurred precisely to capture the imagination of the world.

Sihang Warehouse is located on the bank of Suzhou Creek, which separated the Chinese districts of Shanghai from the International Settlement, dominated by the British and American concessions. Less than 70 metres separated the Eight Hundred from a neutral cosmopolitan metropolis and its large foreign community. Inside the relative safety of the Settlement, the population watched the inferno of destruction across the creek from the rooftops of buildings including the city's most glamorous hotels.[6]

The international press in Shanghai covering the conflict lived a surreal existence, as the American journalist Edgar Snow explained: 'It was as though Verdun had happened on the Seine, in full view of a Right Bank Paris that was neutral; as though a Gettysburg were fought in Harlem, while the rest of Manhattan remained a non-belligerent observer.'[7] The journalist Emily Hahn and her entourage watched the fighting from the roof of the Cathay Hotel before enjoying cocktails at the bar.[8] George Bruce, another

Westerners watch the fighting in Shanghai from a rooftop in the International Settlement. (Author's Collection)

reporter, witnessed the battle from his hotel room on the Bund waterfront and remarked that 'the roofs of buildings in the Settlement near the struggle are lined night and day with watchers'.[9]

The Chinese leadership understood how the war in Shanghai was being reported when it ordered the Eight Hundred to defend Sihang and it hoped to create an international media sensation, which is precisely what occurred. The warehouse was perfectly located to achieve this aim and reporters from the English language *North China Daily News* actually watched the fighting from the roof of their own office building. Reporters had the perfect vantage point to witness the spectacle, as an American newspaper explained in sensationalistic terms when advertising a screening of documentary footage taken during the fighting:

Two westerners watch the fighting in Shanghai from a rooftop in 1937.
(Contributor: Historic Collection/Alamy Stock Photo)

The greatest battle of the Sino-Japanese War ends with the greatest
conflagration the Far East has ever seen — under constant fire,
Movietone's cameramen film sensational fight to the death — for the
first time, actual pictures of hand-to-hand combat — the heroic last
stand of Chinese 'suicide battalion,' trapped and doomed to destruction
in a warehouse — attack and counter-attack amid a hail of bullets
and grenades — Japanese shells and bombs smash a city before your
eyes — fires rage unchecked — an inferno in a city of millions — and
civilians, the innocent victims, fleeing, driven, machine-gunned and
bombed, their homes a shambles, seek shelter from the slaughter, in a
land where terror reigns.[10]

The story of the Eight Hundred naturally transitioned into mythology and,
as Kevin Blackburn and Daniel Chew Ju Ern concluded, their 'heroics
and sacrifices for the motherland were overblown and exaggerated into

legend'.[11] In most accounts, the Eight Hundred are credited with delaying the Japanese advance through Shanghai, allowing other Chinese soldiers to retreat. A Chinese journalist reported during the battle that they 'were ordered to defend critical positions to cover the majority of troops retreating'.[12] More recently a Taiwanese newspaper reported in 2014: 'Defenders of the warehouse held out against numerous waves of Japanese attacks and covered Chinese forces retreating westward during the Battle of Shanghai.'[13] The Eight Hundred certainly fought off numerous Japanese assaults, but their actions did not secure the retreat of their comrades, as Peter Harmsen concluded:

> The battle for the Four Banks [Sihang] Warehouse . . . was one bloody, drawn-out public relations exercise. The battle served no tactical purpose as that part of the city had already been evacuated. Perched near the edge of the International Settlement, a heroic stand at the warehouse simply helped show to the world that there was still fight in the Chinese.[14]

Acknowledging this truth is not disrespectful as the winning of international sympathy for China constituted a higher strategic objective than any potential tactical benefit for soldiers retreating from Shanghai. Furthermore, the Eight Hundred understood that their mission served a symbolic purpose. Zhang Boting, the 88th Division's chief-of-staff who helped coordinate the battle, concluded: 'The "800 warriors" was only a small number for the hundreds of thousands of troops participating in the Shanghai Battle, and therefore, it certainly did not carry significant strategic and tactical value.'[15] However, Zhang did emphasize that their stand 'had a great illuminating effect for the whole nation to rise up to join the anti-Japanese war, as well as for friendly nations' sympathy and support'.[16]

Although Lieutenant Colonel Xie Jinyuan was the central figure at Sihang, Yang Huimin, a 22-year-old Chinese Girl Guide, came to personify the incident more than any other individual and is also the subject of the greatest myth-making concerning the story. Yang delivered a Republic of China flag with its White Sun and Blue Sky to the defenders, which flew over the warehouse as a beacon of hope surrounded by a sea of Rising Sun flags.

The Girl Guide Yang Huimin poses with a Republic of China flag.
(Wikipedia)

Yang's act of bravery, as Kristin Mulready-Stone explained, 'cemented the patriotic fervor surrounding the stand of the eight hundred heroes'.[17]

Yang became an international celebrity who, on a *Kuomintang* sponsored tour, represented China at the World Youth Congress in New York State where she met Eleanor Roosevelt.[18] After this event, she travelled across the American heartland and gave speeches at high schools, churches, Masonic temples and YMCA halls. Yang electrified audiences with tales told with confidence and her events were covered by media giants like *The New York Times* but also by local community newspapers as she passed through small town America.

THE PANTHEON OF LAST STANDS

As an episode of world history, the Eight Hundred Heroes shares similarities with other epic last stands that have become legendary and perhaps the most obvious parallel is the 300 Spartans — a small band led by King Leonidas who defended Thermopylae against an overwhelming force of Persians in 480 BC. Although the Persians defeated the Spartans, who fought with great valour against impossible odds, the Greeks ultimately won the war. In Herodotus's account of the Greco-Persian Wars, Leonidas obtained eternal glory by sacrificing himself for the ultimate victory.[19] To Herodotus, Thermopylae is significant because the battle inspired Greek heroism and the 300 Spartans won a moral victory by helping to unify the Greek city-states against Persia.[20] Thermopylae paved the way for the eventual Greek triumph in much the same way as the Eight Hundred inspired Chinese determination during the Sino-Japanese War.

During antiquity the Romans became fascinated with Thermopylae and Leonidas's last stand in a cross-cultural transfer as they retold the tale to suit their own needs.[21] The Romans adapted the Greek narrative and perceived a connection between Thermopylae and their legend of the 306 Fabii clan members who died heroically while fighting the Etruscans at the Battle of Cremera River in 477 BC.[22] The Romans used Thermopylae as a rhetorical device in their literature to inspire virtue. For example, Valerius Maximus in his *Facta et dicta memorabilia* declared:

> At this point Leonidas, the famous Spartan, comes to mind. Nothing could be braver than his resolve, his act, his death. With three hundred compatriots he had to face all Asia at Thermopylae and by determined valour he reduced Xerxes, that bully of sea and land, not only terrible to men but threatening even Neptune with chains and the sky with darkness, to ultimate desperation.[23]

Just as the Romans drew upon the 300 Spartans to inspire their own heroics, the western Allies found inspiration in the Eight Hundred after Pearl Harbour. Nevertheless, the parallel between Sihang and Thermopylae is seldom made, but the western imagination frequently associates the Chinese last stand with another epic.

During the defence of Sihang Warehouse, western reporters referred to the Eight Hundred as China's 'Lost Battalion' — a reference to a World War I battle. On 2 October 1918, around 690 American soldiers from the 77th 'Statue of Liberty' Division commanded by Major Charles Whittlesey, mostly from the 1st and 2nd Battalions of the 308th Infantry Regiment, marched into the Argonne Forest in France as part of the Meuse-Argonne Offensive. After they advanced into the Charlevaux Ravine, the Germans surrounded their position and for five desperate days this small force fought off repeated attacks from the 254th and 122nd Regiments.

The men became known as the 'Lost Battalion' because they faced a hopeless situation, enduring intense assaults, and their predicament became so desperate they reused blood-soaked bandages taken from their own dead.[24] When the Germans withdrew on 7 October, only 194 Americans walked out of the forest and the remainder were either dead, wounded or captured. The Army awarded the Medal of Honor to seven participants including Whittlesey, who was promoted to lieutenant colonel.[25]

The Army tried to minimize the story of the 'Lost Battalion' during and after the battle. General Robert Alexander, the 77th Division commander, considered their plight embarrassing since they had become surrounded, so he downplayed the fighting during press conferences. Senior officers also suspected that Whittlesey had intentionally gone too far forward in an ego-driven glory quest, but in reality his advance reflected clearly understood orders. Reporters, however, found the saga irresistible and they made

Whittlesey and his men national heroes.[26] As the press propelled the 'Lost Battalion' into popular consciousness, there is an obvious parallel with the Eight Hundred as journalists transformed both battles into myths. However, there is also a critical difference as the American High Command did not want the story to break and the battalion's predicament was an unintended accident. The Eight Hundred in contrast were sent into harm's way by their command hoping to attract media attention.

Another parallel between the 'Lost Battalion' and the Eight Hundred is the extent to which both battles have become the subject of folklore in contradiction to historical evidence. As the story of the 'Lost Battalion' was retold, as Robert Laplander explained, 'so too have the many mistakes and errors that were at first incorrectly associated with the story come to be accepted as fact'.[27] The soldiers in the Argonne Forest were trapped in two separate pockets, but the vast majority of accounts reduced this to a single position. In popular mythology, Whittlesey replied to a German request to surrender with the famous words 'Go to hell!' The press accordingly labelled him 'Go to Hell Whittlesey', but in reality he denied uttering these words and clarified: 'No reply to the demand to surrender seemed necessary.'[28] Despite the romanticized story in the popular imagination, the horrific reality of what the men endured was something else and Whittlesey, completely traumatized by the experience, most likely committed suicide by jumping off a ship bound for Cuba on 26 November 1921.

The 'Lost Battalion' and the Eight Hundred also became widely known in the immediate aftermath of the battles through cinema. The silent film *The Lost Battalion* directed by Burton L. King was released on 2 July 1919, less than a year after the events it depicted. The movie was made with the help of the Army Signal Corps and was partially shot in the Charlevaux Ravine and several survivors played themselves including Whittlesey. Nevertheless, the film depicted the defence of a single pocket and further obscured reality with its over-the-top one-dimensional heroics and most 'Lost Battalion' veterans considered the film ridiculous.[29] In a similar way, two Chinese movies (both titled *Eight Hundred Heroes*) depicted Sihang Warehouse less than a year after the battle and were released in 1938 — one made in the Republic of China and the other in the British colony of Hong Kong. Both films also popularized the legend and the Republic of China version in particular introduced myths into the story that were repeated in two subsequent movies — the Taiwanese film *Eight Hundred Heroes* (1976) and mainland production *The Eight Hundred* (2020).

The 'Lost Battalion' was portrayed as a microcosm of America, as William Terpeluk explained: 'In many ways, the story of the Lost Battalion is the story of America itself in its diversity of social status, nationalities, religions, and political beliefs.'[30] The Eight Hundred is likewise depicted as embodying the unified spirit of China, as a reporter noted during the battle: 'Proud Chinese officials said the besieged warriors all were under 30 years old and came from every province in China. They are fully representative of heroic China's new fighting spirit, said one.'[31] Despite the fame 'Lost Battalion' achieved, memory of the men eventually faded from American society and they became largely forgotten. In contrast, Chinese communities today keep the memory of their 'Lost Battalion' very much alive in a similar way to another American legend.

On 8 November 1937, less than a week after the battle, *Time* magazine labelled Sihang Warehouse 'The Chinese Alamo'.[32] In 1836 during the Texas Revolution, a small band of around 200 soldiers defended the Alamo, a fort outside San Antonio that had once been a mission, against the Mexican dictator General Antonio López de Santa Anna who commanded 1800 soldiers. Lieutenant Colonel William Barret Travis and his second in command Jim Bowie led the mostly Anglo-American defenders, including the famed frontiersman Davy Crockett, fighting for an independent Texas. Santa Anna's forces besieged the Alamo for thirteen days and Travis, knowing all was lost, told his men that they would die if they remained. He drew a line in the ground with his sabre and invited the men to volunteer to stay and fight to the death by crossing the line — all the men crossed and awaited their fate.

On 6 March 1836, the Mexican army launched its final assault and soon most Alamo defenders were dead. A few weeks later a Texan army commanded by General Sam Houston surprised Santa Anna at San Jacinto and defeated him in a fifteen-minute battle. The Texans captured the dictator who agreed to give them independence in exchange for his life.[33] The Alamo may have been a defeat for the Texans, but they won the war and their heroic deeds achieved everlasting immortality with the famous words 'Remember the Alamo'. Texas later joined the United States in 1845 and generations of Americans, particularly Texans, grew up with stories of the Alamo through school plays, books and the popular movie *The Alamo* (1960), directed by John Wayne who also played Davy Crockett.[34] Today, the Alamo is sacred space and a place of pilgrimage to millions of visitors who pay their respects where the heroes met their fate.[35] Sihang Warehouse in Shanghai is likewise sacred space and a popular destination for Chinese pilgrims paying their respects to the Eight Hundred. In this way, both the Alamo and Sihang Warehouse serve current needs. 'For all the visitors,' as Randy Roberts explained, 'the Alamo is both history and memory, as alive today as it was in the nineteenth century.'[36] The same is true in twenty-first-century China.

Despite the Alamo being a foundation myth for Texans, most attention is focused on the battle itself and not the changing narratives of what the battle represents. The historical Alamo is more complex than the legend as the heroes did indeed fight for their own liberty, but they also believed in the institution of slavery.[37] Therefore, African American reflections on the Alamo differ from the dominant white narrative and, in a similar way, Hispanic Texans remember the Alamo differently as the standard narrative casts Mexicans as villains, and given this complexity Randy Roberts reflected:

> The battle cry of Texans during the battle of San Jacinto, and later the Mexican-American War, 'Remember the Alamo,' raises crucial cultural questions: How do we remember? What do we remember? Who governs our memory of historical events? . . . In the end, the quest for the meaning of the Alamo has merged with the struggle to ascribe a meaning for America itself.[38]

The same questions can be asked about Sihang Warehouse because what the Eight Hundred represents has changed over time and is different in each Chinese community. In wartime propaganda the Eight Hundred were portrayed as uncomplicated stoic heroes fighting invaders as a model to emulate to serve the needs of an ongoing war. After Chiang Kai-shek lost the Chinese Civil War in 1949, the Eight Hundred in Taiwan symbolized a bygone age of pure heroism before corruption and incompetence plagued the *Kuomintang* — an ideal that could be rediscovered. The meaning of the Eight Hundred in the People's Republic of China is even more complex. After being airbrushed from history during the Maoist years, the heroes made a comeback as patriots who fought for China against Japanese imperialists, despite being *Kuomintang* soldiers on the wrong side of history. However, no amount of spin can hide the fact that the Eight Hundred were not communist soldiers.

The Easter Rising is another last stand with parallels to the Eight Hundred as they both incorporate a sacrificial rebirth of ancient nations in modern times. On Easter Monday 1916, Irish nationalists launched an insurrection against British rule by seizing key buildings in Dublin, most notably the General Post Office, but skirmishes also took place in Meath, Galway, Louth, Wexford and Cork. Although the British swiftly defeated the rebels after six days of fighting, the Irish Free State was born five years later in 1921. The rising inspired other Irish people to fight for independence and the Easter rebels, despite failing militarily, won a significant moral victory over the British by becoming martyrs.[39]

The rebellion's leadership mostly realized before the rising that they would almost certainly be defeated but made a conscious decision for martyrdom, although the majority of rank and file believed victory was possible.[40] Pádraic Pearse, a key rebel leader who read the 'Proclamation of the Republic' outside the General Post Office, advocated rising during Easter to associate their actions with the Christian feast honouring the sacrifice of Christ.[41] Pearse believed their deaths would be a 'blood sacrifice' to redeem Ireland, echoing Jesus' redemption of humanity. 'We must be ready to die,' he reminded his followers, 'as Christ died on Calvary, so that the people may live.'[42] James Stephens declared a week after the rebellion: 'The day before the rising was Easter Sunday, and they were crying joyfully in the Churches "Christ has risen". On the following day they were saying in the streets "Ireland has risen".'[43] The Easter Rising, therefore, was not an accidental last stand like the American 'Lost Battalion', and the rebel leadership, like the Eight Hundred, mostly knew their sacrifice would be symbolic before the shooting started.

As much of the Irish rebel leadership never expected to win on the battlefield, their symbolic rising had a theatrical element that was not coincidental. Of the seven rebels who signed the 'Proclamation of the Irish Republic', three of them — Pádraic Pearse, Thomas MacDonagh and Joseph Plunkett — were poets. Pearse carried an anachronistic sword during the rising that only had symbolic value and many rebels wore striking costumes and brought various props with them, unsurprising facts as numerous rebels had links to Irish theatre. MacDonagh's play *When the Dawn is Come* concerns an uprising in the near future involving an Irish army confronting the English in a battle to decide the fate of the island. James Connolly, another rebel leader, had recently staged a play, *Under Which Flag*, the tale of the Fenian rebellion of 1867. 'Thomas MacDonagh and James Connolly', as James Moran explained, 'rehearsed the rebellion on the Irish stage before they led troops into the streets of Dublin.'[44]

After the start of the rising, many curious onlookers believed they were witnessing a performance. Joseph Holloway, a citizen of Dublin, read the 'Proclamation of the Irish Republic' and recognized the names of playwrights and assumed it was a theatre advertisement.[45] Another bystander walked into Liberty Hall, famous for hosting stage productions, and noticed rebels handling ammunition. He approached Countess Constance Markievicz, a well-known member of the Theatre of Ireland, and asked, 'Rehearsing, I presume?' After the countess replied 'Yes', the man further enquired, 'Is it for children?' Markievicz responded, 'No, this is for grown-ups.'[46]

The rebels occupied symbolic buildings in Dublin that were militarily indefensible, notably the General Post Office, but these locations provided the ideal stage for their sacrificial production. Michael Collins, who later led republican forces to victory in 1921, declared, 'Looking at it from the inside (I was in the GPO [General Post Office]) it had the air of a Greek tragedy about it.'[47] After the British crushed the rising, many commentators considered the rebellion, as James Moran put it, 'crazed poetic folly' and accordingly viewed the rebels as 'misty-eyed idealists' who were 'obsessed by madcap fictional notions'.[48] Nevertheless, such commentators missed the point as the rebels won in the long run by inspiring the successful Irish War of Independence.

Although the Eight Hundred lacked the flamboyant theatrics of some Easter rebels, Sihang Warehouse was deliberately chosen as an ideal stage to captivate the press in Shanghai's International Settlement who all had front row seats to the drama. However, unlike the Irish rebels, the Eight Hundred had an excellent stage *and* an ideal position to conduct a defensive battle. Sihang was a natural fortress and its close proximity to the International Settlement prevented the Japanese from bombing the warehouse or using heavy artillery due to fear of accidentally attacking the foreign concessions across Suzhou Creek. The Japanese had no choice but to conduct suicidal frontal attacks against determined and well-protected Chinese soldiers.

The Eight Hundred are remembered in China in similar ways to which westerners remember the 300 Spartans, Americans remember their 'Lost Battalion' and the Alamo, and how the Easter Rising is remembered in the Republic of Ireland. Sihang Warehouse deserves a place in world history as a chapter in the universal pantheon of heroic last stands in which history and myth are difficult to separate. The valour of the historic Eight Hundred is real enough and the overblown heroics found in propaganda and legend is unnecessary. This book attempts to separate history from mythology and to present an account of the men who defended Sihang Warehouse that is as accurate as possible. For the first time it provides a comprehensive exposition, bringing together the accounts of the Chinese participants who fought the Japanese from inside Sihang Warehouse and the westerners who witnessed the battle from across Suzhou Creek. However, this is also the story of modern China and begins with the founding of the Republic in 1911 and the emergence of *Kuomintang*'s founder, Sun Yat-sen.

CHAPTER ONE
REVOLUTION AND THE REPUBLIC

SUN YAT-SEN AND WHAMPOA ACADEMY

Xie Jinyuan, the future leader of the Eight Hundred Heroes, was born into an impoverished peasant farming family in Jiankeng village, Guangdong Province on 26 April 1905.[1] Xie Faxiang, his father, married a fisherman's daughter and their eldest son Xie Jinhong died of malaria after immigrating to Southeast Asia.[2] The Xie family descended from the Hakka ethnicity which had disproportionally supported the failed Taiping Rebellion (1850–64), an unorthodox Christian uprising against the Qing Dynasty led by the Hakka rebel Hong Xiuquan. As Xie Jinyuan grew into infancy, he had no way of knowing that the Qing, which had ruled China since 1644, would soon be overthrown and that China was about to enter a turbulent era of massive change and enormous suffering. Sun Yat-sen, the republican revolutionary who would become instrumental in overthrowing the decaying dynasty, would also shape Xie's destiny.

Sun, born in Cuiheng village, Guangdong on 12 November 1866, had Hakka and Yue (Cantonese) ethnicity and his father had participated in the Taiping Rebellion. At twelve years of age, Sun was sent to live with his emigrant elder brother in Hawaii, where he attended the Iolani school run by British missionaries. After four years in Hawaii, he was sent by his brother back to China. As his horizons had been broadened, Sun could not adjust himself to the rural life in his native village. Consequently, in

Sun Yat-sen, founder of the *Kuomintang*. (Wikipedia)

1883, at the age of seventeen, he went to the British colony of Hong Kong and converted to Christianity the following year under the influence of an American missionary and a local pastor. After making a brief trip to Hawaii, he returned to Hong Kong before proceeding to Guangzhou (Canton), where he attended the Medical School of Canton Hospital. Sun later transferred to the College of Medicine for Chinese in Hong Kong, graduating in 1892. However, his heart was never devoted to practising medicine. Instead, he became an anti-Qing revolutionary and travelled frequently, seeking support from overseas Chinese communities. In 1894, Sun organized the Revive China Society in Honolulu with the aim of overthrowing the Qing Dynasty after Japan inflicted a humiliating defeat on China during the First Sino-Japanese War (1894–95). Shortly after, Sun returned to Hong Kong where he organized a similar Revive China Society to plot with several like-minded conspirators. But after the First Guangzhou Uprising failed in 1895, Sun was declared an outlaw and he entered a long period of exile. During this time, he travelled through Europe and America raising funds for the republican cause, helped by his fluent command of English and knowledge of the wider world.

On 22 October 1900, Sun launched the Huizhou Uprising against the Qing but again experienced failure and his exile resumed. In 1905, he founded the United League which advocated republican democracy and he also formulated his political ideology — the 'Three Principles of the People', which consisted of Nationalism, Democracy and People's Livelihood.

'Nationalism' meant developing a modern national consciousness because, according to Sun, the Chinese lacked a cohesive spirit and were a 'sheet of loose sand' because they 'have shown loyalty to family and clan but not the nation'.[3] This process would retain the best aspects of tradition, as Sun the pragmatist declared 'we ought to preserve what is good in our past and throw away the bad', but it was vital to recover China's 'ancient morality'.[4] China had to transcend western materialism to realize its own cultural destiny in the way of the sage kings of ancient China.[5]

'Democracy' initially meant a republican government which seemed the most modern and promising. A republic would reorganize the state and society, allowing the masses to participate in political life under elite leadership. Sun advocated constitutional democracy, but the public would first have to change due to their low cultural and educational levels, although they would eventually be educated into political consciousness.

'People's Livelihood' meant alleviating mass poverty and developing the economy by combining socialism and capitalism as Sun hoped 'these two economic forces of human evolution will work side by side in future civilisation'.[6] Sun advocated a form of state socialism inspired by Bismarckian Germany in which the workers would benefit from regulated workdays and old age pensions. Sun praised Bismarck who 'Practised State Socialism' and 'used the force of state to enable himself to realize the program of the socialists'.[7] Sun's socialism was never communist and he desired to work with the western powers and the international financial system.[8]

On 9 October 1911, a bomb in a revolutionary's house at Hankou exploded accidentally, compelling plotters led by Huang Xing to act promptly to save themselves by launching a premature revolution, but local soldiers joined their rebellion and defeated Qing troops sent from Beijing. The army mutinied and fifteen provinces in south and central China severed ties with the dynasty. Yuan Shikai, the former Viceroy of Zhili in charge of military reforms who had been dismissed by the Empress Dowager in 1908, was recalled to quell the rebellion due to his military connections in northern China. However, he was persuaded to join the revolutionary cause and he opportunistically seized power in Beijing. Sun returned to China from the United States and entered Shanghai in triumph on Christmas Eve and became the provisional president of the new Chinese Republic. However, his presidency would only last six-and-a-half weeks.

At the beginning of 1912, President Sun resided in Nanjing while Prime Minister Yuan ruled from Beijing and the former viceroy sidelined the revolutionary and seized the presidency. On 10 March 1912 Yuan took the oath as president in Beijing and Sun, realizing he had been outmanoeuvred, resigned from government. The 1911 Revolution forced the abdication of the last Qing ruler, the child Emperor Puyi, and formally established the Republic of China, but Yuan failed to bring stability as the new regime had no effective control in the provinces beyond Beijing.

On 25 August 1912, Sun founded the *Kuomintang* with other revolutionary colleagues in opposition to Yuan and the new party won 269 out of 596 seats at the National Assembly elections and 123 out of 274 Senate seats.[9] Yuan became even more authoritarian after crushing an armed rebellion in July 1913 and he outlawed the *Kuomintang*. As the regime became a dictatorship, Yuan restored the monarchy by declaring himself the new Hongxian Emperor in the Forbidden City on 23 December 1915, but numerous southern provinces rebelled, forcing him to abdicate before dying of natural causes on 6 June 1916.

The failure of the 1911 Revolution ushered in the Warlord Era as China fragmented into competing sub-states ruled by local military governors who ignored the weak government in Beijing and fought each other in the pursuit of their own interests. Powerful warlords dominated politics such as the Manchurian Zhang Zuolin, Wu Peifu at Hankou, Yan Xishan in Shanxi and Feng Yuxiang the 'Christian Warlord' in Anhui.

During the chaos, Sun re-evaluated his political theories and developed a new plan for action. He now had misgivings concerning representative democracy and advocated a more authoritarian, executive-dominated government. Sun also developed a three-stage plan to establish constitutional government in China: a period of military conquest to unite the provinces, a period of political tutelage under one-party rule to educate the masses followed by true constitutional government with citizens enjoying full suffrage. Tutelage was necessary to raise the political consciousness of the people under a workable government ruled by dedicated and highly qualified elites.

Sun returned to Guangdong in 1917 in southern China where his message found support among nationalistic youth. As Sun increasingly personified republican aspirations, he founded a new *Kuomintang* party on 10 October 1919. By 1920, the *Kuomintang* had built a power base in Guangdong, the home of Xie Jinyuan who now at fifteen years of age was increasingly politically aware and concerned about China's future.

As the *Kuomintang*'s influence in southern China grew, Sun planned to unite the country as an increasingly opportunistic spirit took hold. In 1921, Sun established a provisional government in Guangdong, but he also realized that the *Kuomintang* could not unify China on its own. After failing to find allies among the Great Powers, the *Kuomintang* forged an alliance with the Chinese Communist Party, which had been founded in 1921, and this partnership set the trajectory of Chinese history for the rest of the twentieth century. The socialist aspects of Sun's philosophy created common ground with the communists and through this United Front he gained an international ally as the Soviet Union believed this alliance would help spread international revolution with the aid of the Comintern.[10]

In 1923 Sun accepted Soviet assistance and a delegation arrived in Guangdong headed by Mikhail Gruzenberg, who operated under the revolutionary alias 'Borodin'. A joint statement declared the need for national unity with a concession that China was not ready for communism.[11] Sun admired Soviet organizational ability: 'If we wish our revolution to succeed, we must learn the methods, organization, and training of the Russians.'[12] Borodin helped Sun reorganize the *Kuomintang* under Leninist principles which elevated the party above government and he became president for life despite the support for democracy found in his Three Principles.[13] The *Kuomintang* adopted some communist traits as every party member had to be prepared to sacrifice their individual freedom for the greater good.

Soviet advisers arrived in China to provide military assistance, notably General Vasily Blyukher, also known as 'Galen', who during the Russian Civil War (1917–23) had successfully defended the Urals and defeated the White Army leader Admiral Alexander Kolchak. In October 1924, Galen became chief military adviser to the *Kuomintang*'s Nationalist Revolutionary Army and he believed in quality over quantity, advocating that three or four well-trained divisions could defeat the warlords. As Soviet ships unloaded armaments for the National Revolutionary Army, more Soviet advisers arrived in Guangdong.

On 6 February 1924, the *Kuomintang* established the Whampoa Military Academy on Changzhou Island in the Pearl River with Soviet assistance.[14] The Qing had earlier established western-style military academies in the late nineteenth century and in 1887 Zhang Zhidong, governor-general of Guangdong and Guangxi, founded an academy that became Whampoa.[15] The new institution would create an elite fighting force using Red Army methods and political education. During the opening ceremony Sun declared, 'our aim in opening this Academy is to create the revolutionary task anew from this day, and students of this Academy . . . will be the bones and trunks of the forthcoming Revolutionary Army'.[16] Sun also had just the right man to make this happen — Chiang Kai-shek.

Chiang, a professional Japanese-trained officer, was born on 31 October 1887 to a middle-class wine merchant. After Chiang toured Whampoa, he noted the dilapidated conditions of the facilities which dated from the late

Sun Yat-sen (third from left) and Chiang Kai-shek (second from left) at the opening of Whampoa Military Academy in 1924. (Wikipedia)

Qing period, but he nevertheless concluded it would be a suitable place to train officers. In May 1924, Chiang became commandant of Whampoa, and he used this position to consolidate his power base by acquiring the loyalty of the academy's graduates.[17] Whampoa in time became a critical pillar in the *Kuomintang* power structure, but in its early days Chiang searched for qualified men to run the academy and personally handpicked its officers. He oversaw the training of around 50 officers who would soon teach the academy's first class.[18]

Whampoa Academy, under the guidance of Soviet advisers, trained cadets through a rigorous and ambitious program which aimed to commission them as officers after a six-month course.[19] The students participated in classroom and field lessons six days a week with Sundays being devoted to political indoctrination focusing on Sun's Three Principles of the People as well as the Confucian values of wisdom, benevolence and

Xie Jinyuan. (Author's Collection)

bravery.[20] Political indoctrination mirrored the Soviet military model and Whampoa produced military commanders and political commissars.[21]

To find students, *Kuomintang* officials searched for suitable candidates across China with middle school or higher primary school education.[22] Prospects had to write an essay on why they wanted to serve and given the party's base in Guangdong, a disproportionate number of cadets came from this province including the future leader of the Eight Hundred.

Xie Jinyuan attended Yumin Primary School before being admitted to Sanzhen Public School and later Fifth Provincial Middle School in Meixian. At age seventeen he studied at Guangdong University (later Sun Yat-sen University) in Guangzhou for three years.[23] In December 1925, Xie was admitted into Whampoa Academy as a typical cadet and his son Xie Jimin later explained the influence Sun had on his father:

> Sun Yat-sen was a person that attached great importance to cultivating talents for national construction, commending Guangdong University as an institution committed to fostering 'wenzhuangyuan' (top talents versed with literature skills) as opposed to Whampoa Military Academy which produced 'wuzhuangyuan' (top military talents). His remarks delivered in meetings at Guangdong University had a profound impact on Xie Jinyuan, who, under the influence of Sun's revolutionary ideas . . . resolved to renounce the pen in pursuit of a military career, and was enrolled in the fourth group of students in Whampoa Military Academy.[24]

Chiang Kai-shek played an active role in the daily activities at Whampoa by supervising the cadets and delivering lectures on loyalty, discipline, obedience and the need to be ready to sacrifice their lives for China. He had the academy's motto, 'Affection with Sincerity', mounted on silk in his office and, as a patriarchal figure, earned the cadet's loyalty and obedience.[25]

Xie and the other cadets lived a Spartan lifestyle, but they were well cared for and provided with good food. The curriculum contained less focus on book learning compared with traditional Chinese military education and instead emphasized combat training, field skills and physical fitness given the urgent need to confront the warlords.[26] Whampoa also adopted some Japanese concepts that Chiang had been exposed to such as a belief that the problem of inferior weapons and equipment can be negated with an aggressive spirit, bold actions and discipline. The students developed a 'Whampoa Spirit' of working together in order to unify China.[27] Chiang believed that the self-sacrifice of his cadets leading the National Revolutionary Army would prevail over the numerically superior warlord armies through unity of purpose, coordinated action and superior strategy.[28] He stressed to his students that they would fight outnumbered as 'each soldier has to be able to fight one hundred enemy soldiers'.[29]

The personal bonds of the Whampoa officers, and their relationship with Chiang, propelled their future careers with many later occupying key positions in the *Kuomintang*.[30] The graduates maintained their special relationships forged at the academy within an army and party system that rewarded personal loyalty in the context of a traditional Confucian hierarchy of human relations and social conventions.[31] The Qing had sent officer candidates to overseas military academics in Japan, Europe and America, and therefore the *Kuomintang* recruited officers with a diversity of training backgrounds. Nevertheless, the Whampoa graduates had a distinct advantage in rising up through the ranks, even against Chinese officers educated at the prestigious United States Military Academy at West Point.

Whampoa produced 645 officers in the academy's first class in 1924 and two years later 3000 students graduated.[32] Not all cadets were Chinese and the faculty included students from Mongolia, Tibet, Thailand, Korea and Vietnam. The Vietnamese revolutionary Nguyen Ai Quoc, who would later become known as Ho Chi Minh, oversaw the academy's Vietnamese students.

THE EASTERN EXPEDITION

In 1920, Chen Jiongming, a soldier from Guangdong known as the 'Hakka General', defeated Sun's enemies and invited the revolutionaries to return to the provincial capital Guangzhou. Chen later disagreed with Sun's planned Northern Expedition to unite China in favour of a southern confederation independent from the rest of China. After relations deteriorated in 1922, Chen forced Sun to flee before declaring himself commander-in-chief in Guangdong and the warlord Wu Peifu recognized him as governor of the province. Sun hired mercenaries who forced Chen to retreat to the east of the province and the revolutionary returned to Guangzhou on 21 February 1923, but Chen marched towards the city later that year until a force of volunteers raised by Borodin defeated this attempt.[33]

The *Kuomintang*'s campaign to defeat Chen once and for all — the Eastern Expedition — marked the first significant test of Chiang Kai-shek and his Whampoa cadets. After learning that Chen intended to launch another attack against Guangzhou, Galen advocated striking first. In February 1925, the National Revolutionary Army advanced east and Whampoa's two training regiments marched despite a shortage of weapons and ammunition. During the intense fighting, the First Training Regiment suffered around 70 per cent casualties but despite strong resistance, the troops captured the port of Shantou and pushed the rebels into Fujian Province, which secured the expedition.[34] The campaign also demonstrated the 'Whampoa Spirit' with bold risk taking, self-sacrifice and discipline as Chiang had preached.[35] The Whampoa soldiers demonstrated restraint, in contrast to warlord behaviour, by not engaging in looting. The English newspaper *North China Daily News* described them as 'a really fine body of troops, well armed and sternly disciplined and, in every way, superior to any who might be expected to oppose them'.[36] Chen later fled to Hong Kong where he died on 22 September 1933.

During the Eastern Expedition, Sun Yat-sen visited Beijing to confer with other leaders hoping for rapprochement between rival groups. During an operation Sun was diagnosed with terminal liver cancer and he died on 12 March 1925. The *Kuomintang* deified Sun, making him the rallying point of its nationalism and desire to unify China.[37] Sun's death, however, left a power vacuum and Wang Jingwei, a left-wing faction leader with the backing of Borodin, became chairman of the National Government. Wang, Chiang and Borodin ruled the *Kuomintang* as a triumvirate but despite the arrangement's leftist direction, Chiang held strong reservations about communism and the Soviet Union. Chiang understood power in revolutionary China: 'If I control the army, I will have the power to control the country. It is my road to leadership.'[38]

THE NORTHERN EXPEDITION

On 1 July 1926, the *Kuomintang* announced the Northern Expedition to destroy warlordism, and Chiang Kai-shek planned the campaign. The outnumbered National Revolutionary Army had a coherent plan for China's future and a centralized political organization capable of making its vision a reality, which generated a broad appeal that no warlord could compete with.[39] The soldiers were also well-trained and burned with self-confidence after the Eastern Expedition. Chiang planned three separate thrusts north towards the Yangtze River. Wang Jingwei would lead the western advance towards Wuhan and Bai Chongxi would command the eastern drive towards Shanghai while Chiang commanded the central advance towards Nanjing. The campaign planned to seize the economically vital Yangtze and its trading ports, giving the *Kuomintang* control of China's commercial lifeblood.

After the expedition commenced on 9 July, Chiang's troops defeated the warlord Wu Peifu and his allies in Hunan before continuing their advance towards the Yangtze. The Whampoa graduates enjoyed higher morale and discipline compared with warlord armies, and Soviet advisers noted their popularity with civilians.[40] As the National Revolutionary Army advanced north, numerous warlord soldiers defected, and Wang Jingwei captured Wuhan in October. In the same month Xie Jinyuan graduated from Whampoa with the fourth class of graduates, majoring in politics. He served as a platoon commander in the 5th Regiment, 2nd Division and participated in the Northern Expedition. After the Battle of Longtan, Xie became a company commander in the 21st Division as the Northern Expedition continued.

On 18 March 1927, Bai's column approached Shanghai and local communists attempted to establish a Soviet council in the city as tensions within the United Front intensified. After Chiang Kai-shek captured Nanjing on 23 March, Borodin advised Wang to displace Chiang as leader. Wang declared Wuhan the new capital, a bold move that Chiang correctly perceived as a challenge to his authority and prompted him to plan a march on the city.[41] Wang backed down and fled China for exile in Europe. Chiang and the right wing of the *Kuomintang* further cemented their power as recent events made many in the party distrustful of their communist allies.

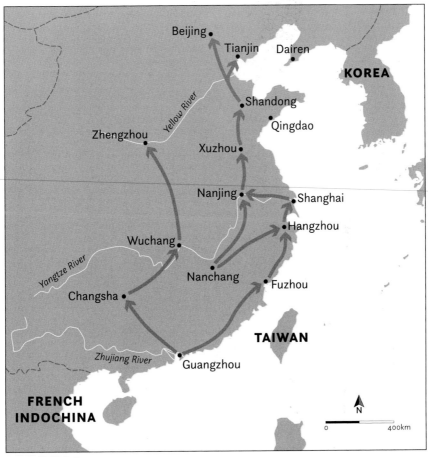

The advance of *Kuomintang* forces during the Northern Expedition, 1926–28.

Chiang feared a communist revolution against foreign capitalists and since he could not afford to fight the Great Powers if they intervened to protect their interests, he faced a dilemma about how to contain his increasingly assertive ally. In late March 1927 tensions arose following the 'Nanjing Incident' after rioters attacked the foreign concessions, resulting in Chiang and the Great Powers fearing a communist takeover. Chiang declared martial law in Shanghai on 9 April and two days later ordered a purge of communists. On 12 April, soldiers began disarming worker militias, triggering large-scale protests and troops opened fire as thugs publicly executed suspected communists. The Shanghai Massacre resulted

Chiang Kai-shek and Soong Mei-ling at their wedding on 1 December 1927.
(Wikipedia)

A portrait of Generalissimo Chiang Kai-shek. (Wikipedia)

in around 5000 deaths and in the aftermath of the bloodshed, Chiang's right-wing clique consolidated a new power base in Nanjing.

The Northern Expedition continued and the National Revolutionary Army advanced towards Beijing. On 6 June 1928, *Kuomintang* soldiers entered the city and, after the warlord Zhang Xueliang declared loyalty to Chiang on 29 December, the expedition successfully reunified China. During the campaign, Chiang's troops suffered 25,000 deaths, but warlord defections caused his ranks to swell with 260,000 more soldiers.[42] The *Kuomintang* declared Nanjing the new capital, ushering in the 'Nanjing Decade', a period of relative peace and prosperity, but in reality Chiang's powerbase was limited to a few provinces in the Yangtze region and he could only rely upon a core force loyal to him as former warlord troops were nominally subordinate to the new regime.[43]

Chiang married Soong Mei-ling at the Majestic Hotel in Shanghai on 1 December 1927, forging a powerful alliance with the influential 'Soong Dynasty'. Soong Mei-ling's sister Soong Ching-ling was the widow of Sun Yat-sen and her brother T.V. Soong was a gifted Harvard graduate who had worked at the International Banking Corporation in New York and was a leading Chinese banker.[44] T.V. Soong became Chiang's finance minister and he reorganized China's financial system in a clear indication to the outside world that foreign capital was welcome. Soong Mei-ling, educated at Wellesley College in Massachusetts, spoke fluent English with a southern accent that dazzled westerners and she became known as Madame Chiang Kai-shek. On 10 October 1928, Chiang became director of the State Council, effectively making him President of China, and he later became known as the 'Generalissimo' in the western world. Chiang and Soong would rule the country as one of the great power couples of history.

In 1928 Xie Jinyuan defended Shandong from a Japanese invasion, following the 'Jinan Incident' of 3 May in which *Kuomintang* and Japanese soldiers clashed in the provincial capital. Following the Northern Expedition, Japanese troops guarding their concession in Jinan maintained tense but peaceful relations with Chinese troops. However, a dispute arose following the death of Japanese civilians resulting in eight days of fighting and over 6000 Chinese deaths. Xie was wounded in the defence and he later commanded a machine-gun battalion in the 5th Regiment. After being promoted to major, he transferred to the staff of the Wuhan Headquarters.

Despite the success of the Northern Expedition, Chiang Kai-shek competed with dangerous rivals in the *Kuomintang*. In 1929, Feng Yuxiang the 'Christian Warlord' challenged his dominance and, after being defeated, Feng allied with Yan Xishan the 'Shanxi Warlord' and *Kuomintang* opponents of Chiang including Wang Jingwei.[45] The rebels declared a new government in Beijing and called for Chiang's overthrow in September 1930. Chiang defeated these enemies in the Great Plains War and he further consolidated power in a conflict claiming 300,000 casualties. As China experienced greater stability, Chiang gained a powerful new ally that would train and equip the Eight Hundred Heroes.

THE GERMAN MISSION

Following Germany's defeat in World War I, the new Weimar Government needed allies and viewed the Chinese Republic as a marketplace to export weapons and military expertise in exchange for rare metals, especially tungsten. As the Treaty of Versailles granted the German concessions in Shandong to Japan instead of China, both countries had been humiliated by the peace settlement and consequently became closer.[46] In May 1921, China re-established diplomatic relations with Germany and officials attempted to deepen political, economic and military ties. Influential groups within German industry, the *Reichswehr* (armed forces) and the Foreign Ministry advocated improving Sino-German relations because, despite the chaos and uncertain political environment, the Germans considered China a land of opportunity.[47]

The *Kuomintang* welcomed cooperation from Germany and a favourable perception of the nation in China originated in the nineteenth century after the Treaty of Tianjin in 1858 and the Convention of Beijing in 1860 consolidated Sino-German trade. As Bismarck focused on domestic politics, Germany was not perceived as a predatory imperialist power and Sun Yat-sen admired the Iron Chancellor who transformed 'a weak Germany into an extremely strong nation'.[48] Although Germany acquired concessions in Hankou, Tianjin and the Shandong Peninsula in the early 1900s, Sun continued to admire Germany. After visiting Shandong in

A Chinese soldier with a German helmet and three *Stielhandgranate* hand grenades during the Battle of Shanghai in 1937.

(Contributor: CPA Media Pte Ltd/Alamy Stock Photo)

1912, he noted German investment in ports, railways, urban development and schools. 'I am impressed,' he declared. 'The city is a true model for China's future.'[49]

During the Northern Expedition Chiang Kai-shek perceived himself as China's Bismarck who would forge the modern nation with 'Blood and Iron'. After Chiang dismissed the Soviet advisers, he wanted German expertise which did not involve political risks, as the traditional Prussian ideal of discipline and the example of the Second Reich demonstrated how a modern nation could be created without revolution.[50]

German advisers came to China as private military contractors who had left the *Reichswehr*, as the Treaty of Versailles forbade Germany from despatching military missions abroad, but their presence had been approved by the Weimar Government.[51] Colonel Max Bauer arrived in China in 1927 after accepting an invitation from Chiang. Bauer had served as an artillery officer during World War I and Ludendorff placed him in charge of the Hindenburg Program in 1916, which coordinated industry and munitions production. After the war, he became a far right-wing conspirator before travelling to Hungary, the Soviet Union, Spain and Argentina, where he worked to secure contracts for German armament industries. As Bauer took a genuine interest in learning about China, he established good relations with Chiang.

Bauer argued for efficiency and against the warlord tendency to raise large armies of dubious quality by advocating a mass demobilization and reorganization of Chiang's forces. Bauer understood that a powerful modern military requires a strong industrial base which China lacked; therefore, he recommended the simultaneous modernization of the country's military and industry, and eventually the country would have its own arms factories, but in the meantime China would import arms from Germany. Bauer used his industrial contacts with concerns such as Junkers and Krupp to produce railroad products and munitions for China.[52] He also advocated modernizing China's military, beginning with a single unit that would become a *Lehrtruppe* (Model Unit), trained with modern weapons and techniques, which would subsequently train other units.[53] After Bauer contracted smallpox, he died on 6 May 1929 after successfully laying the foundation for Sino-German military cooperation.

Lieutenant Colonel Hermann Kriebel, a Nazi Party member who had marched alongside Hitler during the Beer Hall Putsch in 1923, succeeded Bauer but lacked his abilities and he left China in May 1930. Kriebel nevertheless advocated German tactical methods and innovations refined during World War I, such as the need for soldiers to act independently and make judgements using initiative personified by *Stosstruppen* (Stormtrooper) assault squads.[54]

Lieutenant General Georg Wetzell, Ludendorff's chief of operations during World War I, replaced Kriebel and served as Chiang Kai-shek's military adviser from 1930 to 1935. Wetzell developed a rapport with the Chinese general staff, embarking on an ambitious military reconstruction program and he expanded Bauer's small training unit by creating a larger *Lehrdivision* (Model Division).[55] The *Lehrdivision* would train other divisions in modern techniques including the 88th Division — the home unit of the Eight Hundred.

DISEASES OF THE HEART AND SKIN

Following the First Sino-Japanese War, fought over control of Korea, Japan annexed Taiwan and the Liaotung Peninsula in southern Manchuria.[56] After the Japanese won the Russo-Japanese War in 1905, they consolidated their interests in Manchuria, in particular the South Manchurian Railway. In 1914 Japan, as an Allied nation, attacked the German concession of Qingdao and supplanted Germany as the principal imperial power in Shandong. Before 1918, Japan had participated with other nations in the division of China into spheres of influence, but after the war, unable to adjust to post-war notions of self-determination, its government and military could not accept a united China in control of its own destiny.[57]

On the night of 18 September 1931, Japanese guards at Mukden in Manchuria clashed with Chinese troops in retaliation for an attack on the South Manchurian Railway.[58] The 'Mukden Incident' had actually been staged by Japanese officers who sabotaged their own railway as a pretext for intervention. On 19 September, General Shigeru Honjo, commander of the Kwangtung Army, arrived in Mukden and his forces soon seized all Manchuria. Kwantung Army officers believed that control of Manchuria would provide the markets, raw materials and foodstuffs that Japan needed to achieve self-sufficiency.[59]

The Japanese invasion of Manchuria inflamed Chinese nationalism and patriots boycotted Japanese goods in Shanghai, which badly hurt the Japanese economy. On 18 January 1932, five Japanese Buddhist monks from the Hongkou District wandered into the Chinese Zhabei district and began singing their national anthem. A small riot followed which injured three monks and two later died. Japanese officers had planned the incident by arranging the assault on the monks to create another pretext for intervention. Japanese newspapers ran graphic reports and demanded vengeance, and a mob from Hongkou attacked a Chinese factory, killing two people, as Japanese marine reinforcements arrived in the city.

The following day the Japanese Consul General Kuramatsu Murai presented Wu Tiecheng, the Mayor of Shanghai, with demands calling for a formal apology for the attack on the monks, the arrest of their assailants, the payment of hospital expenses and an end to the boycott. An Imperial Japanese Navy fleet commanded by Rear Admiral Koichi Shiozawa arrived at Shanghai on 21 January, and he issued a statement that unless Mayor Wu agreed to the demands his forces would 'take appropriate steps to protect the rights and interests of the Imperial Japanese Government'.[60] On 28 January, Shiozawa's warships bombarded Zhabei while Japanese marines attacked and soon 20,000 more Japanese reinforcements landed. Chinese forces resisted and the ensuing battle became known as the 'Shanghai Incident'.

China's 19th Route Army from Guangdong — commanded by Cai Tingkai and left-leaning Whampoa trained officers not under Chiang Kai-shek's direct control — fought and humiliated the Japanese and temporarily drove them back to the Huangpu River. After the 'Mukden Incident', Chiang had resigned from his posts but with the crisis threatening Shanghai, he resumed leadership in January 1932. By mid-February Chinese reinforcements arrived including Chiang's 5th Army, containing the elite 87th and 88th Divisions, equipped with modern German arms and trained in *Stosstruppen* assault tactics. On 20 February, the 88th Division fiercely repulsed a Japanese offensive at Chiangwan and their counter-attack surrounded numerous Japanese units, forcing the invaders to retreat two days later.[61] The division launched a series of successful attacks against the Japanese but suffered high losses. During the 'Shanghai Incident', the 87th and 88th Divisions fought for over a month and demonstrated considerable skill which shocked the Japanese.[62]

The Japanese deployed superior firepower and their warships shelled Shanghai, making a Chinese victory impossible. The 11th Imperial Japanese Army Division conducted a surprise landing at the Yangtze on 29 February, north of Shanghai, which flanked the defenders and forced the Chinese to retreat, and both sides agreed to a ceasefire. The battle killed 3000 Japanese and 4000 Chinese soldiers, destroying 85 per cent of the buildings in Zhabei and killing 10,000 Chinese civilians.[63] The settlement brokered by the League of Nations favoured the Japanese, and their forces mostly departed Shanghai, but their marines retained a garrison. The Chinese, however, could not station troops in the city but could instead maintain order through the Peace Preservation Corps militia.

Although Japan had triumphed militarily, China won a moral victory by demonstrating that its soldiers could fight modern battles.[64] The Chinese soldiers became heroes and their stand at Shanghai generated a wave of patriotic enthusiasm that helped Chiang consolidate his leadership. As the international press covered the conflict, China gained increasing respect and sympathy as the western democracies became more willing to support China in the League of Nations against Japanese interests.

In 1931 Xie Jinyuan transferred to the 78th Division of the 19th Route Army and later transferred to the 88th Division to command a battalion of the Reserve Regiment. Xie fought the Japanese during the 1932 'Shanghai Incident' and witnessed the Japanese bombing and shelling of the city. Later in the decade, he married Ling Weicheng and they had two daughters, Xie Xuefen and Xie Lanfen, as well as two sons, Xie Youmin and Xie Jimin.

On 18 February 1932, the Japanese established the Manchukuo puppet state and made the Last Emperor Puyi head of state and he later became Emperor of Manchukuo. Japanese forces invaded Jehol in February 1933 and seized the province as international tensions escalated and China yielded more territory.[65] After leaving the League of Nations in March 1933, Japan established another puppet state — the Mongol United Autonomous Government — in May 1933. Although Japanese imperialism continuously threatened China, Chiang did not consider this threat his priority.

After the anti-communist purge, Mao Zedong fled to the countryside of central and northern China with other survivors to the hills of Jiangxi Province. Chiang launched five encirclement campaigns against their bases between 1931 and 1934, prioritizing the destruction of internal enemies before China could face the external threat of Japan. 'The Japanese are a disease of the skin,' Chiang declared. 'The Communists are a disease of the heart.'[66] The last offensive forced Mao and his followers on their epic 'Long March' to Yan'an in Shaanxi Province. After establishing a new base, Mao became the leader of the Communist Party in November 1935.

Sino-German cooperation continued during the 1930s as China received military assistance in exchange for raw materials. The friendly relations survived into the Nazi era despite Hitler's racist worldview as the dictator viewed Chiang as a strong anti-communist and Germany's rearmament program needed vast quantities of Chinese raw materials.[67] Germany accordingly declared neutrality in the ongoing Chinese–Japanese tensions.

General Hans von Seeckt replaced Wetzell as leader of the German Mission in 1933, and by this time three German-trained divisions had been created — the 36th, 87th and 88th. Seeckt had advised the Ottoman Empire during World War I and after the conflict, as Chief of the General Staff, he built the small but elite *Reichswehr* within the restrictions imposed by Versailles. Seeckt recommended large-scale demobilization of poorly trained soldiers in favour of a small elite force based upon the existing *Lehrbrigade*.[68] Although mass demobilization was not possible while Chiang continued to fight rivals and communists, the German advisers continued training the elite divisions and the future Eight Hundred. Seeckt's health collapsed and he left China in March 1935 and later died on 27 December 1936.

General Alexander von Falkenhausen replaced Seeckt and became Chiang's most influential German adviser. Falkenhausen, an expert on China and Japan, had fought in the Boxer Rebellion (1899–1901) and served as military attaché in Tokyo. During World War I, he won the *Pour le Mérite* (Blue Max) for bravery and planned the defence of Jordan in 1918. He later commanded the Dresden Infantry School and retired from the *Reichswehr* in 1930. With extensive experience and interest in Asia, Falkenhausen impressed his Chinese colleagues and established good relations.[69]

Falkenhausen continued the focus on training an elite core and he

Xie Jinyuan and Ling Weicheng on their wedding day. (Author's Collection)

negotiated a large contract to import Rheinmetall artillery, Mauser rifles, Siemens radios, half-trucks and tanks. China's industrial development accelerated as German firms helped establish steelworks, coal mines and factories while arsenals were refurbished and retooled to produce modern small arms and artillery. Falkenhausen arranged large-scale military exercises, the first of their kind in China, to test the progress of Chinese troops.

As Sino-German cooperation intensified, public opinion in China was changing. Although Chiang retained his strategy of yielding to Japanese aggression until China had the strength to resist while focusing on defeating the communists, leaders in northern China increasingly perceived Japan as the greater threat. They questioned the necessity of fighting Mao as an increasingly nationalistic population wanted unity.[70]

In December 1936, the anti-Japanese commander Zhang Xueliang, the 'Young Marshal' from Manchuria, based in Xi'an, refused to fight the communists after being influenced by propaganda calling for all

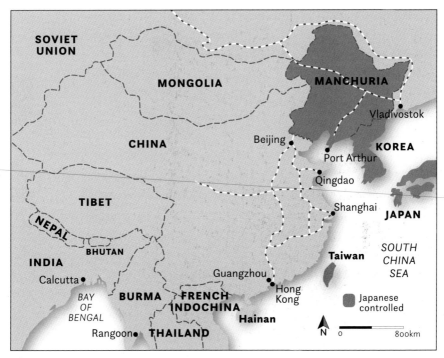

China in 1937.

Chinese factions to unite against Japan.[71] After Chiang travelled to Xi'an to confront Zhang, the Young Marshal kidnapped the Generalissimo on 12 December. Zhang declared that he would release Chiang if he agreed to form a second United Front with the communists.[72] Although Chiang never formally agreed to Zhang's demands, after being released on 25 December, the *Kuomintang* ended the war against the communists and Mao notionally placed his troops under Nanjing's command. Chiang correctly sensed that Chinese public opinion would no longer tolerate any further appeasement of Japan.[73]

The 'Xi'an Incident' generated fear in Tokyo that the second United Front could lead to a Sino-Soviet alliance against Japan, which might allow China to recover Manchuria. In 1937, Japanese strategists developed a contingency plan in which their forces would occupy the five provinces of northern China to secure Manchuria and cut Chinese supply lines, which would be achieved in a swift campaign before the Soviet Union could mobilize and intervene.[74]

As Sino-Japanese tensions increased, Xie Jinyuan celebrated the Spring Festival in 1936 with his family before sending his pregnant wife Ling Weicheng and their daughters Xuefen and Lanfen with their son Youmin to the relative safety of his ancestral home in Guangdong. Xie also wrote parting words to his wife:

> The Japanese invaders show no sign of ceasing their villainous scheme. The Sino-Japanese war looms ahead. Some territories will be seized. The war is bound to last long. Despite that, China will definitely not be defeated, let alone destroyed, as long as each of China's soldiers are determined to defend our country at any cost, even to the last drop of blood. The war is to be extremely fierce and brutal. I have no choice but to arrange you in this remote place. Or otherwise, I will be distracted when combating with enemies. Now the onus is on you to attend upon our elderly parents and foster and educate our little kids. Once the victory is secured, I will personally come here to bring you back to Shanghai and repay your support and dedication to our family that should have been my responsibility. After your delivery, the infant, if a boy, will be called 'Jimin' in the hope that he will inherit the high virtues of our forefathers.[75]

On the evening of 7 July 1937, soldiers from the Imperial Japanese Army conducted manoeuvres in the outskirts of Beijing near Marco Polo Bridge. Under existing treaty agreements, the Japanese could conduct such manoeuvres after receiving permission from local Chinese officials. However, the Japanese had not informed the Chinese of their exercise. After Chinese soldiers heard Japanese soldiers firing training blanks, they replied with real bullets. Although there were no casualties, in the morning a Japanese soldier was missing and a commander ordered his men to attack the town of Wanping to locate the missing man, initiating skirmishes with Chinese troops.[76] The missing soldier returned unharmed after reportedly visiting a brothel, but Japanese officers had already decided to use the incident as a pretext to extract further concessions from China. However, the Chinese would no longer accept violations of their sovereignty and Chiang Kai-shek announced that 'the limits of endurance had been reached'.[77]

The Japanese cabinet reinforced the troops in the Beijing area and Emperor Hirohito declared that his subjects would 'teach China a lesson' by subduing Chinese forces around Beijing and the nearby port of Tianjin.[78] As Japanese officers planned fresh conquests, Chiang announced, 'If we allow one more inch of our territory to be lost, we shall be guilty of an unpardonable offense against our race.'[79] On 16 July, Chiang summoned 150 members of China's political elite to his summer residence at Mount Lu to discuss strategies for dealing with Japan, declaring, 'This time we must fight to the end.'[80]

On 27 July, Japanese soldiers attacked Chinese troops near the Summer Palace and soon intense fighting between the two sides escalated into major conflict. The Japanese occupied Beijing on 28 July and Tianjin the next day. Meanwhile in Tokyo, Emperor Hirohito organized a war meeting and his brother Prince Takamatsu remarked, 'We're really going to smash China so that it will be ten years before it can stand straight again.'[81]

The Sino-Japanese War had begun, an unplanned conflict which Japanese commanders assumed would be another swift and victorious affair in which their troops would occupy northern China to seize its rich deposits of coal and iron ore. As large parts of northern China fell to the invaders, Chiang Kai-shek considered a bold move to strike at the Japanese in Shanghai — a plan that would propel Xie Jinyuan and his Eight Hundred Heroes onto the world stage.

CHAPTER TWO
THE BATTLE OF SHANGHAI

THE SOUTHERN FRONT

In 1937, the Imperial Japanese Army consisted of 247,000 troops in seventeen divisions, four armoured regiments and fifteen aviation squadrons mostly garrisoned in Japan and China. The standard division contained 25,000 soldiers organized in two brigades supported by engineers, artillery, armoured cars and transport units. In contrast, the *Kuomintang*'s National Revolutionary Army consisted of 176 divisions containing approximately 1.7 million troops, but it only had twenty full-strength divisions with 10,000 soldiers while most only contained around 5000 men. Chinese soldiers in general were poorly equipped and trained with little experience in modern coordinated operations. Chinese forces had a critical shortage in artillery and its divisions normally fielded 46 guns compared with a standard Japanese division's 104 guns.[1] Furthermore, Chiang Kai-shek could only count on the loyalty of 31 divisions staffed by Whampoa Academy graduates, including the twenty elite German-trained divisions.[2] The Republic of China Air Force had 600 aircraft but only 268 of them were combat planes and only 91 were modern; therefore, Japan would certainly dominate the skies.[3]

As war raged in the northern Chinese plains, Chiang planned an audacious strategy to open a new front in the densely populated Yangtze provinces centred on Shanghai. The *Kuomintang* in southern China had more effective control over its army and Chiang could deploy his best troops, the 87th and 88th Divisions, against the numerically inferior Japanese marines garrisoned in Shanghai. Chinese forces could also use the city's dense urban environment to reduce the effectiveness of Japanese firepower, just as they had done during the 'Shanghai Incident' of 1932. The Chinese could split Japanese forces and take pressure off their soldiers fighting in the north. A bold move in Shanghai would also send a strong political and psychological message by demonstrating resolve to the Chinese people and the western powers which had significant economic stakes in the city.[4] Operations in Shanghai would get the world's attention and ultimately its sympathy.

By opening a new front in Shanghai, Chinese forces could overwhelm the Japanese marine garrison which normally consisted of 2500 soldiers but could quickly be reinforced with six battalions to raise the troop level to 6300. If the Chinese could rush in troops and expel the Japanese from the city, it would represent a major victory in the eyes of the world. Such an operation would be a race against time as the absolute superiority of the Imperial Japanese Navy meant that additional enemy forces could quickly be shipped to Shanghai but Chinese troops would first have to deploy to the city.[5] In 1937, the Peace Preservation Corps militia was the only Chinese unit inside Shanghai, but six divisions were stationed west of the city, including the 88th Division containing Lieutenant Colonel Xie Jinyuan, who was now the 262nd Brigade's chief-of-staff. Zhang Boting, the 88th Division's chief-of-staff, described Xie as 'a resourceful, far-reaching and highly accomplished staff officer'.[6] Zhang, born on 3 February 1910, grew up in Shanghai before being educated at a Japanese military academy and he would become intimately associated with the Eight Hundred Heroes.

General Alexander von Falkenhausen, head of the German Military Mission, was optimistic about China's chances and advised Chiang Kai-shek that Japan could not afford a total war as the country lacked the finances to sustain a long conflict.[7] 'War on a national scale,' Falkenhausen insisted, 'is a necessary experience for China and will unify her.'[8] Falkenhausen envisaged

Chinese troops fighting the Japanese in Shanghai before conducting a delaying defence from the city to lure the Japanese into the marshes of Lake Tai where strong defensive lines would protect the capital Nanjing.[9] He also recorded his optimism in a signal to Berlin:

> China's chances for victory are not bad because the Japanese — mindful of the threat of Russian intervention — cannot commit all their forces against the Chinese . . . The morale of the Chinese Army is high. They will put up a bitter fight.[10]

On 18 July, Chiang Kai-shek told graduating officers that they could expect the war to spread southwards from Beijing. As the Chinese High Command planned to strike at the exposed Japanese marine garrison in Shanghai, the soldiers of the 88th Division including the Eight Hundred prepared to fight in one of the greatest cities in the world.

METROPOLIS

The First Opium War ended with a British victory at the signing of the Treaty of Nanking on 29 August 1842. The British had demanded land to build trading settlements and the Qing Dynasty ceded territory in Guangzhou, Xiamen, Fuzhou, Ningbo and Shanghai. The British used these settlements to establish their system of 'Treaty Ports', which the Chinese would rightly remember as a violation of their sovereignty ceded by an unequal treaty imposed by British gunboats after suffering an unjust invasion fought for the right to import opium.

Shanghai began as a fishing village in 1074 and as a small cluster of villages grew on a mud flat along the Huangpu River, near the mouth of the mighty Yangtze River, the Chinese unofficially called the place Shanghai or 'Upon the Sea'. Although the small old Chinese walled city of Nanshi, situated next to the British Concession, had been an important port and market town for centuries, the Treaty Port system created modern Shanghai. Over the following decades, international trade created a great port perfectly located near the Yangtze, which became the gateway for global commerce to China's vast interior. Shanghai grew into a grand metropolis as cotton,

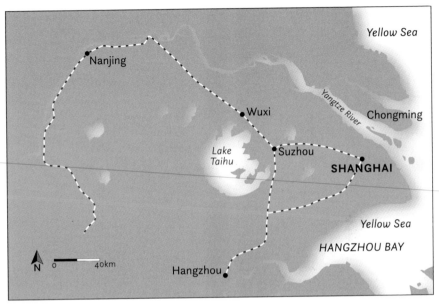

The Shanghai region in 1937.

wood, oil and hides departed on ships while the British mostly imported opium. The city became China's largest port and its main commercial hub through which half of all foreign trade passed and its port could handle 170 ships and 500 junks.[11]

As vast fortunes could be made in Shanghai, other nations established a presence in the city and foreigners enjoyed extraterritoriality as Chinese courts had no jurisdiction over them. The United States created a concession in 1848 and France did the same the following year. The British and American concessions evolved into the International Settlement, governed by the Shanghai Municipal Council, while the French Concession remained independent and was run by a Consul General who exercised the powers of a colonial governor.[12] The British community in Shanghai, known as 'Shanghailanders', dominated the Municipal Council and after the Germans lost their one seat during World War I, Japan obtained it. In 1928 three Chinese members joined the body, giving their community political representation for the first time, and by 1937 there were five British, two American, two Japanese and five Chinese council members.[13]

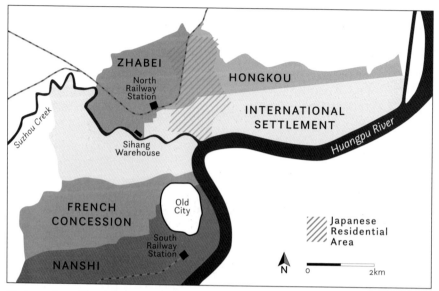

Metropolitan Shanghai in 1937.

The International Settlement represented fourteen nations that obtained treaty port rights from the Qing but only Britain, America, Italy and Japan had land concessions. The Settlement consisted of almost nine square miles while the French Concession, bordering the old Chinese city of Nanshi, was half a square mile and all foreign areas collectively were half the size of Manhattan. The Chinese Municipality of Greater Shanghai was the largest and most populous part of the city. The Chinese suburb Zhabei, located on the northern bank of Suzhou Creek across from the Settlement, contained numerous industrial concerns. After the First Sino-Japanese War, large numbers of Japanese settled in the city and their district, Hongkou, east of Zhabei in northern Shanghai, was known as 'Little Tokyo'. During the 1930s, Shanghai grew to 27 square miles and by the middle of the decade its population exceeded three million, making it one of the most crowded cities in the world. Although only around 70,000 foreigners lived in Shanghai, the city was cosmopolitan and newspapers appeared in English, French, German, Yiddish, Russian and Japanese.

Shanghai was known as the 'Paris of the East' for its economic and

An aerial view of Shanghai in the 1930s.
(Contributor: Sueddeutsche Zeitung Photo/Alamy Stock Photo)

cultural power. In 1937 the city boasted modern high-rise buildings, expensive shops, luxurious hotels, theatres, nightclubs and the Great World Entertainment Centre. The privileged British 'Shanghailanders' conducted their business at the Shanghai Club, worshipped in the city's churches and spent their free time at the racecourse. German businessmen represented their nation's largest firms and they socialized at the German Garden Club. Shanghai was a city of excitement and inequality in which massive wealth, glamour and enormous poverty coexisted.[14]

The famous waterfront area known as 'The Bund' followed the curve of the Huangpu shoreline with impressive hotels, banks and trading houses, and along the majestic river warships from several nations moored in 'Battleship Alley'. Pedestrians walked past villas in the French Concession along boulevards lined with trees.[15] The foreign-educated *Kuomintang* elite entertained themselves in establishments like the Paramount Ballroom and the Black Cat while the rising Chinese middle class increasingly intertwined

The famous Bund waterfront in Shanghai in the 1930s.
(Contributor: Chronicle/Alamy Stock Photo)

with the city's foreigners.

Shanghai was a city of gangsters, political violence, assassinations, kidnappings and extortion. The city's dangerous nightlife involved rich foreigners and Chinese gangsters enjoying exclusive establishments while around one in thirteen women survived through prostitution.[16] The Chinese Communist Party held its first underground Congress in Shanghai in 1921 and used murder and intimidation to control the workers. The *Kuomintang* later hired opium trafficker Du Yuesheng, also known as 'Big-Eared Du', to smash the communist organization and he became the undisputed kingpin of the city's opium trade.[17] Blood Alley in the French Concession was famous for frequent street fights among foreign soldiers and sailors. A Chinese journalist described Shanghai as 'a city of forty-eight-storey skyscrapers built upon twenty-four layers of hell'.[18] As the Sino-Japanese War spread to Shanghai, the burning ruins of the city would soon quite literally appear to be hell on earth.

WAR CLOUDS IN SHANGHAI

In early August 1937, Chinese refugees, sensing the coming conflict, began

Chinese refugees stream across Garden Bridge to the safety of the
International Settlement in Shanghai on 2 September 1937.
(Contributor: Smith Archive/Alamy Stock Photo)

entering Shanghai's International Settlement as the Imperial Japanese
Navy began evacuating its citizens from the city. At a National Defence
Meeting on 7 August, Chiang Kai-shek gained the support of the men
present including his old rival Wang Jingwei.[19] Chiang made it clear that in
Shanghai 'those who retreat without an order will be charged with treason
and no matter what their position, they will be executed without mercy'.[20]
Chinese soldiers in civilian clothing began digging trenches in Zhabei as
50,000 refugees fled into the Settlement.

The final spark occurred on 9 August after Lieutenant Isao Oyama, a
Japanese marine, and Leading Seaman Yozo Saito left the Settlement in a
car and approached a Peace Preservation Corps checkpoint near Hongqiao
Aerodrome. Shots were fired and both men died while a Chinese sentry was
killed.[21] Chinese, Japanese, British, French and American police investigated
the incident the next day. The Chinese account claimed the Japanese car
did not stop at the checkpoint and Lieutenant Oyama opened fire, forcing

the Chinese guards to shoot back, while the Japanese account claimed that Chinese guards fired their weapons without warning. The identity of the dead Chinese guard, who apparently had been shot from behind — an indication he had not died during a firefight — remained unclear, but the incident escalated tensions to boiling point.[22] It is entirely possible that Chinese officials staged the event as a pretext for action and, if so, they had learnt the art of fabricating 'incidents' from the Japanese.

As tension increased on 11 August, the Japanese Consul General Suemasa Okamoto demanded Chinese forces withdraw from Shanghai's demilitarized zone established by the 1932 armistice. Mayor Yu Hongjun dismissed this demand and claimed that Japanese soldiers in Chinese territory had violated the agreement.

Chiang Kai-shek placed Zhang Zhizhong and Feng Yuxiang, the 'Christian Warlord' who had earlier rebelled against him during the Great Plains War, in command of forces in Shanghai. Despite old rivalries Feng declared, 'As long as it serves the purpose of fighting Japan. I'll say yes, no matter what it is.'[23] Zhang Zhizhong, former head of Whampoa Academy, commanded the 9th Army Group west of the Huangpu and the 87th and 88th Divisions made up the bulk of his troops. He planned to seize the initiative and attack the Japanese with an overwhelming assault while Chinese troops had numerical superiority.

As the Chinese planned operations in the city, the Japanese Third Fleet arrived with the cruiser *Idzumo*, the aircraft carrier *Kaga* and fourteen other warships which anchored in the Huangpu River as marines landed to reinforce the small garrison. At the same time General Wang Jingjiu ordered his men in 87th Division to board trucks in Nanjing and drive towards Shanghai while troops from the 88th Division travelled on trains towards the city, as Zhang Boting recalled: 'The great day finally arrived. We received the order on 11 August to set out to Shanghai.'[24]

On 12 August, 50,000 Chinese troops in Shanghai opposed 5000 Japanese marines and Zhang Boting explained their dispositions:

> The enemy took Hongkou District as their base, with their backs to the Huangpu River. Their positions started from Huishan Wharf, and went along Wusong Road and North Sichuan Road to the Japanese Marine

A Chinese soldier and a boy in uniform at a street barricade in Nanshi,
Shanghai in 1937.

(Contributor: Sueddeutsche Zeitung Photo/Alamy Stock Photo)

Corps Command opposite the Hongkou Park on Jiangwan Road. It was
like a long snake with the Navy Command as its head and Huishan
Wharf as its tail.[25]

The 87th and 88th Divisions completed their deployment in northern
Shanghai.[26] The soldiers of the 88th Division established defensive
positions north of Suzhou Creek in Zhabei opposite the Japanese in
Hongkou. Zhabei, an industrial suburb, was a transportation hub where
roads, waterways and the railway converged, making the area strategically
important to both sides.[27] Zhang Boting meanwhile reconnoitred the terrain
and gained intelligence on Japanese positions:

Detailed and repeated reconnaissance was conducted especially at the
bottom of North Sichuan Road and around the Japanese Marine Corps
Command near the Tiantong Temple. I was accompanied by artillery
battalion commander Lieutenant Colonel Wang Jie and Lieutenant
Colonel Xie Jinyuan.[28]

The 88th Division's 34-year-old commander General Sun Yuanliang had
studied at the Tokyo Military Academy and later graduated with the first
class of Whampoa graduates before fighting in the Northern Expedition
and against the Japanese during the 'Shanghai Incident' of 1932.[29] Sun
planned to immediately strike at the Japanese from Zhabei while there was
still an opportunity to drive the Japanese into the sea. At the same time
the 87th Division established positions further north and the 55th Division
deployed to Hongkou opposite the Japanese defenders.[30]

The Shanghai Municipal Council in the International Settlement
mobilized its Shanghai Volunteer Corps and requested support from the
American and British garrison troops.[31] Colonel Charles Price, commander
of the 4th Marine Regiment, deployed his two battalions along Suzhou
Creek to protect the American Concession from any fighting in Zhabei.
Major-General Alexander Telfer-Smollett, commander of British forces,
similarly ordered his men to take up positions opposite Zhabei. As war
seemed inevitable, Anglo-American soldiers built blockhouses and
machine-gun posts protected by barbed wire and sandbags as thousands

of Chinese refugees entered the Settlement to shelter from the coming storm.[32] 'Our assignment was to defend the International Settlement,' the American Marine Ferd Froeschle recalled, but 'our sympathies were with the Chinese'.[33] Admiral Kiyoshi Hasegawa, commander of the Japanese Third Fleet, signalled Tokyo: 'The situation in the area around Shanghai could explode at any moment.'[34]

THE FIRST SHOTS

On 13 August, Japanese and Chinese forces exchanged fire across barricades in Zhabei and Hongkou as two Japanese divisions disembarked at Shanghai. By the afternoon extensive fighting had broken out as Japanese naval gunfire and aircraft attacked Chinese positions. The fighting extended along the northern bank of Suzhou Creek from the North Railway Station to Hongkou and Huangpu River as thousands more refugees entered the Settlement. 'The people were all panic-stricken,' an American Marine observed, 'and were moving their possessions including household furnishings, pigs, chickens and children' and 'the indescribable suffering and widespread destruction grew in horribleness'.[35] After dusk the flames of burning buildings illuminated the skyline of northern Shanghai.

Chiang Kai-shek ordered Zhang Zhizhong to 'drive the enemy in the sea, block off the coast, and resist landings'.[36] Sun Yuanliang planned to assault the Japanese marine headquarters near Hongkou Park — a massive four-storey structure protected from air and artillery bombardment by a double roof of reinforced concrete. The structure was a natural fortress and light tanks, armoured cars and artillery supplemented its already formidable defensive potential. If the Chinese soldiers captured this fortress, it would be possible to secure Shanghai before overwhelming Japanese reinforcements arrived by sea. The 88th Division's attack would be confined to the Hongkou salient and during the conflict both sides respected the foreign concessions as neither wanted to alienate western nations.[37]

The soldiers of the 87th and 88th Divisions were armed with Mauser rifles and stick grenades and wore German-style uniforms with *Stahlhelm* helmets displaying the insignia of the White Sun on the side. *Time* magazine

Chinese soldiers being reviewed in Shanghai in 1937.
(Contributor: CPA Media Pte Ltd/Alamy Stock Photo)

described the German-trained Chinese troops as 'Chiang's grim, steel-helmeted, Prussian-disciplined regulars'.[38]

During the Battle of Shanghai, around 50 German advisers in Chinese uniforms helped plan operations and they were often on the front line directing the fighting against the Japanese.[39] 'We all agreed', Falkenhausen remarked, 'that as private citizens in Chinese employment there could be no question of our leaving our Chinese friends to their fate. Therefore I assigned the German advisers wherever they were needed, and that was often in the frontlines.'[40] Japanese soldiers even referred to the battle as 'the German war'.[41]

On 14 August, the 87th and 88th Divisions assaulted the Japanese positions. The 88th Division made slow progress as the Japanese defended well-prepared strongpoints supported by armoured cars, light tanks and naval gunfire. Chinese infantry suffered heavy casualties after attacking a well-entrenched enemy who called up naval bombardments to smash assaults. Zhang Boting observed that Japanese warships 'firing with intensive naval guns in cooperation with their ground forces' overwhelmed the Chinese 10th Artillery Regiment because 'its firepower was not enough to compete with the enemy's naval guns'.[42] The Chinese dead included the 264th Brigade commander Huang Meixing and all his staff, killed after a shell hit their command post, and one regiment lost seven company commanders in a single attack.[43]

Despite an enormous setback, Zhang Zhizhong planned further attacks, but the Chinese did achieve some success in another sector of the city. The 337th Regiment advanced towards Shanghai from the south-west and attacked Japanese logistics depots in eastern Shanghai. After being reinforced by the 55th and 57th Divisions, the Chinese forced Japanese marines to withdraw to their fleet.[44] The war also reached the International Settlement after Chinese aircraft attacking Japanese ships accidentally bombed the Palace Hotel and Nanking Road, opposite Cathay Hotel, killing over 2000 people — an incident remembered as 'Bloody Saturday'.[45]

On 15 August, the Japanese High Command created the Shanghai Expeditionary Army, consisting of three Imperial Japanese Army divisions, which would soon be shipped to the city to support the marines. General Iwane Matsui, placed in command, had fought in the Russo-Japanese War (1904–05). Before this army arrived, Japanese marines would have to hold out against repeated Chinese attacks and the next day Rear Admiral Denshichi Okawachi, the marine commander, committed his reserves as the outcome hung in the balance. Okawachi, increasingly desperate, informed Tokyo that his forces could hold out for six more days and requested urgent reinforcements.[46]

Zhang Zhizhong meanwhile planned Operation Iron Fist, a full-scale assault in which the 88th Division would attack south of Hongkou Park while the 87th Division attacked further east and both thrusts would reach the Huangpu River, cutting the Japanese position into three sectors. Iron Fist had been conceived by Colonel Hans Vetter, the German adviser assigned to the 88th Division, and Zhang Boting explained its logic:

> Based on the situation of the Shanghai battlefield at that time, the
> German advisor [Hans Vetter] thought the Japanese army's position
> went from Huishan Wharf via Wusong Road and North Sichuan Road
> to Jiangwan Road, which was like a long snake. Therefore, it would
> be good to select a critical point at the waist of the snake, then
> concentrate firepower to launch an assault to cut the snake from its
> waist. This way, the 'head' and the 'tail' would not be able to work
> together. Our troops could then go straight in and out of its 'heart', and
> the enemy's defence organization would naturally collapse.[47]

Zhang Boting also recalled that as Iron Fist would be launched from the
262nd Brigade's position, 'Lieutenant Colonel Xie Jinyuan was appointed
to complete all detailed staff operations, and he would also guide the
implementation. All deployments were completed that night, so he acted as
planned the next day.'[48]

At 0500 h on 17 August, Iron Fist commenced as the 87th and 88th
Divisions attacked Japanese positions. Chinese soldiers initially made good
progress but their artillery support lacked coordination and well-prepared
Japanese positions halted their advance.[49] Zhang Boting lamented
the near success of the operation: 'Although the enemy suffered severe
damage, the plan failed on the verge of success and did not achieve the
desired goal.'[50] Pan Shihua, a soldier in the 88th Division, acknowledged
a lack of proper preparation: 'Because we hadn't done reconnaissance
well enough beforehand, we found ourselves surrounded by Japanese
armor on all sides.'[51] The Japanese even annihilated an entire battalion
from the 88th Division as the doomed men assaulted a building. Once
again, Japanese artillery and naval gunfire proved decisive, as Zhong
Song, a Chinese officer, explained: 'From 9am there was intense Japanese
artillery fire — as if it would level the mountains and wipe out the sea.'[52]
The Chinese had also been forced to attack along narrow and predictable
routes to avoid entering the International Settlement and General Zhang
Fakui, commander of the 8th Army Group, bitterly recalled: 'Without the
protection provided by the foreign concessions they [the Japanese] would
have been wiped out.'[53]

To strike at the Japanese warships, Xie Jinyuan conceived a bold plan

Japanese soldiers manning a barricade in front of a Chinese Coca-Cola billboard during the Battle of Shanghai in 1937.
(Contributor: CPA Media Pte Ltd/Alamy Stock Photo)

to attack the cruiser *Idzumo* docked at Huishan Wharf, the enemy's flagship and command centre, as Zhang Boting explained:

> [Xie Jinyuan] prepared a small fast steamer carrying special explosives. It departed from near Shiliupu in the Southern City, and was expected to explode at three to four hundred meters from the Izumo ship. Unfortunately during the implementation, the executors lacked composure and fired prematurely before reaching the predetermined distance. As a result, they failed to hit the target and only blew up part of the equipment at Huishan Wharf. Our three technicians were shot by enemy fire and could not escape the scene. They died for the country as unknown heroes. At that time, Huishan Wharf was on fire, which newspapers published and cheered everyone greatly. Although Comrade Xie's plan was not achieved, it shocked the enemy and achieved psychological effects.[54]

The ongoing bombardment by Japanese warships also led to a fateful decision. Sun Yuanliang initially located the 88th Division's headquarters at Guanyintang, but this position did not afford sufficient protection from naval gunfire. Sun accordingly moved his headquarters to Sihang Warehouse where the Eight Hundred would soon make their stand.

On 18 August, two Japanese marine battalions from northern China reinforced their comrades in Shanghai. The German-trained 36th Division attacked the next day and Chinese troops reached the waterfront, but a counter-attack by Japanese marines supported by tanks and armoured cars reversed the situation and the Chinese withdrew after suffering massive losses.[55]

On 20 August, the 36th and 87th Divisions advanced south towards

The Chinese districts of Shanghai burning during the fighting in 1937.
(Contributor: CPA Media Pte Ltd/Alamy Stock Photo)

the Huangpu waterfront while the 88th Division attacked in the east but, despite some initial success, Chinese troops sustained 1200 casualties. 'As our army lacked assault weapons, we were unable to achieve full success,' Zhang Boting explained. 'This was the heyday of our army's offensive.'[56] He also recalled the surreal view of the city at night:

One night in late August, I could not sleep. I was leaning against the window and looking at the night view of the battlefield. The enemy's and our tracer bullets fired alternately like shooting stars. Just as our air force was attacking at night, anti-aircraft machine guns began to fire from the enemy's position. The sparks discharged were even more beautiful than celebration fireworks. It was quite spectacular.[57]

As Chinese troops failed to hurl the Japanese into the sea, an officer, Zhong Song, reflected:

> Even though the battles are unbearable, our officers and men's spirits seem very courageous. . . In this war to liberate the people, our army is inferior in every respect, but we have also achieved the spirit of the people's warrior.[58]

However, the Chinese had some good news with the signing of the Sino-Soviet Non-Aggression Pact in Nanjing, allowing Stalin to provide military assistance to China.

ARRIVAL OF THE 'LUCKY DIVISION'

On 23 August, two Imperial Japanese Army divisions from the Shanghai Expeditionary Army landed north of Shanghai. General Matsui intended to outflank Chinese forces by rapidly seizing the towns of Dachang and Nanxiang before executing a complete encirclement of the city.[59] The 11th Division landed near Chuansha and would advance towards Luodian while the 3rd Division landed at Wusong and intended to cut the Shanghai–Wusong Railway and destroy the Chinese guns at Wusong fortress, which had protected Shanghai since the Opium Wars. Afterwards, both divisions would link up and advance south-west.[60] The focus of the battle now shifted from the dense urban streets of Shanghai to the new front north of the city. The 3rd Division, commanded by General Susumu Fujita, was known as the 'Lucky Division' and its men who survived the next two months of savage fighting would face the Eight Hundred at Sihang Warehouse.

Zhang Zhizhong ordered the 11th Division and half the 87th Division to confront these landings and assist the 56th Division in the area. The 11th Division attacked the Japanese in Luodian and retook the town, which controlled the road to Dachang and ultimately to Shanghai. The Japanese counter-attacked and re-entered the town but, after brutal fighting, the Chinese expelled the invaders for a second time.

After landing north of Shanghai, a Japanese soldier Genbei Hamabe, recalled: 'Enemy bullets are falling like rain. I was shocked by our hurried

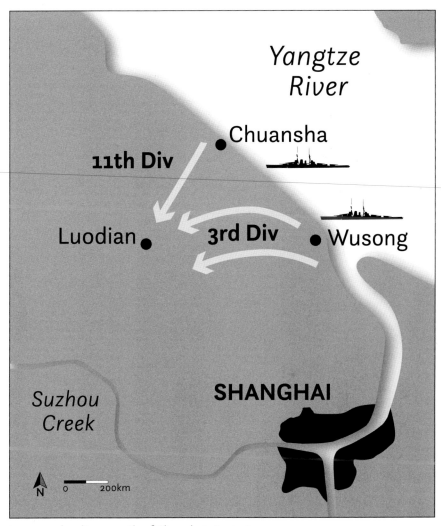

Japanese landings north of Shanghai, August 1937.

landing. The feeling that "this is a war" wells up inside me — much more so than the Manchurian Incident.'[61] Masao Nagatani, another Japanese soldier, similarly reflected:

> I was filled with a sense of fortune and gratitude for having landed safely on this land, taken by the blood and tears of the marines and forward land units. I offered a small prayer to the spirits of the war

dead and faced toward the Emperor in the far, far East. While feeling
how grateful I am for my country Japan, I was able to sense how
horrible this thing called war really is.[62]

The Japanese had seized the initiative and took pressure off the marines
in Shanghai as Chinese troops stopped further attacks in the city as they
redeployed forces to deal with the new threat. Chiang Kai-shek, unhappy
with Zhang Zhizhong's performance, placed Chen Cheng in charge of the
15th Army Group, responsible for dealing with the Japanese landings.

On 24 August, the 3rd Division repulsed two Chinese attacks as
artillery from Wusong fortress harassed Japanese movements. The 3rd
Division captured Yinhang village four days later and the 11th Division
retook Luodian. The Japanese advance stalled the next day, but the
'Lucky Division' eventually captured Wusong and its coastal batteries
on 2 September, and Matsui remarked in his diary: 'I felt boundless
gratification.'[63] The 3rd Division advanced towards Baoshan two days
later and, after Susumu Fujita suggested postponing the attack, Matsui
exploded with anger and ordered an immediate assault. The soldiers of
the 'Lucky Division' attacked in waves and attempted to scale the fortress
walls, sustaining huge casualties without success. After a renewed attack
the next day, the soldiers finally captured Baoshan and they soon reached
the Shanghai–Wusong railway.

By 9 September, the 3rd Division had sustained 589 deaths and 1539
wounded.[64] The men continued to advance, fighting through warehouses,
factories and narrow streets against well-prepared Chinese troops supported
by machine guns and mortars. The 'Lucky Division' lacked heavy artillery
and tank support because the high command considered the soil unsuitable
for such weapons; therefore, the men attacked strongpoints with small-
calibre infantry support weapons.[65]

On 11 September, Chinese forces withdrew towards a new defensive line
that stretched from the North Railway Station to the Yangtze. This retreat
yielded numerous wharfs and docks to the Japanese who could use them
to land reinforcements and heavy equipment. As Chinese forces withdrew,
Zhu Shaoliang replaced Zhang Zhizhong and took command of the 9th
Army Group.

The 3rd Division meanwhile advanced towards the Shanghai racecourse and repulsed strong but poorly coordinated Chinese counter-attacks.[66] Matsui planned a right hook advance across Wusong Creek towards Suzhou Creek. On 25 September, the 3rd Division advanced near Liuhang as Chinese soldiers retreated, and the next day Japanese troops attacked across 20 miles of front, but strongpoints in numerous villages and counter-attacks delayed progress.

On 29 September, Matsui designated Dachang, the gateway to Zhabei, the main objective and ordered his divisions to attack through heavily fortified terrain.[67] The offensive forced the Chinese to retreat south of the Wenzaobin River while the 3rd Division penetrated Chinese lines on the highway to Shanghai on 1 October and, despite the arrival of heavy artillery from Japan, casualties continued to soar.[68] Japanese troops crossed Wusong Creek five days later as the powers of the Nine-Power Pact announced that a conference would attempt to resolve the escalating conflict.[69]

After the Japanese landed north of Shanghai on 23 August, the 88th Division remained in Zhabei fighting defensive battles, as Zhang Boting explained:

> In late August, the enemy attacked our Zhabei position multiple times, but was repeatedly repelled and hit hard by our defenders. The enemy publicly called the 88th Division the 'hateful enemy of Zhabei'. From then on, the enemy was on the front of Zhabei and did not dare to stir up trouble until our army retrograded.[70]

The 88th Division prepared a fresh offensive in mid-October inside Shanghai to cut off Sichuan North Road and isolate the Japanese forces in the northern districts of the city. On 18 October, the Chinese attack commenced near the North Railway Station, which surprised the Japanese and cut the road, disrupting their supply line.[71] Despite this small success, the Japanese approached Dachang the next day, which threatened the 88th Division's position in Zhabei.[72] The Japanese High Command planned a new landing at Hangzhou Bay south of Shanghai with the 10th Army, which would take place in early November to complete the encirclement of the city.

On 25 October, the Japanese finally captured Dachang, only six miles north-west of municipal Shanghai. 'The whole Shanghai front is collapsing,' Chiang Kai-shek observed, 'but we must resist Japan to the bitter end and not turn our backs on our original resolve.'[73] He ordered a withdrawal to the south bank of Suzhou Creek, the last natural obstacle in Shanghai which runs between Zhabei and the International Settlement before joining the Huangpu River. The Japanese 9th Division reached Zoumatang Creek that day and one battalion created a small bridgehead.[74] The 3rd Division crossed the next day and expanded the bridgehead as defeated and exhausted Chinese defenders withdrew from Zhabei. However, the troops in the 'Lucky Division', after being in constant battle for over two months, were barely combat effective and in some cases corporals commanded shattered companies which had been reduced to platoon strength.[75] These fatigued and bloodied troops would soon reach Sihang Warehouse.

CHAPTER THREE
LAST STAND AT SIHANG WAREHOUSE

TUESDAY — THE DAY BEFORE

On the morning of 26 October 1937, General Gu Zhutong, deputy commander of the Third War Zone, telephoned General Sun Yuanliang, commander of the 88th Division, who was at his headquarters inside Sihang Warehouse. Gu confirmed that Chinese forces would soon withdraw from northern Shanghai and that Chiang Kai-shek had ordered him to leave the 88th Division behind in Zhabei as a rearguard to secure the Chinese retreat from the city. Gu then asked, 'What's your opinion?'[1] Sun disagreed with this plan and explained his reservations:

> If the death ratio between us and the enemy is 1 to 1, or even 1 to 10, then I am willing to remain in Zhabei and hold fast to Shanghai. The most worrying thing is that we are isolated here. After a fierce battle, our cadres will be injured or dead and our connections will be cut off. In the situation of a disintegrated organisation, food and ammunition shortages and chaos with no directions, we will be slaughtered by our enemy at will. It is not worth it, and doesn't bring us honour![2]

Gu elaborated that the division would be divided into small independent groups to harass the advancing Japanese from village strongpoints and through guerrilla tactics.[3] Sun, believing this would be a futile waste of experienced troops and that the flat terrain was not suitable for guerrilla warfare, argued against the idea in favour of defending fixed fortified positions. Sun sent Zhang Boting, his chief-of-staff, to the Third War Zone headquarters to ensure that his thoughts would be properly conveyed. Zhang recalled the hazardous journey:

> Things were extremely chaotic. The enemy planes kept hovering in the sky. As soon as targets were discovered, they would fly low and fire at them. I travelled along Zhongshan Avenue by car and was attacked many times . . . and the situation was bleak along the way. Getting off the car near the No. 51 Bridge on Zhongshan Avenue in west Shanghai, I walked westward along the small river and crossed a small bridge about three miles away. I found the deputy chief officer in a hut in the bamboo forest. The deputy chief was looking at the map hanging on the wall. I saluted him.[4]

Gu discussed the general situation in Shanghai with Zhang before explaining that the upcoming Nine-Power Conference in Brussels would consider the Japanese invasion of China and that Chiang Kai-shek wanted the 88th Division to remain in Zhabei as prolonged operations might influence the talks. The troops would fight small-unit actions, as Gu explained:

> Companies, platoons and squads will be dispersed to garrison the strong buildings in the urban area and suburban villages, large and small. We will fight for every inch of land, and get the enemy to pay the price in their blood. We will also watch for opportunities to launch guerrillas, try to buy time and arouse sympathy from friendly nations.[5]

Zhang in disagreement replied:

> Apart from its city streets, the suburbs of Zhabei are flat and there is no concealment. The terrain does not provide the conditions for

guerrilla warfare. In fact, it is even difficult to defend the strongholds separately, because our division has already had reinforcements six times. Currently, only 20–30% are veterans. This situation is just like a cup of tea. The taste is very strong when it is first brewed. After adding water six times, it is more and more diluted, and tastes lighter and lighter. The recruits have not gone through any battles, and some recruits have not even fired their guns. At present, we rely on cadres and veterans to support the recruits on the ground and train them during battles where they gradually exercise their combat skills in practice. With the control of cadres at all levels and the leadership of veterans, the combat system can still be maintained. Once dispersed, the maintenance of force will disappear, and it will be extremely difficult to expect them to fight separately.[6]

Gu listened in silence and eventually nodded in agreement before asking how they could implement Chiang's intent. Zhang explained that the Generalissimo desired a strategic and political outcome. 'It is to emphasize the aggressive acts of the Japanese warlords,' Zhang asserted. 'Shanghai is a cosmopolitan city where facts are seen and heard by both Chinese and foreigners.'[7] He suggested that defending one or two critical strongholds with one elite regiment would bring the reality of the fighting in Shanghai to the conference in Brussels and achieve the desired purpose. Gu agreed with this logic and ordered: 'Time is running out. Please quickly go back and tell division commander Sun that we will do it this way. The deployment has to be completed tonight, and I will report everything to the Chairman.'[8]

Zhang left the headquarters and drove back towards Sihang and during the return journey a platoon commander from the 87th Division warned him that the road ahead was impassable as the Japanese were nearby. After taking a detour through Caohejing, Zhang arrived at the warehouse at 1730 h:

Division commander Sun was pacing back and forth in the room. It was his usual habit to pace and meditate whenever something happened. When he had a decision, he would immediately sit down and write the order, or call necessary personnel to assign tasks. Before I started to speak, he told me that General Gu had phoned with instructions to stay and defend the last position in Zhabei with a regiment.[9]

Sun announced that Sihang Warehouse would be the stronghold, but a regiment was too large for the task as too many troops would create supply and hygiene problems. The general accordingly decided that the 1st battalion from the 524th Regiment would stay behind. The men would defend the warehouse to the death in a demonstration of Chinese determination to influence the upcoming Nine-Power Conference, scheduled to take place in Brussels on 6 November.

Sun ordered Lieutenant Colonel Xie Jinyuan to command the defence of Sihang and he took command of the battalion. During the fighting in Shanghai, Colonel Han Xianyuan commanded the 524th Regiment and Lieutenant Colonel Huang Yonghuai served as his deputy, but after he was wounded, Xie Jinyuan (the 262nd Brigade's chief-of-staff) replaced him in this capacity. Zhang described Xie as a 'tall, handsome, honest and upright' man 'of few words and a person of principle'.[10]

Major Shangguan Zhibiao became Xie's executive officer and adjutant while Major Yang Ruifu, commander of the 1st Battalion, continued to direct the battalion's four companies: 1st Company (Captain Tao Xingchun), 2nd Company (Captain Deng Ying), 3rd Company (Captain Shi Meihao) and Machine Gun Company (Captain Lei Xiong).[11] The exact number of men in the battalion is unclear. Chen Desong, a soldier in the battalion, gave the number as 410.[12] Other accounts often give the number as 452, but Xie's son Xie Jimin later dismissed this figure:

> Books, newspapers and periodicals in Taiwan all adopted the saying of 452 soldiers, because the number of enrolled soldiers in the first battalion of the 524th Regiment was 452. While the fighting was going on day and night, the front-line troops suffered from casualties every day. 420 was the number of soldiers counted up as ordered by Xie Jinyuan while they entered the warehouse.[13]

Peter Harmsen in *Shanghai 1937: Stalingrad on the Yangtze* concluded that 'Xie Jinyuan's force consisted of slightly over 400 officers and soldiers'.[14]

Therefore, the best estimate is that between 410 and 420 soldiers defended Sihang Warehouse.

Major Shangguan was born in Fujian Province on 20 July 1912 and Zhang recalled that he possessed a 'supreme martial spirit' and 'often took the lead and fought hand-to-hand' and 'killed many enemy soldiers'.[15] Zhang added:

> At middle-school age, he [Shangguan] was influenced by revolutionary thoughts, so he quit schooling and joined the army. He started from the grass-roots and graduated from the training class of the [Whampoa] military academy. He was plain, simple, brave and good at fighting. During the tenure of company commander, he was wounded many times but never quit.[16]

Major Yang, born in Tianjin, Hebei Province in 1902, graduated from Whampoa Military Academy. Zhang described him as a 'bold, open and enthusiastic' officer who 'always charged at the head of his troop and was wounded many times'.[17]

At this time the 1st Battalion was deployed near the North Railway Station in the 524th Regiment's defence zone. At 2200 h a messenger reported to Yang Ruifu with orders for him to proceed to regimental headquarters. After arriving, Colonel Han Xianyuan showed him a map and explained that Dachang had fallen and that the division would withdraw that night. Yang, still unaware of the decision to defend Sihang, returned to his battalion headquarters where he delivered orders to his company commanders concerning the withdrawal from Zhabei. 'At that time,' he recalled, 'I was in the room on my own. I could hear that the enemy's artillery fire was a lot stronger than previous days. I felt like losing something precious at the thought of retreat. The pain was indescribable.'[18] At around 2300 h, Colonel Han summoned Yang back to regimental headquarters and he ran through the streets as Japanese artillery exploded nearby, causing shrapnel to rain. After arriving, Yang found Colonel Han in a strange mood:

> I saw the regiment commander, saluted him and looked at him for a long time. However, the regiment commander did not say a word. I

Sihang Warehouse in Shanghai's Zhabei district on the bank of Suzhou Creek.
(Author's Collection)

observed his look and there seemed to be an unspeakable struggle.
I waited for over twenty minutes, but the regiment commander still
did not utter a word. Just as I was baffled and anxious, the division
headquarters suddenly asked the regiment commander to answer the
phone. In the meantime, deputy regiment commander Xie also ran back
from the division headquarters, looking very nervous, which made me
feel even weirder. Deputy regiment commander Xie walked to me and
gave me a small note. This turned out to be an order from the division
commander for our battalion to hold on to Zhabei. Xie said to me,
'Quickly order the troops to gather. I will go to Sihang Warehouse first.'
. . . Tense air filled the whole room at the time. I shook hands with the
regiment commander straight away and farewelled him in tears.[19]

Sihang Warehouse, also known as Four Banks Warehouse and Joint Trust
Warehouse, was designed by the Hungarian architect László Hudec and
built in 1931. The building had been used by four Chinese banks to store
goods.[20] The complex consisted of two six-storey buildings occupying 20,000

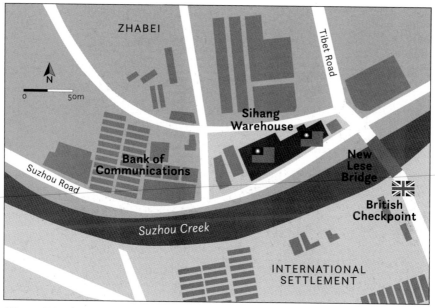

Sihang Warehouse in Shanghai.

square metres on the corner of Tibet Road and North Suzhou Road along the northern bank of the Suzhou Creek — the border of the International Settlement — which was less than 70 metres wide. The warehouse was a natural fortress with ten-foot-thick steel-reinforced concrete walls that could withstand enormous punishment and, as it was one of the tallest structures in Shanghai, the Chinese would have excellent visibility of Japanese troop movements.[21] New Lese Bridge just south-east of the building connected the Chinese position to the British Concession, providing a link to the outside world. The bridge's southern end was guarded by soldiers from the Royal Welsh Fusiliers who would have a clear view of the battle from their sandbags. As the warehouse was the 88th Division's headquarters, it was already stocked with food, ammunition and other supplies, as Shangguan Zhibiao detailed:

There were a lot of grenades and mortar shells. The mortar shells were extremely powerful when thrown from the windows and the roof. Meanwhile, there were thousands of sacks of grain. The first, second and third floors were filled with wheat grains, so there was no shortage of food.²²

The Japanese could easily surround the warehouse on three sides, but they could not attack the building with heavy artillery or bombs due to the risk of accidentally hitting the British or American concessions and creating an international incident. The Japanese, with their firepower negated, had no easy means of attacking Sihang. The warehouse would provide the Chinese the same advantages the Japanese marines had when they defended their headquarters in Hongkou during the first phase of the battle — a massive fortress that could not be assaulted in a tactically sound manner given its proximity to the International Settlement.

Xie Jinyuan proceeded directly to the warehouse and, after arriving, noted its fortress-like qualities and the dozens of slots through the walls which his well-protected men could use to fire at Japanese troops. As the battalion's companies were located in different positions across Zhabei, runners had been despatched with orders for the men to rally at Sihang. Yang Ruifu arrived at the warehouse with the 2nd Company and noticed that Xie and the 1st Company had already arrived. After learning that the 3rd Company and the Machine Gun Company had not yet arrived, Yang despatched two more messengers to find them. 'In the meantime,' he recalled, 'I ordered the 2nd Company to send some people to participate in the requisition of water tanks and cooking utensils, and to serve as a security on the periphery of Sihang Warehouse.'²³

During the night, the men strengthened their position by creating defences out of sandbags and sacks filled with wheat or corn as well as blocking all doors and windows on the ground floor and half of the higher level windows. They also created a killing field around the warehouse by clearing away debris. Xie posted a lookout to watch for the Japanese and after midnight he addressed the men. 'Despite enemy encirclement underway,' he reminded them, 'we will never ever cease fighting as long as there is still one person alive . . . no matter what this warehouse will be our base or graves.'²⁴

The remainder of the 88th Division and other Chinese troops meanwhile withdrew from Zhabei in an orderly manner and set fire to the neighbourhood as part of a scorched earth policy. They departed the district as orange and yellow flames from burning buildings lit the night sky. The Japanese could have advanced through the deserted streets unopposed, but they halted at sunset as their reconnaissance failed to detect the Chinese withdrawal. 'The enormous Chinese army', as a foreign journalist observed, 'simply melted away and at dawn the Japanese found themselves facing empty positions. The two armies were no longer in contact.'[25]

WEDNESDAY — THE FIRST ATTACK

At dawn on 27 October, smoke rose across Zhabei and a reporter from the *North China Herald* witnessed 'the awful aftermath of hostilities' with fires burning 'all through the day, until the whole of its northern Chinese city was wrapped in flame'.[26] Dr Johannes Bernard Thiersch, a German professor in Shanghai, also witnessed the devastation:

> I saw the burning of Chapei [Zhabei], the fighting and bombing, the capture of the city by the Japanese . . . There were some terrible scenes in Shanghai — mutilated bodies, starving refugees pleading for help in the settlement and then cholera and other diseases. We did what we could to help.[27]

Soldiers from the Japanese 3rd 'Lucky' Division, commanded by General Susumu Fujita, advanced through abandoned Chinese positions in a triumphal spirit and hoisted thousands of Rising Sun flags from the ruined buildings. However, their mood shifted after hearing rumours that Chinese soldiers inside Sihang Warehouse had taken oaths to fight to the last man.[28] By not advancing during the night, the invaders had lost the opportunity to storm the warehouse before the Chinese were prepared. 'The only explanation for this,' the German adviser Robert Borchardt concluded, 'was a lack of independent thinking by junior officers.'[29]

Before dawn Yang Ruifu anxiously waited inside Sihang Warehouse for the Japanese to arrive. 'I was deeply worried that the enemy would approach,' he recalled. 'I could not just wait there, so I ordered the messenger to destroy all the lights in the building, so that it would be easy for our army to take cover.'[30] At 0730 h an outpost at the Han Bridge reported that Japanese soldiers were approaching the North Railway Station and Yang ordered the platoon not to retreat without orders. The men reported 45 minutes later that the Japanese had captured the station and that a Rising Sun flag could be seen on the building. Yang ordered his troops to open fire and the platoon engaged a Japanese patrol, initiating a two-hour fighting retreat to the warehouse.

The 3rd Company, the Machine Gun Company and the 3rd Platoon of the 1st Company finally reached Sihang around 0900 h and Yang Ruifu angrily enquired into their late arrival. The men explained that they had retreated with the other battalions from the regiment as originally ordered until staff from the regimental headquarters informed them of their new mission.[31]

Xie Jinyuan and Yang studied the terrain and deployed the battalion, placing the 1st Company on the east facing Tibet Road, the 3rd Company on the west opposite the Bank of Communications and the 2nd Company on the northern and southern sides. In addition, they positioned two Type 24 Maxim heavy machine guns on the roof in an anti-aircraft role and distributed the other machine guns among the 1st and 3rd Companies. As the men made their final preparations, some took up defensive positions along the outer wall surrounding the building and others watched for enemy movement through the slots from inside the warehouse.

The first Japanese troops reached Sihang at 1300 h — a column proudly marching with a Rising Sun flag. As these troops came within effective range, Chinese officers ordered their men to open fire. 'Those aggressive enemies,' Yang Ruifu observed, 'were given head-on blows by the defence force on the periphery of our position. Four or five people were shot dead and the rest all fled.'[32] The Japanese tightened their grip around the warehouse by occupying the adjacent Bank of Communications, but their troops that entered abandoned fortifications walked into a trap as Chinese soldiers had rigged a bunker with grenades and a mortar round. 'As I had expected,' Yang recalled, 'four or five devils got in not long after. Our garrison soldiers pulled the grenade rope, which made a few bangs and caused heavy casualties to the enemy.'[33]

The soldiers inside Sihang Warehouse continued to develop their

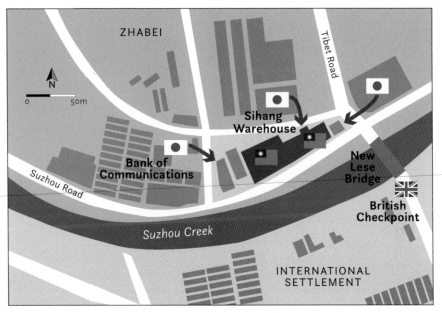

Japanese attacks against Sihang Warehouse.

defences by sealing all doors and windows as well as placing tall bundles of sacks at the south wall and northern doorways to block entry points. The defenders also made dummy positions on the perimeter outside the warehouse to draw Japanese fire and waste their ammunition. Chinese sentries watched for signs of enemy movement while soldiers on the fifth floor carefully observed the Bank of Communications from a higher vantage point as they suspected Japanese officers would use the building as a command post to plan their attacks against the warehouse.

In the early afternoon the Japanese launched their first assault on Sihang as a company attacked the western side of the warehouse. A full-strength Japanese company consisted of 194 soldiers supported by light and heavy machine guns, grenade launchers and two Type 41 mountain guns.[34] However, after the attrition experienced since the 'Lucky Division' landed at Wusong two months previously, the company was far from full strength and its men were exhausted. By this time reporters in the International Settlement had become drawn to the fighting, as a Chinese journalist observed:

Japanese soldiers assaulting Sihang Warehouse. (Author's Collection)

> It was noticed that three enemies, each holding two Chinese civilians
> in their hands, were strutting through the nearby Wuzhen Bridge. All of
> a sudden, the two enemies in the front were shot dead by one of our
> soldiers appearing from nowhere, while the remaining one, dashing
> with a gun towards our soldier, was also killed in an instant after being
> stopped by the brave civilians he pushed away. Moreover, an enemy
> lurking in a tall building was shot down by a precise bullet from another
> building before attempting to shoot our passing soldiers.[35]

Captain Shi Meihao and his troops from the 3rd Company defended
Sihang from charging Japanese troops. Xie remained in the warehouse
to oversee the construction of fortifications while his executive officer
Shangguan Zhibiao directed the soldiers outside the warehouse who were
resisting the enemy attacks. At 1430 h a group of around 50 Japanese
soldiers forced the defenders at the outer wall to retreat inside the
warehouse, as Shangguan witnessed:

> Eventually, our outpost troops that were outnumbered were ordered to

retreat back into the warehouse after realizing the purposes of whittling down enemies at the minimum cost and buying sufficient time. Enemies following behind were finally repelled by us after we swiftly blocked the gate of the warehouse.[36]

Yang Ruifu meanwhile fought the Japanese from inside the warehouse:

Although the enemy's fierce attack was not interrupted for a moment, fortunately, our brothers took turns to fight in resistance. They fought hard and fiercely, which was worth commending. We lay on the ground, wiping the dust from our faces and eyes, while fighting back at the enemy. At this time, I personally led the 3rd Company's bloody battle with the enemy.[37]

At 1500 h Captain Shi Meihao was shot in the face, but he covered his wound with a towel and refused to relinquish command. Shortly afterwards a machine-gun bullet hit his leg. Yang removed him from the battle and Captain Tang Di took command of the 3rd Company.

After failing to storm Sihang, the Japanese set fire to the north-west section of the warehouse where fuel and wood was stored. 'In an instant,' Chen Desong witnessed, 'thick plumes of smoke billowed as if the entire building was blazing. All soldiers of the regiment embarked on extinguishing the fire with hydrants and meanwhile blocking enemies.'[38] The Chinese later extinguished the flames in the early evening.

During the fighting observers inside the International Settlement noticed a small group of around 70 Japanese soldiers slowly crawling towards the warehouse through rubble and it took them almost an hour to move 45 metres.[39] These Japanese believed they could not be seen from the warehouse, but defenders on the upper levels spotted them and Yang Ruifu had an idea:

It suddenly occurred to me that we could throw grenades from upstairs, so I ordered platoon leader Yin to lead ten soldiers to the top of the building to drop grenades. At this time, there were as many as 70 or 80 enemy soldiers gathered under the foot of the south-west wall like

Sihang Warehouse seen from the International Settlement during the fighting with battle damage visible on the building's west wall. (Author's Collection)

hedgehog quills. Two mortar shells and a few grenades were immediately dropped. Seven enemy soldiers were killed and 20 or 30 injured.[40]

The grenades halted the attack and the Japanese withdrew. A Chinese journalist witnessed Chinese machine-gun fire and grenades kill around 60 Japanese soldiers: 'The correspondent found such heroic scenes moving and startling.'[41] Yang realized that the actions of his men had been noticed in the Settlement and he heard Chinese civilians shouting with joy after the Japanese retreated. After sunset the Chinese defenders observed dogs dragging away Japanese corpses. Yang forbade the men from sleeping that night and ordered all troops not on sentry duty to build fortifications as the flames from burning buildings in the distance illuminated the night sky.

THURSDAY — THE FIGHTING INTENSIFIES

At 0700 h on 28 October, Japanese bombers circled Sihang and the two Chinese anti-aircraft machine guns kept them at bay. The planes did not attack the warehouse as the close proximity to the International Settlement likely convinced the pilots not to return fire. By this time the additional fortifications constructed during the night, particularly at the main gate, were well-established. One hour later Yang Ruifu gave a speech to all officers and squad leaders to explain why they were defending Sihang as there had been insufficient time beforehand to emphasize the importance of their mission, and he noted that the men 'were very excited and vowed to fight the Japanese enemy to the finish'.[42]

Yang visited each company later that morning to talk to the wounded and afterwards he accompanied Xie Jinyuan to the roof where they witnessed the burning ruins of Zhabei as thick black smoke obscured their view. As machine guns strafed the warehouse, they noticed a group of Japanese troops walking on Suzhou North Road. Xie grabbed a rifle from a sentry and took careful aim before squeezing the trigger and the single bullet hit a Japanese soldier who fell to the ground. Yang remarked to Xie, 'You proved yourself to be a first-class shooter.'[43] Xie returned to battalion headquarters while Yang inspected the companies:

> I saw soldiers wearing short clothes, as if crawling out of the soil. Although they were sweaty all over, their courage and spirit were still very good, even though they had not slept for two days and two nights, or had one good meal. When I saw this kind of industrious and persevering spirit, I felt more certain to be able to resist for a long time.[44]

At midday Xie addressed the men during an inspection of the warehouse, patting them on their shoulders and asking if they were hungry.

At 1500 h the Japanese launched their second major attack on Sihang after rain had extinguished the flames around the warehouse. Yang Ruifu witnessed the assault:

> I saw the enemy bandits in the northwest of Sihang Warehouse, moving four or five flat-firing cannons in a concealed manner, and placing them towards us. I ordered the machine guns to shoot at the enemy to stop them, and the enemy bandits' machine guns on the roof of the Bank of Communications also immediately returned fire. Thus, we started the second bloody battle with the enemy.[45]

The Japanese fire was fiercer than the previous day and, as bullets struck the building and smoke hindered vision, Yang ordered all soldiers to stop working on fortifications and to fight the enemy onslaught. Xie commanded the defence on the eastern side of the warehouse while Yang directed the fighting at the western side in the 3rd Company's position where Chinese and Japanese troops were locked in a deadly stalemate.[46]

A crowd of around 30,000 Chinese and foreigners watched the battle from across Suzhou Creek and any success the defenders experienced resulted in loud cheers from the masses.[47] Chinese citizens also held up large signs with messages indicating Japanese troop movements, as Chen Desong explained:

> Thousands of people watching the battle on the top of buildings constructed on the south bank of the Suzhou Creek waved their caps and towels and shouted towards us to send their greetings. They also informed us of enemy assembly locations and their operations through words written on blackboards.[48]

A reporter from the *North China Daily News* observed the action:

> The Japanese riddled several window panes of one of the godown [warehouses] with machine-guns — to which the defenders made no reply. As they attempted to come nearer to the building, several hand grenades were thrown at them.[49]

Another western journalist reported the drama:

> Despite a shower of machine gun bullets which spattered the settlement pavements, crowds of Chinese and foreigners gathered on the rooftops of nearby buildings to see the battle to the end in the heart of a modern city.[50]

The fighting lasted two hours and the Chinese defence became more desperate than the previous day, but the Japanese eventually withdrew around 1700 h. The Japanese had one success after cutting off the warehouse's electricity and water supply, causing Yang Ruifu to order rationing. He also ordered soldiers to guard the drinking water supply and from now on all urine would be kept and used to fight fires.

After sunset crowds gathered on the south bank to support the defenders who were heavily fatigued from the recent fighting. Yang Ruifu used the relative calm of night to formally introduce the men to Xie Jinyuan, who had only been their commander for two days, before again stressing the importance of their mission:

> Due to time constraints, I did not have the opportunity to clearly inform everyone in advance why our battalion stayed in Zhabei this time. Now everyone has fully understood. I hope all patriotic men here hold their determination to die, and die together with deputy commander Xie and me the battalion commander! You can write a very simple letter to notify your family. After you finish writing, collect them to be sent to the post office in the future. This is to demonstrate everyone's determination to sacrifice.[51]

Chinese civilians inside the Settlement had meanwhile organized a collection of food, clothing, medicine and other supplies for the battalion through the Shanghai Chamber of Commerce.[52] Yu Hongjun, the Mayor of Shanghai, explained during a press conference that his officials received numerous messages from Chinese and foreigner citizens asking for the battalion to be allowed to withdraw. As the conference continued a request arrived from Sihang: 'Send us 500lb of flour, 500lb of salt, 50,000 bean cakes,' before adding that 'we will hold out for a week.'[53] After a reporter asked Mayor Yu how the Chinese would get the supplies to the warehouse, he replied, 'Never you mind. I will find a way.'[54]

Volunteers from the All-Shanghai Federation for the Support of Armed Resistance drove ten truckloads of supplies across New Lese Bridge that night under the cover of darkness and unloaded them in a building next to the warehouse where the defenders could collect the goods. Yang Ruifu inspected the supplies which included fruit, bread and cigarettes and he established a rationing system to ensure all men received their fair share. He also noted that newspapers and letters arrived, which the men read with interest and emotion.

During the night Yang located a telephone and established communications with the outside world. He arranged for the wounded to be evacuated across the bridge to hospitals inside the Settlement and ten severely injured Chinese soldiers were evacuated to the British Concession under an arrangement made with the Royal Welsh Fusiliers.[55] British soldiers on the southern bank aimed their rifles at any approaching Japanese troops to discourage them from interfering with the evacuation.[56] Before the medics took the wounded away, Yang instructed them:

> . . . when you get outside, remember that the number of our soldiers defending Sihang Warehouse, whoever asks, should be asserted as eight hundred instead of one battalion's soldiers, lest enemies ascertain our understrength predicament and attack us more furiously.[57]

Yang's ruse succeeded and Shanghai newspapers soon announced that 800 soldiers defended the warehouse, instigating the legend of 'Eight Hundred Heroes'.[58] In perhaps the first transmission of the growing mythology, a cable from the Central News Agency announced:

> When checking the opposite side from the south bank of Suzhou Creek . . . the staff correspondent witnessed a startling scene amidst scattered gunshots from all directions. It turned out that 800 strong fighters from the 1st Battalion, the 524th Regiment, the 88th Division, led by the Regimental Commander Xie Jinyuan along with the Battalion Commander Yang Ruifu, was combating with enemies with their last drop of blood and last bullet, engaging in a heroic, intense battle that would remain immortal in history.[59]

By this time the battle had grabbed the attention of media across the world. In America *The New York Times* reported 'a Chinese dare-to-die detachment' had 'engaged today in a fight to the finish with Japanese'.[60] In Britain, *The Guardian* announced that 'the doomed Chinese battalion . . . is still holding out' before adding that the Royal Welsh Fusiliers had posted letters Chinese soldiers had written to their families and loved ones.[61] In Australia, *The Sydney Morning Herald* similarly declared, 'One battalion of Chinese remains in Chapei [Zhabei]. They have converted a warehouse into a fortress and have sworn to die rather than surrender.'[62]

Most Chinese accounts claim that two western military officers entered the warehouse that night and made Xie Jinyuan an offer: 'If you are willing to put down your weapons and come to our concession, we can guarantee your safety and we can also send you back to your unit.'[63] However, Anglo-American officers would not likely have made such an offer as allowing Chinese soldiers to rejoin the war would have given the Japanese a pretext to intervene inside the British and American concessions.[64] The _North China Daily News_ reported that western military officers and the Shanghai Municipal Council had unsuccessfully tried five times to persuade Xie to accept internment within the Settlement.[65] _The New York Times_ similarly announced that the Chinese 'refused the offer of a British messenger, who had braved machine-gun fire to reach them, to permit the Chinese detachment to enter the International Settlement on condition that they lay down their arms.'[66] A Chinese newspaper even backed up these accounts: 'British soldiers in the concession of Tibet Road, sympathizing with them in danger of being besieged, requested them to disarm and pass via the concession. Our soldiers, however, resolutely declined such offer.'[67]

During the night Yang Ruifu inspected the platoons repairing the defences and kicked any soldier he found sleeping. 'Will you choose to be asleep or alive?' he asked. 'From now on, anyone that sleeps in disregard of my order will suffer severe punishment with zero tolerance.'[68] As the men continued strengthening their defences, another visitor arrived at Sihang Warehouse, the Girl Guide Yang Huimin who would soon become an integral part of the legend of the Eight Hundred Heroes.

CHAPTER FOUR
ARRIVAL OF THE FLAG

GIRL GUIDE NUMBER 41

The Chinese Boy Scout movement began in 1912 at schools and universities under the sponsorship of Christian missionaries. A Chinese student, Zhang Zhaonan, later became acquainted with the Girl Guide movement in England and, after returning to China in 1919, she founded a Girl Guide troop in Shanghai.[1] The Boy Scout and Girl Guide movements encouraged patriotism in early Republican China and members of both organizations guarded the interment ceremony during the burial of Sun Yat-sen in Nanjing.[2] As the *Kuomintang* consolidated power, the new government brought these youth movements under its control and perceived the Boy Scouts as a precursor to military training. The Girl Guides encouraged women to have more freedom compared to traditional society, increasing its popularity, and Soong Mei-ling, the wife of Chiang Kai-shek, patronised the movement and often inspected troops and awarded ribbons. After the commencement of hostilities in Shanghai in 1937, Boy Scouts and Girl Guides performed civil defence duties and around 3000 of them served in the city during the battle.[3] As part of the Wartime Service Corps, they maintained order in refugee camps and helped wounded soldiers.

Yang Huimin from Jiangsu Province, born on 6 March 1915, had studied at Sun Yat-sen University before joining the Shanghai Wartime Service Scouts. The 22-year-old, also known as 'Girl Guide Number 41', became swept up in the monumental events taking place in the city:

> By early August, enemies' gunfire had approached Shanghai. At that time,
> not much time had lapsed since I graduated from my senior high school.
> I was working in the Meidi Candy Company, which had suspended. I,
> together with many other patriotic youths, committed to the cause of
> safeguarding our homeland, joined the field service group of Shanghai
> Girl Guides. The over three-month defence eventually failed to prevent
> Shanghai from being occupied. Members of the service group either
> retreated along with our troops or entered the concession with refugees.
> In the Shanghai International Settlement, there was a nunnery beside
> the Suzhou Creek accommodating more than one thousand refugees, for
> whom I together with the other seven Boy Scouts and Girl Guides under
> my leadership tried to provide assistance.[4]

As news of Sihang Warehouse spread through the city, Yang learned
about the Eight Hundred Heroes still fighting in Zhabei. 'We were thrilled
because they marooned themselves deliberately to hold strategic ground,'
she recalled. 'I guess I was just too curious.'[5] On the night of 27 October
1937, she approached the sound of fighting before being challenged by a
British soldier at New Lese Bridge:

> In the dim star light, a big and tall British soldier stood on the other
> side of the barbed wire. He asked me in his stiff Chinese, 'Who are
> you?' Instead of answering him, I raised three fingers to salute him. He
> shouted in English, 'Boy Scout'. I told him that I wanted to investigate
> the source of the gunshot. He saw that I spoke with a relaxed and
> careless attitude, plus I was wearing the Boy Scout uniform but talked
> in a sissy manner, and he could not find any appropriate Chinese words
> to question me, and therefore had to just follow me. We . . . entered the
> British guard pillbox at the end of the bridge. Through the embrasure
> was clearly seen Sihang Warehouse which was only a street away.[6]

The following day Yang noticed the Japanese flags in Zhabei and became
troubled by the absence of a Chinese flag: 'I felt a haunting urge to help

The Girl Guide Yang Huimin in her uniform. (Author's Collection)

An American bubble gum card illustration depicting Yang Huimin bringing the Republic of China flag to Sihang Warehouse. (Author's Collection)

hoist a Blue Sky with a White Sun, our national flag, on the roof of Sihang Warehouse, to lift the morale of Shanghai citizens and highlight our national august righteousness.'[7] She reported her observations to the Shanghai Chamber of Commerce and its leaders gave her a large Republic of China flag to deliver to the defenders.[8] After returning home in the evening, Yang removed her uniform and wrapped the flag around her body before putting the uniform back on.

Yang returned to the British bunker and sneaked across New Lese Bridge under the cover of darkness. 'I ran like everything across the bridge which everybody in the world it seemed like was shooting at,' she recalled. 'A bullet went through my scout cap but I cannot be afraid because I had volunteered and it became my duty not to be afraid but I ran fast.'[9] After reaching the northern bank, Yang continued forward:

I lay on the ground and crawled across the road. My beating heart had just settled down when gunfire suddenly broke out loudly. I thought I was spotted by the enemy or the guards, so I hid in the fortification on the road side and did not dare move. Overhead were sparkled burning flares which appeared red and green in colour. It was actually the enemy who were attacking Sihang Warehouse again.[10]

After the gunfire died down, Yang slowly crawled forward while taking cover behind sandbags as Japanese bullets could be heard landing nearby. She ran towards the warehouse and waited in a trench for the fighting to die down and after reaching the building, she climbed a rope lowered by soldiers and entered through a window. 'When the heroes saw me arrive,' Yang remembered, 'they were full of smiles as they spoke freely with me about the cowardice of the Japanese troops.'[11]

The news of Yang Huimin's arrival spread through the warehouse, and she delivered the flag to Xie Jinyuan and the men:

I took off my jacket and solemnly presented the sweat-drenched national flag to them. In the dim light, the heroes who defended their country were all moved to tears! Regiment commander Xie said, 'Brave comrades, what you presented to us was not only a sacred national flag, but also the Chinese nation's unyielding spirit!'[12]

The soldiers gave her messages written in Chinese calligraphy on handkerchiefs which would later remind her of their courage.[13] Major Yang Ruifu, the battalion commander, realizing that the battalion did not have a flagpole, ordered his men to make one and they did so using bamboo poles and rope.

FRIDAY — THE DAY OF THE FLAG

On the morning of 29 October, a small group of Chinese soldiers raised the flag on the roof of Sihang Warehouse during a brief ceremony while dawn broke, as Yang Ruifu remembered:

Around six a.m., I appointed the orderlies and buglers led by the probational officer to hoist the national flag presented by Miss Yang last

The Republic of China flag provided by Yang Huimin flies over Sihang Warehouse as a beacon of hope. (Author's Collection)

night on the roof of Sihang Warehouse amidst salutes and the sound of a clarion. Our national flag featuring Blue Sky and White Sun flies high in the sky of Zhabei District, instantly leaving many surrounding [Rising] Sun Flags eclipsed.[14]

Xie gave a brief speech: 'My fellows, as long as we survive, we will permit no damage to our flag. We would rather die than surrender. We will relentlessly eliminate enemies.'[15] Yang Huimin also witnessed the event:

At that moment, the first whitish rays had appeared in the east. In the faint early dawn light, ten or twenty people stood on the platform, raising their hands solemnly to salute the national flag. There was neither music, nor splendid display, only a cold shot or two. However, the solemn and respectful atmosphere, and the pure, sad and heroic scene, were deeply moving. I will never forget it in my life.[16]

Although Yang Huimin offered to stay to help care for the wounded, Xie declined and instructed her to leave the warehouse immediately: 'Race across the road and jump into the river!'[17] Major Shangguan Zhibiao, the executive officer, recalled her courage: 'We admired her aspiration, but a girl was not able to do much in a fierce battle and there were many inconveniences. Therefore, we asked her to return to the concession.'[18] Yang departed the warehouse and jumped into Suzhou Creek before swimming back to the International Settlement. 'I looked up and saw that Suzhou Riverside was full of people,' she recalled. 'One after another, they waved and cheered at the beautiful national flag that was fluttering in the morning sunshine on the roof of Sihang Warehouse!'[19]

A Chinese crowd in the International Settlement watched the lone flag standing out among countless Rising Suns and shouted, 'Long Live the

The Republic of China flag provided by Yang Huimin flies over Sihang Warehouse seen from the British Concession of the International Settlement across Suzhou Creek. Note the sandbags of the British Army positions facing the building.

(Image courtesy of Special Collections, University of Bristol Library: www.hpcbristol.net)

Chinese Republic!'[20] Shangguan Zhibiao noticed Chinese and foreigners applauding as the flag 'fluttered in the wind and looked particularly dazzling' while the 'enemy was shocked and suffered a psychological blow'.[21] The American reporter Keane Arundel observed the event and immediately drew a parallel to the Alamo, as the mythology intensified:

> A lone Chinese flag fluttered in the smoky dawn today high over shell-torn Chapei [Zhabei], heart of China's ruined metropolis, as proof that a 'doomed battalion' of Chinese soldiers was still there in the roaring hell of bombs, bullets and shrapnel. All China, figuratively, watched that flag. It has become a symbol of China's heroic resolution to accept annihilation rather than Japanese conquest. To Shanghai's Americans it recalled Texas' historic Alamo, where Americans died in 1836 rather than yield to Mexico.[22]

In the morning Xie Jinyuan wrote a letter to General Sun Yuanliang, commander of the 88th Division, who received it later that day:

> I resolve to sacrifice my life and fight without any imprudence and neglect strictly in compliance with the supreme order until all the task is completed. I have made up my mind to win or to die. Three days and nights of effort have reinforced the fortifications as solid as expected, which will frustrate any enemy attacks.
>
> On 27 October enemies waged another assault but suffered over eighty fatalities according to the report of our sentries.
>
> Around 6 a.m. yesterday (28 October), I myself sniped at enemies and killed one, at the sight of which our compatriots at the south bank of Suzhou Creek all applauded and cheered. I am determined to die heroically when completing the task. Everything will be handled fine. Please be reassured!
>
> Sincerely yours,
> Xie Jinyuan[23]

Sun Yuanliang replied with his own letter the same day:

> Deputy Regimental Commander Xie, Deputy Regimental Commander Shangguan, Battalion Commander Yang, and each of our allegiant and brave soldiers,
>
> Though recently I have been staying in the front of western Shanghai, my mind and soul are closely connected with each of you garrisoning Zhabei District. I am ordered to defend the axis of the battlefield in Zhabei District and safeguard our territory, while each of you fights courageously and hold on for two and a half months during which enemies have never realized their attempt to transgress the bounds. You repay our country in such deeds and perform exceedingly well.
>
> Nevertheless, all fronts recently moved westward, given the whole situation affected by the partial change. Our army is also ordered to move the camp, while the onus of defending the last battlefield of Zhabei District is on you, my loyal and brave soldiers.
>
> Each of you indomitably defends your positions in compliance with

the order and swear to share the same fate with Zhabei, remaining tenacious and taking responsibility at the critical juncture, the spirit of which everyone in our army revere tremendously.

Warriors resolutely sacrificing their lives for a righteous cause are never scarce in the Chinese nation. Yue Fei's army remained steadfast, and the army led by Qi Jiguang courageously resisted enemies and dedicated their lives to our country, leaving their noble spirit immortal.

Bearing our Generalissimo's teachings in mind, our National Revolutionary Army that is endowed with such virtues has no hesitation in sacrificing their lives and have long been determined to die for our country.

The results attained in this battle are truly extraordinary feats in history, which is a glorious page that will be respectfully and earnestly perused by billions of Chinese descendants and millions of future generations worldwide.

Your three days and nights of defence has made our soldiers' bravery, and enemies' flinch plain for the world to see, and earned commendation and admiration from both Chinese and foreigners in Shanghai. The populace goes around providing support and hoping to 'keep a soldier alive at the cost of hundreds of their own lives', which is indeed the honour of the Chinese nation, the honour of the Republic of China, and the honour of each soldier in the National Revolutionary Army.

You are expected to continue fighting to complete your task of resisting enemies to the last drop of your blood.

Our Generalissimo sends extremely high praise and deep condolences to the heroically sacrificed comrades, which I respectfully relay to you.

By Sun Yuanliang in western Shanghai on 29 October[24]

The Japanese 3rd 'Lucky' Division, led by General Susumu Fujita, humiliated by the defiant flag, planned an all-out assault to capture the warehouse that day. At 0700 h Yang Ruifu noticed that 'enemies, at the sight of our national flag flying high on the top of the building, becomes more exasperated, furiously shooting us through windows of the Bank of Communications'.[25] Japanese planes also harassed their position, as Yang continued:

Meanwhile, numerous enemy aircraft hover overhead all day,
attempting to bomb our field, whereas our air defence forces on the
roof heighten their vigilance, taking aiming at and shooting them
with anti-aircraft machine guns as long as they lower their altitude a
little. In consequence, enemy aircrafts are repelled four or five times
successively, and havoc is ultimately forestalled.[26]

At midday Japanese light tanks, most likely Type 94 Te-Ke tankettes, joined
the siege in support of the infantry.[27] Yang Ruifu noticed the enemy's
tightening grip around the fortress as 'four or five enemy tanks balk at every
major traffic intersection along Guoqing Road on the north of the Suzhou
Creek and northern areas of Sihang Warehouse, threatening and intending
to cover their infantry besieging'.[28]

In the afternoon, the defenders received a warning over the telephone
that patriotic Chinese had spotted hundreds of Japanese soldiers converging
on their position who intended to attack at 1400 h.[29] Shortly afterwards the
Royal Welsh Fusiliers guarding New Lese Bridge provided another warning
as the 'final enemy assault looms ahead'.[30]

At 1400 h Japanese soldiers attacked Sihang supported by intense
machine-gun fire and, as Chinese soldiers resisted from their excellent
defensive positions, shells pounded the warehouse for over an hour and
the air smelled of cordite and dust.[31] However, the defenders repulsed the
enemy infantry but continued assaults forced the 3rd Company, guarding
the perimeter, back into the warehouse. Japanese troops rushed forward and
attempted to climb inside using ladders like a medieval siege, but Chinese
defenders pushed them over and returned fire with rifles and machine
guns.[32] As Chinese crowds watched the action from across Suzhou Creek,
the journalist Keane Arundel observed that 'Chinese guns blazed defiantly
at Japanese who surrounded the building on three sides'.[33] A reporter from
the *North China Daily News* also watched the battle:

Rifle-grenades and rifle bullets had peppered the massive grey godown
[warehouse] since early in the day, but shortly after 3 p.m. the Japanese
attack became more vigorous although apparently the continued
shooting had little effect. Japanese during the afternoon improved

Japanese soldiers attacking Sihang Warehouse in a manner resembling a medieval siege. (Author's Collection)

on their machine-gun emplacement in North Suzhou Road by adding sandbags and sheets of steel and corrugated iron. They also moved two additional machine-guns into position on the west wall of the tall godown. The Chinese replied from perilous posts in the upper windows of the building, facing the Creek. Late in the afternoon the Japanese used rifle-grenades, apparently without effect. One 'do-or-die' member of the Japanese attacking force came out into the open at about 4 p.m. and fired a number of rifle shots at the corner of the godown, causing Chinese heads to withdraw with lightning speed.[34]

A Japanese field gun shelled the warehouse while Chinese soldiers on the roof opened fire with their rifles. Another journalist who witnessed the drama observed the bravery of the Chinese but considered their position hopeless:

While hundreds of spectators, including women with tears running down their cheeks, are looking on from the International Settlement,

Two Japanese soldiers climb a ladder during their assault on Sihang Warehouse. (Author's Collection)

the Japanese are launching violent assaults against the 'lost battalion' of Chinese . . . Spectators saw the Japanese assault the position again and again, only to be met with showers of hand grenades and withering machine-gun fire. The Japanese tried to dynamite the warehouse, but failed. They have now brought up three-inch guns to fire at point-blank range, so that this is likely to be the 'Suicide Legion's' last day.[35]

According to some Chinese sources, as the Japanese seemed to be on the verge of victory, the Chinese soldier Chen Shusheng wrapped grenades around his body and jumped from the warehouse into a group of enemy soldiers and died in the explosion along with twenty Japanese troops.[36] Desperate Chinese suicide attacks had earlier taken place during the Battle of Shanghai; therefore, the truth of this story is plausible. For example, Xiong Xinmin, an officer from the 36th Division, saw a Chinese soldier with several grenades run towards a Japanese tank which the man successfully destroyed at the cost of his life.[37]

Although the attack continued, Japanese troops made no progress and suffered heavy casualties. Some Chinese soldiers with restored morale balanced their helmets inside window frames using bamboo poles to draw enemy fire, which resulted in much macabre laughter from inside the warehouse.[38]

As the fighting for the warehouse raged, Japanese marines on two naval pinnaces proceeded along Suzhou Creek hoping to attack the warehouse but were stopped by an improvised boom consisting of Chinese junks at the Zhejiang Road Bridge.[39] The Japanese sailors announced to the British soldiers on the bridge that they were on their way to help the Shanghai Fire Brigade extinguish fires in Zhabei. The British troops replied that their continued voyage would violate the British Defence Sector and refused to move the boom.[40] The British Military Headquarters meanwhile asked Japanese authorities to withdraw the boats.[41] In the afternoon, the Japanese sailors agreed to withdraw and a platoon of Royal Welsh Fusiliers escorted the gunboats back to the Huangpu River.

The British became increasingly hostile to the Japanese that day after four soldiers from the Royal Ulster Rifles — Mallon Howard, Jack McGuire, Robert Delaney and Joseph O'Toole — were killed by Japanese shells falling in the International Settlement. Reporters observed that British soldiers expressed pro-Chinese sympathies and one journalist noted that 'British soldiers in the vicinity of the warehouse are sharing their rations with the besieged garrison'.[42]

After sunset, Japanese gunfire died down, only to later resume its original intensity as their troops launched a night attack, as Yang Ruifu recalled:

> Enemies attempt to approach our battlefield by taking advantage of the darkness, preparing on the northwestern side to dig a tunnel with excavators to bomb the walls of Sihang Warehouse and to crash through the gate with tanks. Fortunately, such a malicious scheme is detected by our observation post.[43]

After this assault, Xie Jinyuan ordered Yang improve the defences and he explained the new procedures:

> I. Firing signal flares towards nearby enemies and shooting any exposed enemy with light and heavy machine guns.
> II. When enemies approach Sihang Warehouse, a large-size flashlight tied on a bamboo pole will be stretched out of the window by a soldier to serve as a searchlight, while his partner will observe through another window shrouded in darkness, throwing grenades at any approaching enemy detected.
> III. Making thick cotton wicks, soaking them in kerosene, and lighting before throwing onto the ground.[44]

British and American officers meanwhile continued their attempts to persuade the Chinese to leave the warehouse and accept internment. 'I offered to allow them sanctuary in the settlement, provided that they laid down their arms,' declared Major Harrison of the Royal Welsh Fusiliers. 'They replied that they preferred to die.'[45] Brigadier General John Beaumont, commander of the United States Marines, also offered them sanctuary, but a Chinese soldier replied, 'Let the Japanese try to escort us to safety.'[46] Major-General Alexander Telfer-Smollett, commander of British forces, made a similar appeal through a Shanghai Municipal policeman who crossed Suzhou Creek and reached the warehouse, but Xie Jinyuan announced, 'We came here to die and we are going to stay. We have decided not to join the retreat.'[47] After receiving another appeal to retreat, Xie declared, 'We stand to the last. Only if Marshal Chiang Kai-shek orders us to do so will we leave.'[48]

By this time Chiang had received hundreds of telegrams urging him to save the battalion and Anglo-American commanders pleaded with him to not sacrifice his troops. These appeals, as the *North China Daily News* concluded, 'illustrate the city-wide concern and sympathy for the gallant defenders. Tributes to the heroism of the men were forthcoming from practically all circles.'[49] The League of Chinese Women asked Chiang's wife Soong Mei-ling to save these 'patriotic heroes for our campaign of resistance'.[50] Soong allegedly responded, 'They must die so China may live!'[51]

The stand of the Eight Hundred at Sihang had successfully aroused Chinese nationalism. During a press conference, a *Kuomintang* military spokesman announced that the 'heroic stand' of the battalion indicated China's 'inspired unity' and constituted 'living proof that we will never surrender'.[52] Mr Y.M. Chien of the Joint Savings Society declared, 'Our godown [warehouse] is glorified by the presence of the lone battalion who are resolved to fight to the last. We will never regret even if the structure should be completely destroyed by the Japanese.'[53] The defenders inside the warehouse became increasingly resigned to dying in battle. 'Death is not an important issue,' Xie Jinyuan expressed to Sun Yuanliang, 'but we wish to inform you that before our mission is accomplished we will not make our sacrifices lightly.'[54] A foreign correspondent talked to the defenders during a lull in the fighting and a Chinese soldier told him, 'This place is our tomb.'[55]

SATURDAY — BOMBARDMENT AND INFERNO

At 0700 h on 30 October, Japanese artillery commenced a bombardment of Sihang Warehouse which lasted all day and aimed to obliterate the Chinese defenders without any further costly infantry attacks. Yang Ruifu recalled the intensity of the shelling and how the fortress absorbed the punishment:

> The gunfire is more violent than ever before. . . Three-meter thick
> sacks have been laid along walls from the first, second and third floor

of Sihang Warehouse to the roof, while each major entrance has also been reinforced in the same way. Enemies' flat trajectory artillery and machine guns become useless.[56]

Yang also observed how the Japanese shells created holes in the windowless western wall which allowed the Chinese defenders to fire at Japanese troops. A journalist from the *North China Daily News* witnessed the fighting and noted the presence of a second flag:

> [After dawn] it was noticed that another, though smaller, Chinese flag had joined the big one floating on the west wing. . . An occasional shrapnel shell burst near and just above the large national Chinese flag, which continued to float merrily, and apparently suffered no damage. Japanese machine-guns in the road and from the north peppered the walls and windows of the godown [warehouse], the Chinese inside replying with rifle-fire. An occasional soldier could be seen moving about on the roof of the godown.[57]

After three days of unsuccessful attacks, a Japanese naval officer announced at a press conference inside the International Settlement that every effort has been made to persuade the Chinese troops to surrender but 'all overtures tendered in a spirit of humanitarianism had been disregarded'.[58] As the Japanese planned the annihilation of the defenders, a military spokesman declared, 'They must be destroyed' and another officer similarly boasted, 'We will never let them escape alive.'[59]

Rear Admiral Tadao Honda, a Japanese naval attaché, declared at a press conference that the Japanese would dislodge the Chinese from the warehouse because of their 'stout, stubborn refusal to surrender'.[60] 'Our patience is exhausted,' he added. 'We have done our utmost to spare the lives of the defenders in the true Samurai spirit, but we must make a final assault now.'[61] Honda warned residents in the Settlement to take precautions against the fighting, but he also conceded that the Chinese battalion had conducted a 'more or less heroic stand'.[62] *Time* magazine, in a clear indication of where its sympathies lay, described Honda as a 'news ogre' who 'sneers'.[63]

Earlier that day Xie Jinyuan wrote a letter to Soong Mei-ling:

An American bubble gum card illustration depicting the Japanese bombardment of Sihang Warehouse. (Author's Collection)

Unless fate ordains otherwise at the last minute, we shall not have the honor of seeing your Excellency again. . . So we ask you to tell the Chinese people that we are the happiest men in all China. To us has been given the great honor and privilege of showing to the enemy the Chinese spirit toward the invasion of our beloved country. We would ask your Excellency to convey to the British forces of the International Settlement our deepest appreciation of their help and inspiration in our ordeal. We feel sure that if British soldiers were in our place they would as willingly die for their country. I am most thankful that these men have been able to prove their valor and yet live. . . Although we were harassed day and night by snipers, our casualties were small until the Japanese turned on their heavy artillery. Then as many died from wounds inflicted by ricochets as from direct hits. Dust, gases from bursting shells and the cordite fumes from our own cartridges made the atmosphere stifling. We were forced to crawl from place to place as a steady rain of bullets poured in the windows and cavities in the walls. We are most grateful for the co-operation of the British troops, who did their utmost to alleviate our suffering by supplying us with food and bandages at grave risk to their own lives. On Friday and Saturday, the walls of the warehouse were threatening to collapse under the heavy Japanese bombardment.[64]

In response, Soong Mei-ling wrote an article for the international press:

I am keeping in hourly touch by telephone with the activities of the 'Death Brigade' at Shanghai. My prayers are offered for the gallant Col. Hsieh Ching Yuan [Xie Jinyuan], the commander, and his gallant men. Their sacrifices exemplify the spirit of China today and they will go down in Chinese history as among the greatest national heroes of the war. Col. Hsieh Ching Yuan [Xie Jinyuan] states that he will not surrender unless by orders of the generalissimo. I am torn between the desire to save the lives of these brave men by persuading the generalissimo to give the necessary orders and my loyalty to China. Their sacrifice will greatly inspire our people and stiffen the morale of the country. The wives and the families of these brave men remain silent when they might be petitioning the generalissimo to stay the massacre of their husbands and their sons. However, the generalissimo knows that Col. Hsieh Ching Yuan [Xie Jinyuan] and his men do not want the order to surrender as they prefer to die for China.[65]

By this time Chiang Kai-shek had decided that the Eight Hundred were 'too valuable to spare' and that they should be saved: 'In thinking about whether the Xie Jinyuan unit in Zhabei's Sihang Warehouse should advance or retreat, live or die, I decided today [to have them] withdraw, because their objective and duty have already been fulfilled.'[66]

Zhang Boting, the 88th Division's chief-of-staff, had been maintaining communications with the Eight Hundred from Weida Hotel in the French Concession. After Zhang received Chiang's retreat order, he realized that as Sihang Warehouse was surrounded on three sides by the Japanese, the only escape route would be across New Lese Bridge. However, a breakout into the International Settlement would have to be coordinated with the British.

In the afternoon Zhang met Yu Hongjun (Mayor of Shanghai), Feng Shengfa (Deputy Commander of the 88th Division), Yang Hu (Shanghai Foreign Commissioner) and Major-General Alexander Telfer-Smollett (Commander of British Forces) in a villa on Huanlong Road inside the French Concession. Yang Hu explained Chiang Kai-shek's order and the need to obtain assistance from the British Army. Telfer-Smollet announced that his soldiers had established good relations with the troops inside Sihang Warehouse and asked how he could help. Zhang Boting replied that as the men would have to cross Suzhou Creek, they would have to pass through the British soldiers and procedures were needed as the breakout would attract the attention of Japanese searchlights and machine guns.[67] Telfer-Smollett agreed to provide assistance and the men developed evacuation procedures, discussed communication and considered how to counter Japanese machine-gun fire. Afterwards Zhang returned to Weida Hotel and telephoned Sun Yuanliang to update him on the plan.

In the afternoon, the Royal Welsh Fusiliers stopped patrolling the area around New Lese Bridge, given the intensity of the Japanese artillery fire. Staff at the British-owned Shanghai Gas Company feared a catastrophe if Japanese shells hit the storage tanks, containing an enormous quantity of gas, located less than 300 metres from the warehouse.[68] Meanwhile in the neighbouring American Concession, Brigadier-General John Beaumont ordered his Marines near the tanks, east of the British position on New Lese Bridge, to take precautions and, if necessary, withdraw from the danger area.[69] The shelling continued into the night as Japanese searchlights lit up the warehouse.[70]

Despite the conversations between the Chinese and British governments concerning the withdrawal from Sihang, Xie Jinyuan had not yet been informed of the decision to retreat. At 2100 h Zhang Boting phoned him and explained the new order, but the commander did not wish to obey:

All heroes have already made a will and vowed to defend the last
position of Sihang to death, as long as the death is meaningful! As long

as it is a worthy death! Chief of staff, please report this to the division commander, and ask the chairman to allow us to achieve this![71]

In response, Zhang and Feng Shengfa attempted to convince Xie and Shangguan Zhibiao to withdraw, without success. In the end Zhang had to firmly order Xie to obey Chiang's instruction:

> Your determination to die for a just cause is certainly admired, but this is the order of the Supreme Commander. I am only conveying the order and it is the bounden duty of soldiers to obey orders. This is not the only opportunity to fight the Japanese devil. In the future, there may be an even more important mission for you than defending Sihang Warehouse! If you disobey the order, then your bravery and sacrifice will become mere physical courage and meaningless![72]

Xie discussed the order with his officers. 'Upon receipt of the order,' Yang Ruifu recalled, 'we gathered for a conference. Realizing that the main duty of a soldier is to obey we could not but act as ordered by the high authorities.'[73] After Xie accepted the order, Zhang explained the breakout procedures he had arranged with the British and the operation would start at midnight the following night. Zhang's account of the conversation included a claim that British soldiers would suppress the Japanese machine guns and that they would later allow the Chinese soldiers to rejoin their division.[74]

Xie did not immediately inform his soldiers about the breakout, fearing they might revolt if ordered to leave the warehouse.[75] However, after learning the news their minds turned away from thoughts of martyrdom and focused on survival and reaching safety inside the International Settlement. Nevertheless the men experienced guilt, as Shangguan Zhibiao explained:

> Every single person had regrets in their heart, because we were already mentally prepared to fight to the end. In just three days, we established an invisible relationship with the warehouse. We felt that we had not fulfilled our aspiration to kill the enemy, and we were unreconciled.[76]

After sunset the Japanese bombarded Sihang Warehouse with greater intensity than during the day. Four Japanese 75-mm guns fired a steady rain of shells presumably in an attempt to smash a hole in the northern side of the structure to allow their soldiers to charge inside.[77] Yang Ruifu watched the bombardment:

> Their gunfire intensifies around ten p.m. About one hour later, Sihang Warehouse comes under heavy bombardment from flat trajectory artillery and mortars. The most intense bombing is at a frequency of one round per second, and roars sweep through the silent night.[78]

As the Japanese shells were being fired in a southerly direction, some rounds missed the Sihang Warehouse and went over Suzhou Creek and landed inside the Settlement. A few projectiles hit the *North China Daily News* building, injuring three Chinese civilians, and flames could be seen coming from the warehouse as the Eight Hundred awaited their final day in the fortress.[79]

CHAPTER FIVE
BREAKOUT AND AFTERMATH

SUNDAY — THE LAST DAY

On the morning of 31 October, soldiers of the 3rd 'Lucky' Division, commanded by General Susumu Fujita, continued their siege of Sihang Warehouse and Japanese artillery shelled the building. A journalist from the *North China Daily News* witnessed the onslaught:

> Although sporadic machine-gun and rifle duels throughout the day seemed to show that the Chinese soldiers within the building were almost a match for the Japanese outside, the first few shells fired from a battery to the north-west of the godown [warehouse] not only turned the tide, but almost made it a flood. The issue was a foregone one, the only question being, how long?[1]

The bombardment endangered the foreign concessions and around twenty 75-mm projectiles hit in the International Settlement and Huangpu River, including one round that landed 6 metres from the cruiser USS *Augusta*.[2]

As the British expected the Chinese to break out into the Settlement, the Municipal Police drove ten trucks close to New Lese Bridge on standby to transport any survivors into internment. The Eight Hundred meanwhile prepared to escape. A platoon from the 1st Company with a heavy machine gun led by Platoon Commander Yang Deyu would cover the retreat and the wounded would be sent across the bridge first. The Machine Gun Company and a part of the 1st Company would retreat in small groups under Xie Jinyuan's direction. The 2nd and 3rd Companies would next cross the bridge under the command of the battalion commander Major Yang Ruifu. As the men waited, the Japanese bombardment continued and a reporter from the *North China Daily News* watched the spectacle:

> The terrific concussion of 4-inch shells fired at almost point blank range into concrete walls, the sharp crack of rifles, the dull thud and momentary flash of hand-grenades, the awe-inspiring sudden flash of steel projectiles tearing their deadly way through the building, the staccato chatter of heavy machine-guns, the 'dot-dot-dot' of tracer bullets, and finally the blood-red glow of fire in an upper storey.[3]

At midnight the Chinese breakout commenced, as Yang Ruifu recalled:

> Around twelve o'clock in the evening, our troops commenced retreating into British concession as requested by orders. However, Tibet Road, for which no alternative route is available, is subject to a tight blockade with a floodlight and four machine guns since our attempt has been exposed to enemies. Despite the concentrated firepower and hails of bullets, our tenacious soldiers still struggle to suppress the fire and manage to rush out courageously during the slight interval of enemies ceasing fire.[4]

Over the next four hours the men raced across the bridge in small groups to safety under the cover of darkness. Japanese shells pounded the western wall and Chinese defenders inside the warehouse fired at Japanese troops until 0200 h, as a journalist from the *North China Daily News* observed:

> From the seven 'rifle ports' made in the west wall by the Chinese soldiers, shots were exchanged with Japanese soldiers on the roof-top of a low, two-storey red brick godown [warehouse] to the west and with

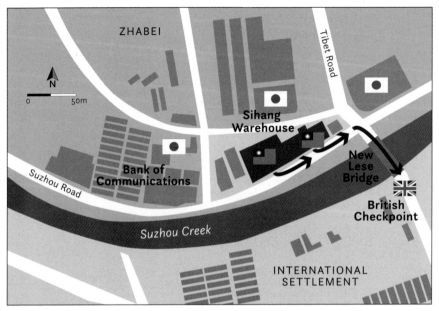

The breakout of the Eight Hundred Heroes from Sihang Warehouse.

a machine-gun post on North Suzhou Road. Occasionally, a small flash and a thud showed where a hand-grenade had been dropped from the building, apparently at Japanese soldiers trying to gain an entry.[5]

A short lull in the Japanese bombardment occurred at around 0100 h before searchlights lit up the western wall and two Japanese field guns fired at almost point-blank range. One Chinese soldier threw a grenade at a searchlight, but it landed short of the target and caused no damage as Japanese tracer-bullets ricocheted off the wall.[6]

As searchlights illuminated Tibet Road, Japanese machine-gun crews near the northern end of the bridge watched for signs of Chinese soldiers and opened fire at their moving shadows. The *North China Daily News* correspondent witnessed the unfolding drama as 'every now and again, some of the besieged would make a dash from the godown [warehouse] for the British lines, and with a savage crackle, tracer bullets would come racing after them'.[7] Lloyd Lehrbas, an American journalist, observed the breakout from the American Concession:

I was an eye-witness to the thrilling deadly drama from beginning to end, watching from a United States marine sandbag about 50 yards directly across Soochow [Suzhou] creek from the doomed fortress. Terrific roars of Japanese big guns rocked the sandbags as shells hurtled through the entire structure . . . When the Japanese onslaught was most furious I peered over the sandbags and suddenly saw dim shapes slipping from the warehouse and running for cover. Divining the escape, Japanese sweep the exit with searchlights and laid down a curtain of machine gun bullets. The dugout telephone tinkled and the report came in that 'approximately 50 had made it in dribbles of twos and threes'.[8]

A British reporter from *The Observer* also watched the flight of Chinese soldiers from the warehouse from a Royal Welsh Fusiliers position near the bridge:

For three hours early to-day I witnessed a tense drama, as 300 men dashed across a 20 yard strip of road in which it seemed that nothing could live. . . Two machine-guns trained on the illuminated road were continuously spraying the men's only possible exit, and British soldiers watching from behind sandbags believed it was inevitable that the besieged would be mowed down as they crossed. It was a tense moment when the first man dashed across the road, machine-gun bullets spattering round him. Soon afterwards men came in small groups through a hail of bullets. Some fell. As they stumbled into the British post they smiled and shook hands with the British soldiers, who congratulated them on their courage.[9]

During the breakout a group of Japanese troops supported by a light tank engaged the retreating soldiers. Platoon Commander Yang Yangzheng returned fire, but a shell from the tank caused a piece of shrapnel to hit his face, injuring his left eye, and his comrades dragged him half-conscious to safety. After passing out, Yang awoke in a hospital where a doctor explained that his left eye had been removed.[10]

As Japanese shells bombarded Sihang Warehouse and machine-gun fire became more intense, the volume of return fire from the Chinese defenders inside decreased. Thousands of Chinese civilians cheered as the Eight Hundred ran into the Settlement. Yang Ruifu recalled the desperate fighting:

> The enemy, as if they had already learned of our purpose, posted machine-guns on the east and south sides of the godowns [warehouses] and a powerful searchlight on the west side.
> Thus during our retreat we were directly in their line of fire.
> However, we withdrew safely, while a small detachment of our soldiers were fighting a gallant rearguard action. Several times we thought of rushing toward the enemy to engage them in a hand-to-hand battle, but we held ourselves in check in view of the order from our highest command.[11]

A Japanese bullet hit Yang's leg, but he managed to drag himself across the bridge despite intense pain and he watched the last Chinese soldiers cross the bridge:

> By two a.m., the clean-up troop had safely retreated, while dozens of the wounded, as well as the national flag previously flying high on the top of the warehouse, have all been carried out, which makes me feel enormously delighted and relieved.[12]

Lieutenant Leon Lane, an American Marine, also witnessed the breakout and later recalled helping the Chinese:

> I sort of stuck my neck out and it was a little against regulations but I helped a lot of them across who might have been killed. Some of the other fellows did too. . . Of course the Japs were shooting at the Chinese we were helping and didn't care who they hit.[13]

The British travellers W.H. Auden and Christopher Isherwood, who visited China in early 1938, encountered rumours about the Royal Welsh Fusiliers firing at the Japanese during the breakout, as they detailed in their book *Journey to a War*:

Some people will tell you that the British troops in their pill-box, tired of being shot at, returned the Japanese fire, and even put a machine-gun out of action. This is officially denied. Anyhow, the Japanese, in the darkness and confusion, could hardly be certain where the bullets were coming from.[14]

Zhang Boting's account of his meeting with Major-General Alexander Telfer-Smollett claimed that covering fire from British troops was a prearranged part of the plan. Major Shangguan Zhibiao, the executive officer, also asserted:

The enemy had set up four machine guns and two searchlights near the North Railway Station. When we were ordered to evacuate, the British troops on the southern end of the New Lese Bridge assisted us in destroying one of them.[15]

British soldiers probably did open fire as their sympathies were certainly with the Chinese and they had been angered by the deaths of the four soldiers from the Royal Ulster Rifles by Japanese shells only two days earlier.

Major-General Telfer-Smollett, who personally commanded the Royal Welsh Fusiliers at the bridge, received the Chinese soldiers as they ran across the bridge in small groups and he remarked, 'I have never seen anything greater.'[16] In 1939, Telfer-Smollett became Lieutenant Governor of Guernsey in the Channel Islands and served as a District Commander in the United Kingdom from 1940 until retiring in 1942. Afterwards, he lived at Cameron House in Scotland and became Lord Lieutenant of Dunbartonshire. He died in 1954.

During the fighting Japanese artillery finally penetrated the western wall of Sihang Warehouse. Observers on the southern bank noticed that a light on the warehouse's first floor, which had been seen since Tuesday night, went out after 0130 h, which suggested the Chinese position was collapsing. Another lull commenced around 0230 h and fire consumed the small one-storey building between the warehouse and Tibet Road. At around 0400 h the roof collapsed as the warehouse burned and a red glow was seen coming from the western side as flames flickered around

An American bubble gum card depicting Xie Jinyuan leading his soldiers during their breakout from Sihang Warehouse. Note: the American artist who created this image depicted Xie Jinyuan as left-handed without realizing that at that time being left-handed was culturally unacceptable in China. (Author's Collection)

the eastern side. The *North China Daily News* reported that Xie Jinyuan returned to the warehouse to rescue some men trapped in the burning building.[17] Once in the Settlement, Xie told the British, 'We have lost face,' and that if it was not for Chiang Kai-shek's order to withdraw 'we would have fought there until the last man'.[18]

After the sound of fighting ceased, Sihang went quiet until observers noticed red and white lights on the rooftop as triumphant shouts of 'Banzai!' could be heard. The reporter from the *North China Daily News* noticed that a 'sun-rayed flag of the Japanese Army floated from every pole where only the day before a huge Chinese Nationalist flag had flaunted its defiance'.[19] The defence of Sihang Warehouse had ended and Yang Ruifu later reflected: 'This battle ends up with neither victory nor my sacrifice for the righteous cause, except "unconditional obedience to orders". Our compatriots' compliments and care fill me with both gratitude and shame.'[20]

SANCTUARY IN THE CONCESSIONS

British soldiers and Shanghai Municipal Police assisted the 377 Chinese survivors immediately after they arrived inside the International Settlement and they cared for the wounded. The Chinese had retreated with around 400 rifles, 24 light machine guns, six heavy machine guns and ammunition boxes.[21] As British soldiers disarmed the Chinese they noted that their rifles were still hot from combat, and one journalist reported: 'The Chinese brought out in triumph the huge Chinese flag which had flown over their warehouse fortress.'[22]

The British drove the Chinese soldiers in trucks and police riot vans to the Race Course before moving them to a camp behind Jiaozhou Park where they would be guarded during their internment by soldiers from the Shanghai Volunteer Corps. At the same time 50 wounded were taken to various hospitals including Yang Ruifu who declared from a bed, 'I hope I shall speedily recover so that I can return to the front.'[23]

Chinese accounts usually contain a narrative of British betrayal. For example, Shangguan Zhibiao insisted: 'It was agreed in advance that the commander of the British army had promised to assist the isolated troop to evacuate and return to west Shanghai through the concession to join their teams.'[24] Zhang Boting claimed that the 'concession authorities broke their promises' because they were 'frightened by the ruthlessness of the Japanese and did not dare to release the isolated troop back to their units'.[25] Xie later insisted that he had been promised that his men would be allowed to return to the 88th Division.

There are three main possibilities concerning the accounts of British betrayal. Telfer-Smollett may have indeed promised the Chinese that the Eight Hundred would be allowed to rejoin the war. However, this notion lacks credibility as he would have been aware that allowing Chinese soldiers to leave the Settlement would violate international law and give the Japanese a pretext to intervene in the British Concession. Another possibility is that the discussion between Telfer-Smollett and the Chinese officials, which was facilitated through an interpreter, became the subject of accidental misunderstanding. However, a more likely scenario is that Zhang Boting misled Xie Jinyuan during his difficult phone conversation when trying to persuade him to accept the orders to withdraw. The notion of a British

Members of the Eight Hundred Heroes in internment immediately after their breakout from Sihang Warehouse. (Author's Collection)

Members of the Eight Hundred Heroes being interned by the British Army. (Author's Collection)

promise to allow the Eight Hundred to rejoin their division would have made it easier for Xie to overcome his reluctance to leave the warehouse. Although there can be no absolute certainty regarding what happened, Xie and his men genuinely believed in the promise and legitimately *felt* betrayed by the British. As such, they initially refused to hand over their weapons and accept internment until Xie ordered them to do so, but he also reminded them, 'We must be patient and one day we will stand up again!'[26]

The exact number of Chinese casualties sustained at Sihang Warehouse is disputed. Immediately after the breakout, *The New York Times* reported that the Chinese left behind 200 dead in the warehouse.[27] The reporter Lloyd Lehrbas stated that 26 survivors were gravely wounded (who were not necessarily wounded during the withdrawal) and the Chinese claimed that 200 of their men had been killed.[28] Other newspapers in the immediate aftermath reported that around 100 Chinese soldiers had died in total (and between two and six were killed while between ten and 24 were wounded during the breakout).[29] Japanese marines later reported finding around 100 dead Chinese soldiers in the warehouse.[30] During an interview on 2 November, Xie Jinyuan stated that he commanded 410 soldiers who entered the warehouse and that ten died and 30 were wounded.[31] Xie later claimed: 'Actually the total number of soldiers was 420, of whom more than 10 sacrificed, and some were injured and admitted to the hospital for medical treatment, so finally 377 soldiers retreated.'[32] If it is accepted that between 410 and 420 Chinese soldiers defended the warehouse and that 377 of them were interned, then 33 to 43 are unaccounted for, but at least ten wounded troops were evacuated before the breakout so not all these men were killed. Therefore, it is possible that only ten Chinese died, but the death toll was likely higher although probably fewer than 50 men were killed.

Over 200 Japanese are believed to have died at Sihang Warehouse, mostly from the 3rd 'Lucky' Division as well as some marines. Sun Yuanliang claimed: 'Enemy corpses in the vicinity of Sihang Warehouse totalled over two hundred approximately.'[33] Xie Jimin in *My Father, General Xie Jinyuan* gave the same figure:

> . . . more than 200 enemy soldiers were killed and countless ones were wounded. Two enemy tanks were also destroyed and two more

were damaged. The number of enemies killed was the sum of the daily counts obtained by observation posts.[34]

The 3rd Division commenced the Shanghai campaign with 14,624 soldiers and during the entire battle suffered 3013 deaths and 8578 wounded — a staggering casualty rate experienced by the supposed 'Lucky' troops.[35] Therefore, the Eight Hundred only accounted for a small number of their overall losses during a long and brutal ordeal.

A Japanese press statement claimed that their marines found large quantities of fresh food including bread and milk inside Sihang Warehouse. The statement concluded: 'The Landing Party cannot repress a feeling of wonder and displeasure at the presence of these provisions which must have been smuggled through the British defence lines.'[36] The Japanese Foreign Office in Tokyo similarly declared:

> It is alleged that the Japanese found the buildings connected with the British sector by way of an adjacent house. The Chinese troops, in offering their last resistance, apparently had free access to the British sector, from which, provisions and water were supplied.[37]

Xie Jinyuan denied the Japanese reports of foreign food in the warehouse: 'Our food consisted mainly of rice, biscuits and vegetables furnished by Chinese sympathizers.'[38] However, Xie was obviously lying to cover up the role the British played in helping get these supplies to his troops.

Chiang Kai-shek promoted each surviving officer and soldier one rank and granted posthumous honours on the dead and pensions to their families.[39] Xie Jinyuan learned about his promotion from a journalist during a press conference, as *The New York Times* reported: 'He blushed like a child when The Associated Press told him for the first time that Generalissimo Chiang Kai-shek had promoted him.' Xie then replied, 'But I don't deserve such an honor.'[40] The reporter also referred to him as 'dignified but simple and modest'.[41] The Executive Yuan of the *Kuomintang* awarded Xie and Yang Ruifu the Blue Sky and White Sun Medal.[42]

Chinese newspapers in Shanghai immediately glorified Xie Jinyuan and the Eight Hundred as mythology became central to the way their story was told. For example, an article titled 'Ode to You' appeared in *Ta Kung Pao* the same day of the breakout:

> The 1st Battalion, the 524th Regiment stationed in Sihang Warehouse has caused nationwide and even worldwide sensation over the past few days. . . The glorious morals of integrity and righteousness are underlying their fearlessness of death and determination to sacrifice their lives despite awareness of the inexorable fate and lack of approach to withdrawal. They lift the characters of China's new generation of soldiers from obscurity to prominence and serve as paragons for Chinese compatriots. We owe them enormous respect and praise.[43]

Another Chinese newspaper similarly praised Xie: 'Your action (persisting in the anti-Japanese war) has undoubtedly represented the will of the Chinese people to fight to the end of the war and has broken the peace dream of the pro-Japanese traitors.'[44]

The breakout of the Eight Hundred left a deep impression within the Settlement. Mary Matteson Wilbur from a family of American missionaries considered the news 'more exciting than any for weeks' and that the Chinese braved Japanese machine guns and escaped to the 'intense admiration of all foreigners'.[45] Nina Troy, an American Methodist missionary in China, recalled passing by Sihang Warehouse in the aftermath of the battle:

> Going to the camp we pass the great shell of the building where the 'Lone Battalion' held out for so long and so bravely. Blackened and bombed with falling walls and great shell holes give proof of the terrific struggle that went on there for days. Just beyond that is a vast section, block after block of devastated city. Not one whole undamaged structure stands. Torn broken and shattered roofs broken windows great shell holes and gashes in the walls pile of furniture upon pile of debris everywhere pieces of furniture torn books and pictures and yes human bones all cry out the awful news of shells bombs war and death.[46]

The damaged Sihang Warehouse after the fighting. (Author's Collection)

The internment of the Eight Hundred in the International Settlement did not end the hostilities in Shanghai and fighting continued in the southern sectors of the city, although to all observers the outcome was not in doubt.

THE END IN SHANGHAI

On 31 October 1937, the Japanese attacked across Suzhou Creek and created two bridgeheads on its southern bank. They further consolidated their position the next day as additional troops crossed the stream.[47] On 3 November, the Nine-Power Pact conference began in Brussels without Japanese representation and the Chinese hoped for foreign intervention to aid their perilous situation. As the diplomats spoke in the splendour of a European capital, the violence continued in Shanghai without interruption.

The Japanese commenced their landing at Hangzhou Bay, 150 kilometres south of Shanghai, on 5 November. The high command had committed 70,000 troops to this operation and, after the 6th and 18th Divisions disembarked, Japanese troops advanced towards Songjiang to cut the Hangzhou–Shanghai railway line. The 114th Division landed five days

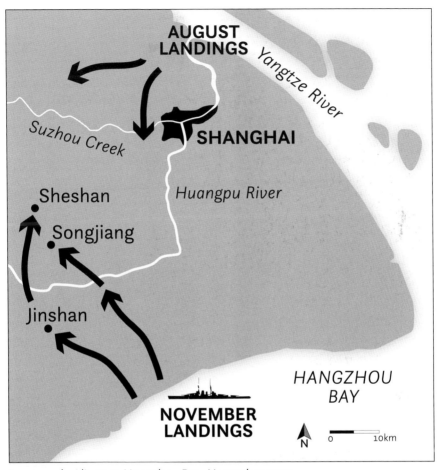

Japanese landings at Hangzhou Bay, November 1937.

later and the Japanese threatened to surround Shanghai. As the Chinese had depleted their forces in this sector to reinforce their positions north of the city, they had insufficient forces to contain the new Japanese beachhead. Chiang Kai-shek, realizing that a total collapse in Shanghai was only a matter of time, decided to abandon the city, but he wanted to hold out until at least 16 November as there would be propaganda value if Chinese soldiers had resisted for three months. The newly arrived 107th and 108th Divisions attempted to hold Songjiang, but the soldiers began withdrawing on 9 November. Chiang had ordered the formation of a new defensive line at Suzhou further west and in a speech apologized for failing to predict the

Victorious Japanese soldiers during the Battle of Shanghai in 1937.
(Contributor: CPA Media Pte Ltd/Alamy Stock Photo)

landing at Hangzhou Bay: 'It's a responsibility that I, as supreme leader, should take upon myself! I truly ask forgiveness of the motherland!'[48]

As Chinese soldiers retreated from Shanghai, the Japanese advanced through empty streets and captured Hongqiao Aerodrome. The Japanese now effectively controlled the city and General Iwane Matsui, commander of the Shanghai Expeditionary Army, dubiously announced at a press conference on 11 November: 'The fundamental thing to understand is that Japan is not an aggressor but came here to restore order among the civilian population of China.'[49]

Chiang Kai-shek had committed between 500,000 and 700,000 soldiers to his Shanghai gamble, including his best German-trained divisions. Despite some initial success in pushing the Japanese marine garrison back, the enemy committed 300,000 troops and their superior organization and technology — in particular artillery and naval gunfire support — proved to be decisive. The exact casualties of the battle are disputed but the best estimate, according to Hans van de Ven, is 9115 Japanese killed and 31,257 wounded as well as 187,000 Chinese casualties.[50] The German advisers including Alexander von Falkenhausen noted Chinese valour in the face of overwhelming odds but were disturbed by their willingness to sacrifice their lives.[51] China lost its best troops in Shanghai as the elite 87th and 88th Divisions had effectively been destroyed. General Sun Yuanliang with a handful of men from the 88th Division escaped Shanghai and he began re-raising his shattered unit.[52] Zhang Boting recalled: 'We were ordered to retrograde westward, and then ordered to rush to Nanjing to take part in the battle to defend the capital.'[53]

During the fighting, over 100,000 refugees fled into the foreign concessions and another 350,000 left the city.[54] Shanghai's refugees experienced an enormous humanitarian catastrophe and 7000 civilians sought assistance around the Catholic St Ignatius Cathedral in the French Concession. Father Jacquinot de Basange, a Jesuit priest and vice chairman of the Shanghai Red Cross, created the Nanshi Safety Zone where a quarter of a million refugees found sanctuary.[55]

The League of Nations, due to the effort of Chinese diplomats, issued a unanimous condemnation of Japanese aggression but took no concrete action. On 24 November, the Brussels Conference ended with no decision to intervene and no plan for peace.[56] Although a Chinese submission had requested economic sanctions against Japan, the parties refrained from implementing this measure. The conference issued a weak statement declaring that direct negotiation between the Chinese and Japanese would not end the conflict, although it urged a peaceful resolution of hostilities.

Although the Great Powers failed to take action against Japan, world leaders were nevertheless alarmed at Japanese foreign policy and in this way Chinese sacrifices in Shanghai were not in vain. Previously, during the Japanese invasion of Manchuria in 1931 and the 'Shanghai Incident' of 1932, the British Foreign Secretary John Simon noted that Japan was 'widely seen to have a strong case against China'.[57] During the 1930s large numbers of westerners in the Treaty Ports continued to perceive Japanese actions as a stabilising cure for Chinese disorder. After the start of fighting in July 1937, the British financier Vandeleur Grayburn declared with colonial arrogance: 'It's just the natives fighting.'[58] The Chinese stand at Shanghai changed these perceptions and their nation was perceived to be on the right side of international treaties and norms.[59] On 4 November 1937, three days after the Eight Hundred escaped from Sihang Warehouse, *The Boston Globe* declared, 'The world can no longer belittle the fighting ability and bravery of the Chinese soldier, but must applaud him, for in sheer heroism he is a match against any soldier in the world.'[60]

Although the Japanese captured Nanjing on 13 December, the *Kuomintang* Government retreated to Wuhan and Chinese resistance survived the fall of the capital. During the subsequent 'Rape of Nanking', the Japanese murdered 200,000 civilians, further solidifying international sympathy towards China and hatred of the Japanese Empire.[61] Despite being shocked by the excesses of his troops, Matsui did not restrain his officers, notably Prince Yasuhiko Asaka who ordered the barbarism. After World War II, the International Military Tribunal for the Far East convicted Matsui for his role in the 'Rape of Nanking' and he was hanged as a war criminal in Tokyo's Sugamo Prison on 23 December 1948.

Following the Battle of Shanghai, substantial overseas aid began arriving in China as the nation was not entirely alone. Following the signing of the Sino-Soviet Non-Aggression Pact in August 1937, Soviet military aid arrived from Turkistan carried by a caravan of 20,000 camels. After trucks began supplementing this effort, between 2000 and 3000 tons of supplies arrived each month including gasoline, rifles and artillery.[62] Stalin also sent an aviation unit — the Soviet Volunteer Group — consisting of four fighter squadrons, two bomber squadrons and 200 airmen, which arrived at Nanchang on 12 January 1938.[63] On 26 January, the Soviets conducted their first air raid and hit Japanese airfields at Nanjing, destroying over 30 enemy planes.

After 1937, the British Foreign Office allowed vast quantities of arms to enter China through Hong Kong to help keep *Kuomintang* soldiers fighting. These shipments travelled across the Hong Kong–Hankou railway, and an American officer reported on this trade in June 1938: 'The Chinese are bringing more munitions and war supplies into China than ever before. The Hong Kong Harbor has never in its history berthed so many steamers.'[64] During the first sixteen months of the war, 700,000 tons of supplies reached Hankou from Hong Kong. The Burma Road also became a significant British lifeline to China as were French arms shipments which arrived from Europe

Major Japanese offensives in China in 1937.

at Haiphong in Indochina and were transported overland to China.[65]

During this time German armament exports to China continued. Germany sent two arms shipments worth 44 million marks to China in December 1937 and the country delivered 144 million marks in arms to China during the early stages of the Sino-Japanese War.[66] German advisers continued to assist Chiang Kai-shek in Wuhan and Falkenhausen oversaw the raising of new divisions and helped the Chinese High Command plan operations. In the first half of 1938, the Chinese won a series of battles against the overextended Japanese during the Xuzhou campaign, which restored morale.[67] During the Battle of Taierzhuang, the most notable victory to date, Chinese forces with German assistance executed a crushing encirclement battle that annihilated the Japanese 10th Division and only 2000 enemy troops escaped the pocket, leaving behind 16,000 dead.[68]

Hitler had kept Germany neutral during the Sino-Japanese War despite the Anti-Comintern Pact of 1936 and a desire for closer cooperation with Tokyo, although Foreign Minister Joachim von Ribbentrop urged the dictator to break ties with China in favour of a Japanese alliance. During economic negotiations, the Japanese informed Berlin that in order to gain access to markets in their puppet state of Manchukuo, Germany would have to cease supporting China. In April 1938, Ribbentrop, after consulting with Hitler, ordered the withdrawal of German advisers from China. Falkenhausen and his men delayed their departure by noting their contractual obligations, causing the Nazis to threaten them with treason trials.[69] After Falkenhausen informed Chiang of Nazi threats to their families, the Generalissimo allowed them to leave. On 5 July, the German Mission — the men who had trained the Eight Hundred Heroes — departed Wuhan on a special train and Falkenhausen, in a final address, declared:

> We can look back on our work and achievements with pride and satisfaction . . . knowing that we, as old German soldiers, have done our duty. . . The activities of the German advisors in China will go down in the history of Germandom in the Far East as a further glorious chapter of hard work and German efficiency.[70]

Falkenhausen later planned to overthrow Hitler as part of the conspiracy of Generals Hans Oster and Ludwig Beck in 1938. After being recalled to active duty, he became military governor of Belgium during World War II and oversaw a relatively benevolent occupation, which at times collaborated with the resistance, before being replaced by the Nazi Reich Commissar Josef Grohe in July 1944.[71] The Gestapo arrested Falkenhausen for suspected involvement in Claus von Stauffenberg's July plot on Hitler's life and he was sent to Dachau.[72] After the war, Falkenhausen stood trial in Belgium for not stopping the deportation of over 25,000 Jews and for executing hostages. The court sentenced him to twelve years in prison, but he was paroled three weeks later as he had protected the bulk of the Belgian population from the Nazi terror.[73] Chiang Kai-shek sent Falkenhausen his best wishes through the Chinese ambassador and the former German general thanked the Generalissimo for helping him in prison and he declared his 'loyal devotion

The German Mission in China departing Hankou in a special train with a swastika flag to protect it from Japanese air raids. (Author's Collection)

and expression of fidelity which I never changed and never shall change'.[74] Falkenhausen died in West Germany on 31 July 1966.[75]

The Chinese stand at Shanghai prevented the early capture of Wuhan and the temporary capital held out until October 1938, after which the *Kuomintang* Government withdrew deeper into the interior to Chongqing with its remaining industrial base where it would be secure for the rest of the war. The Chinese strategic withdrawal from Wuhan up the Yangtze created an epic that raised morale and a defiant spirit often referred to as 'China's Dunkirk'.[76] In November 1938, Chiang conferred with his High

Command at Nanyue in Hunan Province where he announced a strategy of trading space for time in which the Japanese, at the limits of their supply lines, would be defeated in the interior.[77] Although Japan now controlled China's main cities and ports as well as its most important railroads and the fertile lower Yangtze, the *Kuomintang* refused to concede defeat.[78] The war entered a stalemate that Japan, lacking an effective strategy, could not win. As the war continued, the legend of the Eight Hundred Heroes continued to inspire the Chinese people until their eventual victory in 1945, but it would also inspire other *Kuomintang* troops to conduct their own last stands.

OTHER DOOMED BATTALIONS

On 10 November 1937, ten days after the breakout of the Eight Hundred, a press report from Taiyuan, capital of Shanxi Province, claimed that 10,000 Chinese defenders were emulating Shanghai's 'Doomed Battalion' by refusing to surrender.[79] Before the fall of Shanghai, the Chinese spymaster Dai Li had fled into the French Concession where he hoped to rally his men in the Special Action Corps, a clandestine *Kuomintang* militia and intelligence unit recruited from the city's underworld. Dai had been inspired by Sihang Warehouse to conduct a heroic defence of Nanshi, the small old Chinese walled city inside Shanghai, but his cadres abandoned their posts and sought refuge in the foreign concessions.[80] However, another Chinese force did defend Nanshi on 11 November. The 165th Brigade, comprising mostly naval military police, made a stand under the leadership of Regimental Commander Jiao Changfu.[81] The drama took place on the border of the French Concession in full view of spectators inside neutral territory across Siccawei Creek. The men fought against Japanese soldiers and light tanks before breaking out across the stream. One Chinese soldier carried a wounded comrade into the concession and French guards helped Chinese troops who made it across.[82] The foreign press covered the action just as they had done at Sihang and the American correspondent Edgar Snow witnessed the fighting:

> Never again, I think, will it be possible for any mere spectator to get
> such a close-up but wide-angled view of a battle in progress, as we got

of the last stand of the defenders of Nantao [Nanshi]. Only a ribbon of 50 feet of sluggish Siccawei Creek, which formed the boundary between the French Concession and Chinese territory, separated us from the battlefield. I climbed up to the rickety balcony of a Chinese lodging, which fronted on the Creek, to join a half dozen camera men who must have got the most complete movies of a battle ever filmed outside a Hollywood movie set.[83]

During a press conference Mayor Yu Hongjun spoke about these defenders. 'I was once Mayor of Greater Shanghai,' he stated. 'But I am still Mayor of this,' he declared while drawing a circle on a map around Nanshi. A reporter at the conference concluded that the Chinese soldiers were 'making a last stand and emulating the "doomed battalion" of Chapei [Zhabei]'.[84]

On 3 December 1937, as Chinese soldiers resisted the Japanese advance in Jiangsu Province, the press reported that a Chinese detachment was fighting from the Jiangyin Forts and 'it appears that the defenders have decided to emulate Shanghai's "doomed battalion"'.[85] Another report emerged on 20 May 1938 of a Chinese battalion fighting to the death on the Yellow River in Henan Province:

The heroism and vivid details contained in the story of the second 'doomed battalion' are stated by the Chinese to rival that of the first, which won renown in the Joint Savings Godown [warehouse] during the Shanghai hostilities. On the night of April 10, it is related, one Chinese battalion stormed the city walls of Chiyuan and occupied Kwangtimiao (the temple of the God of War) inside the east gate of the city. Without reinforcements, however, the battalion was immediately surrounded inside the temple. Inspired by the bravery and patriotism immortalized by Kwang Ti, the famous General of the Three Kingdoms who was later worshipped as the Chinese God of War, the battalion is said to be still holding out in the temple after nine days of 'desperate fighting with only 100 men left of the original number.'[86]

The press reported yet another 'doomed battalion' story on 20 December 1938:

It would appear that Shanghai will have another 'lone battalion' as a source of inspiration because according to Chinese evening reports yesterday, there are 600 guerrillas still fighting in the war-ravaged walled district of Nanhwei [Nanhui] despite fierce attacks repeatedly launched by the Japanese in their attempt to wipe out all guerrillas on the peninsula.[87]

Xie Jinyuan and the Eight Hundred Heroes certainly inspired other 'lost battalions', but while these other battles took place, they endured a mundane existence interned within the British Concession.

CHAPTER SIX
BETRAYAL AND THE LAST DAYS OF OLD SHANGHAI

INTERNMENT AND RIOTS

After the Eight Hundred Heroes retreated into the International Settlement, the Shanghai Volunteer Corps, acting upon instructions from the Shanghai Municipal Council, interned them as required by international law. The soldiers now lived at Jiaozhou Park, a former Public Works Department camp consisting of rudimentary sheds at the corner of Jiaozhou Road and Singapore Road. The facility became known as 'Lone Battalion Barracks'.[1] The Russian Regiment of the Shanghai Volunteer Corps, a force mostly raised from the descendants of White Russians who had fled the Reds during the Civil War, guarded the men under the command of British officers. The guards, as the executive officer Shangguan Zhibiao remembered, 'were quite polite' but their 'surveillance was quite strict'.[2] Shangguan referred to the barracks as 'a lonely island within a lonely island'.[3] Zhang Boting, the 88th Division's chief-of-staff, similarly described the barracks as 'a spiritual fortress at the enemy's rear, and a beacon of hope in the heart of compatriots in the enemy-occupied areas'.[4]

The internees initially established good relations with the guards — a development made easier by Japanese blundering. In a failed public relations exercise, Japanese officials attempted to send wreaths to the funeral of the four British soldiers from the Royal Ulster Rifles who had been killed by their shells. A Japanese spokesman in a press conference denied that his countrymen had fired the projectiles and blamed the incident on Chinese artillery, a laughable accusation as thousands of witnesses in the Settlement had watched the Japanese bombardment of Sihang Warehouse.[5] British authorities naturally declined the Japanese offer, but thousands of Chinese people attended the funeral at the Bubbling Well Cemetery and Xie Jinyuan sent wreaths with a banner declaring, 'Long live the friendship of China and Britain. Righteousness will never perish. They shall survive after death.'[6]

The Japanese further alienated public opinion on 21 November 1937 after Major Haradu, an attaché, demanded the Shanghai Municipal Council hand over the 377 internees to Japanese forces.[7] The Council ignored the illegal request; however, the Australian communist newspaper *The Workers Star* reported incorrect rumours to the contrary:

> The Municipal Council of the International Settlement at Shanghai, established as the government of the settlement by a treaty forced on China by the 'civilised' European nations at the point of the gun, and now consisting of five Chinese, five Britishers of the 'old school tie' tradition, two Americans and two Japanese fascists, has virtually declared itself on the side of Japan against China, by weakly submitting to the Japanese fascists' insolent demands for virtual control of the settlement. These demands include . . . handing over of all interned Chinese, including the 377 survivors of the heroic 'Doomed Battalion,' who held back the invaders by their magnificent stand at Chapei [Zhabei] until defences behind them could be strengthened. This is the cowardly and treacherous level to which our rulers have sunk: to be willing to hand over these heroes to the most bloodthirsty barbarians the world has ever seen, for almost certain execution.[8]

Although this story got its facts wrong as the Council never contemplated handing the Eight Hundred over to the Japanese, it did illustrate that their

Xie Jinyuan (centre) reading a newspaper while interned inside the 'Lone Battalion Barracks'. (Author's Collection)

saga had resonated with people on another continent who emotionally identified with their plight.

On New Year's Day 1938, Xie Jinyuan began to write a diary about life in the 'Lone Battalion Barracks' which contained his thoughts on daily life in captivity, the ongoing war, China's future and international events. In a typical diary entry, Xie wrote:

> I did some exercise after getting up early in the morning, and then I wrote a report. The report consisted of three parts: (1) reporting my indignation for being besieged here; (2) expressing my opinions for regaining freedom; and (3) reporting the procedures for handover of the supplies provided by the Municipal Council in the future. I finished lecturing the military drills and disciplines in the morning, and I wrote the report with a pen at 4:00 p.m. and I was hesitating about who would hand it over. At about 3:00 p.m., I attended a basketball match with the basketball team of Changzhou Private Middle School, and won by the score of 26:15.[9]

Xie also established a daily routine for his men:

> All officers and soldiers rise at four thirty in the morning before
> spending half an hour washing up, getting houses in order and doing
> the cleaning. From five to seven thirty a.m. we do morning exercises
> and training in the playground. At eight, Russian guards of Shanghai
> Volunteer Corps spend about ten minutes counting noses. Breakfast
> begins at nine, and a lecture is given from ten to eleven, after which the
> time from eleven to two thirty p.m. is for duty arrangement, diagnosis,
> doing laundry, taking a bath and free moving. Another lecture is given
> from two thirty to three thirty. Supper begins at four p.m. The time for
> teaching and practising Chinese boxing, singing songs or playing games
> is from five to seven thirty p.m. Then we take a shower and rest at eight
> to eight thirty before going to bed at nine.[10]

Chen Desong, a Chinese soldier, remembered that in internment the
men 'retained their army life schedule invariably, including morning
exercises, being on duty and standing guard, and making soap, towels and
woodworking on their own'.[11] Shangguan Zhibiao similarly recalled:

> Xie Jinyuan, with his consistent revolutionary military demeanour, asked
> everyone to strengthen their conviction and consolidate unity. . . He
> also asked me to be in charge of establishing a school for the isolated
> troop, so that soldiers with low-level of education would have the
> opportunity for further education. A factory of the isolated troop was
> established, which was divided into a hosiery and towel team, a rattan
> work team, a soap team as well as a driving team, so that each officer
> and soldier would acquire a skill.[12]

The Eight Hundred lived a mundane existence but were nevertheless
grateful to have escaped Japanese captivity. However, their good relations
with the guards broke down in mid-1938, as Xie alluded to in a lecture he
gave in the barracks:

> What I would like to talk about today is the issue of our legal status

during this time. According to international law and the 'Hague Rules of Land Warfare', the disposal of prisoners of a belligerent country should belong to the power of the government of the enemy country, not the power of the individual or army who captured the captives. Therefore, the prisoners cannot be regarded as criminals. It is also expressly stipulated that prisoners should be treated humanely and their private rights and religious beliefs should be retained. As long as it does not go beyond the scope of order and discipline, there should be considerable freedom. . . I appeal to all peace-loving people around the world, please uphold truth and justice, awaken the Shanghai International Settlement authorities, get them to mind their neutral attitude, fulfil their promises and give us freedom.[13]

As relations soured, tensions bubbling under the surface threatened to explode and one issue provided the spark. The British officers did not permit the internees to raise the Republic of China flag in the barracks so they instead held symbolic 'spiritual' flag-raising ceremonies every morning without an actual flag.[14] However, Xie Jinyuan negotiated with Colonel J.W. Hornby, Commander of the Shanghai Volunteer Corps, who gave permission for two genuine flag-raising ceremonies to take place on 11 August (the 27th anniversary of the Republic of China) and on 13 August (one year after fighting commenced in Shanghai).

On 9 August the internees received the flagpole and Xie ordered soldiers to plant it in front of the auditorium. Hornby, however, insisted that the flagpole must be shortened so the flag could not be seen from outside to avoid complications with Japanese authorities. Xie agreed but the Chinese became increasingly suspicious that their rights were being infringed.[15] The flagpole was cut to the agreed length the next day.

At 0600 h on 11 August, Xie and his men raised the flag, which attracted unwanted attention, as Shangguan Zhibiao explained:

. . . commander Xie and I raised the flag with all comrades of the isolated troop, making the beautiful and magnificent Republic of China flag waving on the lonely island. A few hours later, the Municipal Council saw our 'Blue Sky, White Sun, and a Wholly Red Earth' national flag fluttering in the wind in the barracks of the isolated troop. They immediately sent over 300 British soldiers to surround the barracks and Jiaozhou Park.[16]

After Xie was informed that guards would soon take the flag down, he ordered his men to protect their national symbol. Russian guards moved forward and came under attack from internees armed with bottles, stones, bamboo and other improvised weapons.[17] The guards requested reinforcements and the other members of the Russian Regiment arrived in trucks. The Russians refrained from opening fire and fought back with batons and rifle butts before seizing the flagpole, as Chen Desong recalled: 'we were outnumbered and eventually compelled to leave the playground with the flag confiscated by them.'[18] A reporter from the *North China Herald* witnessed the aftermath:

Lorries waiting to convey the injured to hospital then drew up to the small gate and a 'North-China Daily News' reporter witnessed the removal of members of the Russian Regiment, bleeding from wounds caused by the bottles and sticks of the rioters, and many soldiers, mostly young fellows who appeared to have had the worst of the exchanges with the Russians. Several were carried out in blankets with blood spattered all over their faces. When they had been placed in the lorry it was seen that they were marched out between fixed bayonets of the Russian Regiment and put into the vehicle where an armed Volunteer stood on guard. . . When the camp was cleaned up after the rioting, the Russian Regiment seized a large quantity of improvised arms, such as bamboo poles, rakes and choppers, and also a number of German-type helmets, as worn by most Chinese soldiers.[19]

Four Russian guards had been wounded while 50 internees were taken to the hospital and four died from injuries — Liu Shangcai, You Changqing, Wu Zude and Wang Wenyi — and Shangguan Zhibiao reflected: 'They were wounded by the White Russian army and died for the national flag.'[20] The British travellers W.H. Auden and Christopher Isherwood when visiting a hospital met injured members of the Eight Hundred, as they detailed in their book *Journey to a War*:

Tucked away in unobtrusive comers, unnoticed and almost forgotten, are the crippled remains of the soldiers who fought to defend Shanghai. . . The soldiers were astonishingly cheerful, and all anxious to be photographed. One boy was a remarkable artist. He drew portraits and caricatures. He had fought in the 'Doomed Battalion'. His younger brother, he told us, had been eaten alive in Shan-si [Shanxi] Province by a wolf.[21]

In the evening Xie asked his men for their opinions and the internees commenced a hunger strike and vowed not to eat until the camp authorities returned their flag.

On the morning of 12 August, the Eight Hundred conducted a 'spiritual' flag-raising ceremony as their hunger strike continued. Tensions remained high and at night Xie and Hornby negotiated, but relations between internees and guards remained hostile the next day as the men conducted another 'spiritual' flag-raising ceremony.

After news of the incident spread through the Settlement, sixteen Chinese organizations protested to the Council over its refusal to allow the flag raising and the 'drastic measures' taken by the Russian Regiment as the incident could have been resolved peacefully.[22] After Xie and other officers were relocated to the Russian Regiment quarters on the Bund waterfront, he negotiated with Mr Yu Ya-ching, a Council member, and tensions eased. The Chinese soldiers ended their hunger strike and the officers returned to the camp on 7 October. The Council gave $1000 to the families of the four dead soldiers through the Chinese Ratepayers Association. The Council also appealed to the officers to help 'in carrying out the extraordinary difficult and delicate task imposed on the Council through no wish of its own, of keeping order and discipline in the camp'.[23]

The Japanese meanwhile attempted to exploit the riot and turn public opinion in the Settlement against the Eight Hundred. The pro-Japanese *Manchuria Daily News* accordingly reported that the 'precious lost battalion' was 'thoroughly thrashed and trounced by truncheons' during a 'hearty Sino-Russian tussle'.[24] The newspaper also republished editorials from the *Shanghai Evening Post* and *Mercury* which labelled the incident a 'childish affair' instigated by ungrateful internees who had 'enjoyed the Settlement's hospitality for long months' but had developed a 'touchy patriotism' and 'a state of mind quite out of line with realities'.[25]

After life in the 'Lone Battalion Barracks' returned to normal, Xie received numerous visitors including journalists and Chinese students from Shanghai's Gonzaga College.[26] On 25 October the *North China Daily News* reported a positive story about the internees after relations with the guards improved:

> The 'Doomed Battalion' have taken up athletics ever since last spring and they are at present as keen as any sportsmen. The soldiers first learned to play basketball which is extremely popular among Chinese. Not long ago they were staged an exhibition of volleyball by the Russian Regiment, Foreign Y.M.C.A. League champions.[27]

As the internees continued their mundane existence, significant events occurred around them. In late 1938, German and Austrian Jews fleeing the Nazi terror began arriving in the International Settlement in large numbers and eventually 18,000 Jewish refugees from Central and Eastern Europe found sanctuary in the city, which required no passport or visa to enter.[28]

On 21 February 1939, Private Shao Gongqi, a 22-year-old soldier, escaped from the camp and disappeared. After he was found absent during morning roll call, the guards searched the camp but found no clue concerning how he had evaded the sentries or crossed the eight-foot wall surrounding the camp. Detectives from Gordon Road police station concluded that he did not scale the walls since no traces of blood or clothing were found on the barbed wire, and the *North China Daily News* reported:

> . . . police stations in the Settlement and the Concession have all been given a description of the soldier and are on the lookout for him but it is doubtful as to whether he will ever be found, it being felt that he will find safe refuge practically in any Chinese home, as members of the Battalion are considered national heroes.[29]

On the night on 31 March, three Chinese soldiers escaped in heavy fog and, once again, there was no indication of how they exited the camp and another investigation by detectives found no clues.[30] The three men presumably found sanctuary with the Chinese community and police patrols in the Settlement had no luck tracking them down.

Yang Ruifu, the battalion commander, also escaped from internment and planned to rejoin the war, although he still suffered from the bullet wound to his leg sustained during the breakout. After being smuggled out of Shanghai by the Chinese resistance, he settled with his family in Chongqing to recover in May 1939. Meanwhile back in the barracks, Lei Xiong, commander of the Machine Gun Company, became the new battalion commander.[31] The *Kuomintang* promoted Yang to colonel, but wartime shortages prevented proper medical treatment and his wound became infected. Yang died in Chongqing on 3 February 1940, aged 38 years. He did leave behind an important legacy with his 'Account of the Lone Unit's Four Days of Battle', the most accurate account of the Eight Hundred, which was originally published in the *Dasheng Daily* in Sichuan Province on 12 June 1939.

On 5 May 1939, Xie Jinyuan noted the continued practice of 'spiritual' flag-raising ceremonies in his diary: 'All officers and soldiers muster at twenty to six in the morning to hold the "spirit flag" raising ceremony in our mind because of the lack of a national flag.'[32] He did not record any concerns regarding the absence of a real flag and four days later his diary mentioned sport as camp life continued as normal:

> In order to prepare the basketball match against the Chizhi alumni team on 14 May, the practice time of Group A basketball team was changed to last from 5:30 a.m. to 7:30 a.m. The donation of a silver cup for the charity basketball match and the proposed collection of one silver dollar and the autograph album for refugee relief have been published in today's Wen Wei Po. . . Zibin Wu arrived and gathered the basketball players of Group A and Group B in the lecture hall of the third company, and the training was finished at about four o'clock. I read the History of Napoleon Bonaparte until 5:30 p.m.[33]

Xie and his men, as active-duty but interned soldiers, in theory were supposed to receive pay sent by the *Kuomintang* in Chongqing, but the funds did not always arrive on time. The money was required to pay for food and everyday items while the Shanghai Municipal Council covered the costs of medical care, clothing and maintaining the barracks. Although the internees received donations of food and other supplies from the Chinese community, money from Chongqing was still required to cover most of their basic needs and an arrangement was made in which the Council covered these costs, which the Chinese Ministry of Finance would reimburse. By March 1939, the Council had spent $43,600 maintaining the battalion, but the financial situation became worse after Chinese philanthropic organizations stopped subsidising expenses due to a lack of funds.[34]

The financial difficulties provided the Japanese with another pretext to turn public opinion against the Eight Hundred. In August, Japanese ratepayers threatened to stop paying taxes because of a supposed heavy drain on the Council's finances caused by the cost of interning the soldiers.[35] The Japanese presented a solution to this problem by offering to take custody of the Chinese internees.[36] In response, Xie issued a press statement declaring that in April his government reimbursed the Council with $43,000 and added that neutral nations are normally only repaid the cost of interning belligerents after an armistice, as France had repaid Switzerland the cost of interning its soldiers only after the Franco-Prussian War ended.[37] Xie also suggested that the Council could increase its revenue by taking control of the Japanese district of Hongkou.

On 11 August, Xie commented in his diary on the one-year anniversary of the riot over the raising of the flag:

> The 'spirit flag' raising ceremony is held at five thirty, starting with the chanting of our slogan. Subsequently, I remark that we should sacrifice our lives for our country, and put the freedom and survival of our country before individual freedom and lives. I also talked about the meaning of life and death, saying that death, if necessary, should be readily accepted and living on in disgrace rather than dying honourably is utterly worthless.[38]

Later that month Xie's thoughts focused on international relations as the Nazi-Soviet Pact altered diplomatic norms across the world and he noted potential advantages for China: 'Japan is the most affected and isolated

Xie Jinyuan (centre) in front of the Eight Hundred Heroes while interned inside the 'Lone Battalion Barracks'. (Author's Collection)

country. The axis powers Germany and Italy betrayed Japan and gave it a spiritually fatal blow.'[39] On 4 September Xie reflected upon the start of World War II in Europe: 'if the war no longer expands, Britain, France and Poland will have the advantage in fighting against Germany. China is in a weak position. Most of the industrial properties are in the hands of the imperialists, and Chinese people are cruelly oppressed.'[40]

On the second anniversary of Sihang Warehouse, Xie presided over a ceremony with representatives from Chinese civic bodies and a 'spiritual' flag-raising ceremony took place beside a portrait of Sun Yat-sen. After the men sang the *Kuomintang* anthem, Xie gave a speech on their last stand and expressed regret that they were still interned.[41] The men also received a telegram from the Girl Guide Yang Huimin, who was recovering in a hospital in Chengdu following a car accident.[42]

In January 1940, the Chinese community in the Philippines raised funds to supply the Eight Hundred with winter coats.[43] The men had also decided to become more self-sufficient by establishing a factory to make craft goods for sale to the public and requested funds from a government relief organization in Hong Kong to start the project.[44] However, tensions returned to the camp on 12 February, after Russian guards started erecting barbed wire, resulting in a crowd of civilian onlookers on the other side throwing stones. Despite the commotion, no guards were injured and police reinforcements soon dispersed the crowd.[45] Normal life resumed and the camp remained quiet for the next few months.

On 18 May Xie agonized over his mother's death in his diary:

> To date, I have never taken even the slightest filial responsibility to repay her devotion while bringing me up. I do hope I will have a chance to attend my father in the days to come. For the sake of my allegiance to our country, even God should sympathize with my situation and allow my parents to die content. To alleviate my mental pain, I spent the whole morning sorting out the roster in which tests taken by officers and soldiers are recorded until the time of lunch.[46]

Ten days later Xie received a telegram from Chiang Kai-shek: 'I've known your situation. I hope you will be patient and self-respected. Please do not be irritated by the harsh attitude of others; please be neither humble nor pushy. Instead you should be determined and persistent.'[47]

On 13 September, Chinese workers from the Public Works Department began repairing the gate leading to the football field. After Xie objected, over 100 soldiers marched to the gate, causing the work to stop. Major G.H. Mann, the camp commandant, arrived on the scene and enquired into the basis of the objection. Xie refused to see Major Mann who ordered his guard commander not to allow anybody in or out of the camp until Xie explained his conduct. During the stand-off, the internees entered the guard room yard and unsuccessfully attempted to disarm the Russians. After reinforcements arrived, tensions eased and Xie began talks with Major Mann and both sides made concessions.[48]

The workers returned to repair the gate the next day, but they also constructed additional barbed-wire barricades. Chinese soldiers protested and again attempted to disarm the guards without success, but they assaulted Colonel Hornby who had arrived to negotiate with Xie. The

Russian Regiment sent reinforcements to the camp while a police riot squad and two fire engines also arrived. The internees gathered near the Jiaozhou Park fence and after the protesters refused to leave, the guards attempted to disperse them with water cannons. The guards restored order after throwing tear gas canisters at the crowd. Following the drama, the internees demanded release since they had surrendered to the British Army and not the Shanghai Volunteer Corps, as the *Japan Chronicle* reported while attempting to score propaganda points:

> The men of the 'Doomed Battalion,' . . . have begun to clamour for their
> release. They argue that they surrendered to the British garrison, and as
> the British garrison has now left Shanghai their continued internment
> is illegal. It is not an argument which appeals, for their surrender was
> really to the Settlement authorities. Three years behind barbed wire,
> however, perhaps is not calculated to sharpen the intellect.[49]

The tensions died down for a few days until 18 September. In the afternoon, Chinese workers from nearby factories gathered at the camp entrance and were allegedly agitated by internees to attack the sentry. The workers approached the guard and threatened to free the soldiers, while internees began throwing stones. In the chaos, internees surrounded the sentry who shot and killed Sergeant He Yuxiang in self-defence after a warning was ignored.[50] After the crowd dispersed, sixteen internees surrounded another guard who also opened fire without injuring anybody. After the riot, doctors from the Public Health Department cared for the wounded and Xie released a press statement announcing that one of his soldiers had died and 26 men were wounded, including two who had been bayoneted. He also claimed that electricity had been turned off and that Chinese civilians throwing food over the wall had been beaten by guards. Xie added that his men had been well-treated over the past three years, but the situation had recently deteriorated. 'I believe in Heavenly justice and retribution,' he declared, 'and I trust that consequences must be faced some day. Now I appeal to the Settlement authorities for justice and nothing else and please consider the consequences of the high-handed manner.'[51]

Chiang Kai-shek ordered an investigation into the shooting and the

Chinese Foreign Ministry protested to the British and American embassies, demanding those responsible for the shooting be punished.[52] Chinese newspapers in Shanghai called for conditions in the camp to be improved to reduce the potential for violence but incorrectly alleged that guards had opened fire with machine guns.[53] The Japanese attempted to exploit the riots to generate ill-will and a letter supposedly written by a 'Shanghai Englishman' appeared in the *Japan News Week*:

> At the end of October 1937 the world was being thrilled by stories of the so-called 'doomed battalion'. . . Since then they have periodically given trouble. They have attacked their guards and strong measures have had to be adopted to maintain order, the last occasion being this week. As is to be expected they have always alleged ill-treatment of one kind or another, but there seems never to have been reasonable ground for complaint. . . The inevitable fractiousness and lack of mental balance of men under such restraint is probably responsible.[54]

Camp life returned to normal after discussions with Mr T.K. Ho, Deputy Secretary of the Shanghai Municipal Council. The authorities agreed to remove the contentious barbed-wire barricades while four Chinese wounded remained in Lester Chinese Hospital and the less wounded received first aid in the camp. The men also buried Sergeant He Yuxiang. Disciplined morning roll calls resumed as did regular food deliveries and the electricity supply was turned on.[55] Xie told the press that the positive developments occurred due to discussions with the Council and a telegram from Chiang Kai-shek instructing him not to aggravate the situation.[56] After the return of normality, visitors again visited the camp and Ma Nyein Tha, a Burmese journalist, interviewed Xie:

> One little thing I noticed about him was this, he was wearing a button-photo of the Generalissimo and hanging in his house he had a photograph of the Generalissimo and Madam. In the smallest Chinese tea shop in the remotest parts of Burma I have seen similar evidence of loyalty.[57]

On the morning of 7 October, a Chinese soldier climbed on top of a barracks building, through a hole he had made in the roof, close to the main gate on Singapore Road.[58] A Russian sentry urged him to come down, but the man jumped over the wall before running down the road and hiding among the pedestrians. The pursuing sentry ordered him to stop and opened fire after the escapee ignored the instruction. The bullet hit the man in the neck and guards detained him in the camp until an ambulance took him to Lester Chinese Hospital. The bullet also slightly wounded two pedestrians who only required first aid.[59] No further incidents took place and Xie announced that the shooting affair had been settled, although he did not know why the man had attempted escape but speculated that after three years of internment he was in a terrible state.[60]

Xie announced later that month that the men would hold a track and field competition inside the camp and invitations were sent to local Chinese sporting clubs.[61] Chiang Kai-shek got involved and ordered a banner to be awarded to the soldiers at the event as a token of encouragement.[62] The competition marked the third anniversary of the battalion's stand at Sihang Warehouse and in the evening the men watched the film *Brave Soul on the Battlefield* before Xie delivered an address.[63]

On New Year's Day 1941, Xie urged his men to be more diligent and to prepare for a victorious year.[64] Despite an appeal to optimism, life in the camp remained hard and men suffered from tuberculosis and vitamin deficiencies.[65] However, the situation in the camp was about to become much worse.

MURDER AND FUNERAL RITES

As the Eight Hundred Heroes experienced internment, a rift developed within the *Kuomintang* that would eventually have profound consequences for them. Wang Jingwei, Chiang Kai-shek's old rival and the second highest ranking official in the party, had become increasingly defeatist and concluded that western imperialism constituted a greater threat to China than Japan. Wang departed Chongqing in December 1938 and travelled to Hanoi in French Indochina where he publicly called for China to negotiate with Japan to end the war. After surviving assassination attempts by

Wang Jingwei (seated middle) at the Signing of Japan-Manchukuo-China Joint Declaration in Nanjing on 30 November 1940. (Wikipedia)

Wang Jingwei (third from the right) meeting the Japanese Prime Minister Hideki Tojo (third from left) in 1942. (Wikipedia)

Kuomintang agents, Wang arrived in occupied Shanghai three months later where he negotiated with Japanese officials on the establishment of a new government. Wang formally became the head of state of the 'Reorganized National Government of the Republic of China' on 30 March 1940, a puppet government based in Nanjing that became widely known as the Wang Jingwei regime and his name in China became a byword for traitor.[66]

In January 1939, Xie Jinyuan denounced Wang in a press statement, emphasizing that the all-front resistance policy against Japan was decided upon by the Chinese Government and could not be altered by a disgraced traitor. Xie also urged all Chinese people to ignore Wang's appeals and support Chiang Kai-shek.[67] On 10 October 1940, the *North China Daily News* reported that most Chinese inside the International Settlement remained loyal to Chiang:

> That the Chinese population in the foreign areas of the city are still loyal to the Chungking [Chongqing] Government was clearly demonstrated yesterday when China celebrated Double Tenth, the anniversary of the National Independence Day. All the streets in the International Settlement and French Concession were beflagged, and but on a very few buildings were yellow pendants, the distinction between the Chungking [Chongqing] and Nanking [Nanjing] Governments, seen.[68]

Visitors to the 'Lone Battalion Barracks' included agents of Wang Jingwei's regime who unsuccessfully attempted to convince Xie to switch sides. Chen Gongbo, Wang Jingwei's mayor of Shanghai, allegedly offered to make Xie the puppet regime army's chief-of-staff.[69] After giving up on these attempts, the conspirators decided to assassinate the commander and they recruited four disgruntled soldiers from inside the camp.

At 0555 h on 24 April 1941, the internees in the camp finished a 'spiritual' flag-raising ceremony as the men sang the national anthem. According to the commonly accepted account of what happened next, officers on duty discovered that four men — Private Zhang Guoshun and Corporals He Dingcheng, Zhang Wenqing and You Diliang — were absent. Another soldier found them in their living quarters and told them to proceed to the drill field. After they arrived, Xie reprimanded them for not following discipline. One of the four produced a dagger and stabbed Xie in the chest and the other three men stabbed his throat and head with sharp blades. The assassins stabbed Xie over eight times and the commander fell to the ground with blood pouring from his body and he soon died. Shangguan Zhibiao intervened to stop the attack and was also stabbed:

> Suddenly, He Dingcheng, Zhang Guoshun, You Diliang, Zhang Wenqing charged toward the side of commander Xie and attacked him with knives. When I saw this, I rushed over to intercept, and had my left arm and waist stabbed six times. However, unfortunately, commander Xie was stabbed in the head, fell to the ground on the spot and died for the country. Although I was bleeding all over the ground, I was grateful for the greatness of the regiment commander, and I was able to leave the scene in a state of unconsciousness, with his body on my back. . . Although I was fortunate enough to have the rest of my life, I always regretted not being able to rescue commander Xie. A great national hero of the generation passed away.[70]

A group of soldiers detained the four assassins until the police arrived who took them to the central police station while an ambulance took Shangguan Zhibiao to hospital. Chen Desong remembered that day: 'All officers and soldiers of the regiment sobbed hysterically.'[71] News of Xie's murder shocked the Chinese in Shanghai and in the rest of the country. General Sun Yuanliang, commander of the 88th Division, reflected that the four men 'had succumbed to the temptation of evil people'.[72] Xie Jimin, Xie Jinyuan's son who was three years old at the time, later recalled how his family reacted to the news:

> My mother, Ling Weicheng, had just suffered from the death of her mother-in-law one year ago. Now she was hit by such a tremendous blow, so she cried bitterly and fainted several times. Thinking of comforting the old and frail father-in-law and taking care of the young children, she once said, 'I really don't know how to live in the future.' Zhu Haohuai, the head of Jiaoling County, officials from various organizations, my father's relatives and friends, and people from all walks of life came to offer their condolences.[73]

A *Kuomintang* investigation concluded that the murderers had acted upon the wishes of Wang Jingwei's agents.[74] The four men had been experiencing hardship caused by the lack of funds which increased tension in the camp. He Dingcheng claimed that Xie had greedily hoarded money while the men went without, but investigators concluded that there was no basis for this belief. The investigation concluded that the frustration the four experienced due to financial hardship 'was the underlying cause of the unforeseen incident'. The report continued:

> Therefore given the fact that on the average day, Regimental Commander Xie received visitors . . . no matter whether they were collaborationists or other party members, or anyone else who came to the barracks to express sympathy and solicitude, they were famous people and he had no way of refusing [to see] them; he thought he could help to change them through the example of his character. The result was that unstable people took advantage of this opening to mix with those on the inside [of the barracks] and were able to entice the criminal He [Dingcheng] and the others to go against their superiors by staging an armed rebellion which brought about this unfortunate incident. These are the important, true, underlying causes.[75]

Kuomintang officials also noted that He Dingcheng had 'repeatedly violated military discipline' and Xie had accordingly punished him, but in internment the commander 'could not punish him in accordance with military law'.[76]

The murder presented the *Kuomintang* with an opportunity to use the public outrage over Xie's assassination to rally their supporters and discredit Wang Jingwei.[77] Wu Shaoshu, director of the Three Principles of the People Youth Corps in the International Settlement, reported to Chongqing that he would use Xie's murder to rally support by 'arousing patriotic sentiments' and that his cadres had 'expanded propagandizing and called youth circles into action to go to the lone battalion barracks'.[78] This Youth Corps, a *Kuomintang* organization with a well-organized presence inside the Settlement, turned the assassination into a propaganda coup which revitalized morale inside Shanghai, after the populace had experienced three-and-a-half years of brutal Japanese occupation.[79]

The Chinese press unsurprisingly denounced the murderers and Wang Jingwei.[80] The Shanghai papers *Zhengyanbao* and *Zhongmei ribao*, published in the Settlement, reported on the assassination and generated public outrage. Patriotic citizens also established a fund to care for Xie's family and the *Zhengyanbao* remarked:

> This kind of spirit is of course the result of each person's recognition of Xie Jinyuan's willingness to die for his country. But the actual significance is really for people to show their love and protective feelings for their motherland.[81]

Chinese reporters recalled their high esteem of the dead commander and one journalist remembered him as 'gentle and polite, with an erudite style of conversation' who 'was worthy of admiration'.[82]

The English language newspapers followed a similar line as the *North China Daily News* reported on 26 April:

> In the presence of about 3,000 Chinese, mostly students and admirers of the 'national hero', the remains of Colonel Hsieh Ching-yuan [Xie Jinyuan], late commander of the 'Lone Battalion', were encoffined at a ceremony held yesterday inside the camp. . . Indicating that the late colonel was held in high esteem by the Chinese, many attending the meeting wept. Colonel Hsieh's [Xie] body was dressed in the official Chinese gown covered with the Chinese national flag and after a simple ceremony at which those attending the meeting paid their last tribute to the dead Chinese hero of Chapei [Zhabei] fame, the remains were carried by his subordinates and friends and placed inside the coffin said to be valued at $6,000.[83]

Crowds flocked to the camp to pay their respects to Xie's remains, as the *North China Daily News* reported two days later:

> Forming a long queue, about 15,000 Chinese of all walks of life went to the 'Lone Battalion' camp in Singapore Road throughout Saturday to pay their last tribute to the late Colonel Hsieh Ching-yuan [Xie Jinyuan]

... The same hero-worshipping spirit was kept up yesterday by the Chinese here. Most of them had a glimpse at the casket partially made of glass.[84]

Chiang Kai-shek conferred posthumous honours on Xie and promoted him to major general. Chiang also ordered a $50,000 grant be given to his family and his children would receive free education at government expense.[85] Chiang's wife Soong Mei-ling sent a message of condolence to Xie's family on behalf of the Chinese Women's Civilian Relief Association and the Generalissimo telegraphed a message to the whole country:

The Regimental Commander Xie Jinyuan sacrificed his life for our righteous cause, leaving soldiers of the Republic of China a glorious symbol and adding a solemn and stirring page to our history of resistance against aggression. When leading eight hundred isolated soldiers to defend Zhabei District, he swore to fulfil his duty till death, to defend our national flag and the last battlefield and never retreat. His loyalty, bravery and fearlessness have earned worldwide commendation. He remained steadfast and consistent during over three-year incarceration in the 'Lost Battalion Barracks' despite various difficulties and hardships, and maintained the quality of independence and self-reliance our National Revolutionary Army should possess. Such long-term hard and bitter struggle, rare and commendable, is not inferior to the dauntless fighting and sacrifice of the officers and soldiers exposed to gunfire and bombs in the front. His sacrifice caused by the attack is apparently a long-cherished plot of enemies and their puppets who brought over ruffians and instigated the murderous scheme, whereas our brave officers and soldiers in the 'Lost Battalion Barracks', though unarmed, captured the traitors, preventing their collective honour being damaged. Despite his unfortunate decease, his spirit will remain immortal.[86]

By 29 April, a staggering 40,000 people had paid tribute to Xie at the 'Lone Battalion Barracks' with a notable number of students wearing *Kuomintang* uniforms and armbands.[87] Shangguan Zhibiao, now leader

Xie Jinyuan's funeral led by Shangguan Zhibiao (centre front).
(Wikipedia)

of the Eight Hundred, despite his serious wounds inflicted during the assassination, returned to the camp to pay his respects. The size of the crowds increased while a memorial was planned for 3 May and Chinese newspapers received large donations to fund the event. In order to hold back masses of mourners, only registered individuals and organizations could be present at the memorial. Inside the camp people prepared by gathering 100,000 mourning scrolls and wreaths as crowds bowed before a portrait of Xie.[88]

The Gordon Road police meanwhile continued their investigation of the four assassins who would be tried by the First Special District Court presided over by Judge Chiang.[89] The *North China Daily News* reported on 22 June that ten soldiers from the 'Lone Battalion Camp' had been charged with murder and were being tried by the First Special District Court and that 'some of them confessed to the crime others denied that they had anything to do with the plot'.[90] The identities of the other six men were not stated. Shangguan Zhibiao testified during the trial that Zhang Guoshun stabbed him five times when he was trying to save Xie. The coverage of the trial centred on the undisputed ringleader He Dingcheng who claimed that Xie whipped him after he stole food from the camp kitchen, but he admitted to stabbing Xie. Zhang Guoshun admitted to carrying a knife but denied attacking Xie, although he did confess to stabbing Shangguan Zhibiao. The *North China Daily News* explained that establishing precisely what happened was difficult:

> The case is very complicated. While several witnesses alleged that they were attacked while trying to rescue deceased, accused tried to exonerate themselves by saying that they also tried to save him and mistook a witness to be a bad character. Interest was centred round the knife used in the murder. One witness confessed having brought a knife with him in the camp but that the knife had been stolen by an accused who in turn passed it on to another accused.[91]

On 1 November 1941, the press announced that three of the four assassins had been sentenced to death. Zhang Wenqing's death sentence was commuted to life imprisonment after an appeal. Two other soldiers were sentenced to life imprisonment and two others received nine-year sentences.[92] However, it is unknown if the death sentences were carried out before the Japanese attacked Pearl Harbor on 7 December. The ultimate fate of the assassins is unknown, although Shangguan Zhibiao claimed that two hangings took place after Japan invaded the British Concession:

> In order to win people's hearts and suppress the anger of the compatriots across the country, Wang's Puppet Regime severely punished the murderer who assassinated Xie. In the 32nd year of the Republic of China calendar, the two murderers He Dingcheng and Zhang Guoshun were hanged in Suzhou, and the remaining two murderers were also sentenced to life imprisonment.[93]

It is not possible to verify this story and Xie Jimin later lamented on the mystery surrounding the fate of his father's assassins:

In the wake of the outbreak of the Pacific War, Japanese armies seized the settlement. A broadcast program once stated that these four were sentenced to death, but whether execution happened or not remained unknown.[94]

As the Japanese Empire now controlled the International Settlement, its soldiers would finally exact revenge on the Eight Hundred Heroes for the humiliation they received at Sihang Warehouse after years of patient waiting.

CHAPTER SEVEN
CAPTIVITY AND VICTORY

ENDURANCE AND ESCAPE

Before dawn on 8 December 1941, the Japanese invaded the International Settlement. All British and American troops had already been withdrawn from Shanghai, but the river gunboats USS *Wake* and HMS *Peterel* were in the city. A Japanese boarding party seized the *Wake* after overpowering the skeleton crew but the *Peterel*, commanded by Lieutenant Stephen Polkinghorn, fought back courageously. After a Japanese officer boarded the warship and demanded its surrender, Polkinghorn responded, 'Get off my bloody ship!'[1] The Japanese opened fire from shore batteries and nearby warships as the *Peterel* returned fire with two machine guns, but after suffering several direct hits, the ship exploded and keeled over. Six of the eighteen crew members died and the Japanese captured most of the survivors, but sympathetic Chinese civilians hid some of the British sailors.[2]

Japanese soldiers supported by light tanks and armoured cars advanced through the Settlement and secured key buildings including the Cathay Hotel. Wang Jingwei's regime established a presence in the Settlement and his secret police planned murder and kidnappings from a house on Jessfield Road.[3] Japanese soldiers also surrounded the 'Lone Battalion Barracks'. According to Sun Yuanliang, commander of the 88th Division, Wang

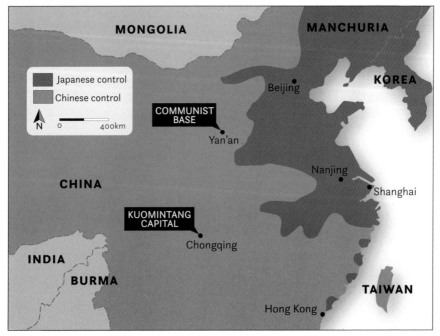

Japanese control of China in 1940.

Jingwei's agents initially attempted to persuade the Eight Hundred to defect:

> On 10 December, Chen Gongbo, the puppet mayor of Shanghai, wrote
> to comrade Lei Xiong, deputy regiment commander of the isolated
> troop, requesting everyone in his troop participate in the 'Peace
> Movement'. Comrade Lei refused sternly. On 28 December, hundreds
> of Japanese soldiers broke into the barracks of the isolated troop,
> escorting the unarmed troop to Baoshan Yuepu Airport for detention.[4]

On 9 February 1942, the Japanese transferred the prisoners to a camp in
Xinlonghua where they performed hard manual labour before moving
them to Laohuqiao Prison in Nanjing, as the soldier Chen Desong recalled:

> They transferred us from Jiaozhou Park to Wusong Kou and later to
> a railway station in the northern suburbs of Shanghai to imprison us.
> Even though unarmed, we fought twice by using stones and wooden

sticks with enemies whose misdeeds in China remained inhumane. The Japanese were concerned about international opinion, daring not to kill us at will and imprisoning us in the Laohuqiao Prison of Nanjing, where we continued our struggle. One day, the Japanese demanded we carry dung, which irritated a soldier of Hubei so much that he broke an enemy's arm. Hundreds of enemies marshalled together immediately and encircled us with machine guns positioned all around, threatening to shoot all of us dead.[5]

As the Eight Hundred retained their discipline and displayed a defiant spirit, the Japanese dispersed them to different camps in Guanghua Gate, Xiaolingwei, Hangzhou, Yuxikou and New Guinea while others remained in Laohuqiao Prison.[6] The men in captivity were ruled over by cruel new masters with no regard for the Geneva Convention and they now spent their days performing hard manual labour. Shangguan Zhibiao, who took command of the Eight Hundred after Xie Jinyuan's murder, remembered their plight as the men were forced 'to do hard work such as digging roads and carrying coal' and they 'lived a life of slavery like cows and horses'.[7]

British, American and Dutch civilians, now under Japanese occupation, had to wear red armbands in public, but some aspects of normal life remained and the Anglo-American members of the Shanghai Municipal Council continued to provide services. Japanese policy changed in 1943 and they interned 7600 Allied civilians in Shanghai within concentration camps referred to as 'civilian assembly centres' where the prisoners endured harsh conditions.[8] James Graham Ballard, a twelve-year-old prisoner, later wrote his classic novel *Empire of the Sun* (1984) based on his experiences in captivity during this time.

On 6 November 1942 the majority of the prisoners at Guanghua Gate near Nanjing escaped and fled to Xiaomao Mountain where most of them stayed after joining a local guerrilla unit while nine of the group headed to Chongqing to rejoin *Kuomintang* forces.[9] News of the escape reached the outside world in December 1942 after *The New York Times* reported that escapees had established contact with the Chinese government:

Seventeen Chinese soldiers, sole survivors of the 'Lone Battalion' which

fought a valiant rear-guard action at Shanghai in 1937, have escaped
from a Japanese concentration camp at Nanking [Nanjing], front
dispatches from East China reported today.[10]

Another newspaper announced: 'The soldiers are awaiting orders from
the ministry of war here and all have signified their desire for action
against the enemy.'[11]

In November 1942 another group of Chinese prisoners escaped from
Xiaolingwei, as Chen Desong recalled:

One night in November of 1942, eight of our soldiers successfully
escaped when we accidentally discovered the absence of electricity in
the electrified wire fence. With the help of local people and the New
Fourth Army, we safely reached Chongqing by way of Anhui, Jiangxi,
Guangdong, and Guangxi Province, and along the way we were greeted
enthusiastically by both soldiers and civilians. After finding the rear
office of the 88th Division established in Chongqing, we finally realized
our wish to rejoin the unit. I was appointed as a Platoon Commander
and received three-month intensified training before leaving for the
Myanmar [Burma] battlefield along with the expeditionary forces.[12]

In July 1943 the press reported that the nine soldiers from the Eight Hundred
had reached Chongqing and Corporal Li told his story:

We were taken by truck to a prison camp, with seven Japanese guarding
each 10 of us. They tried to make some of us turn traitors, and when
they failed, they lined us up and fired machine gun bullets an inch
above our heads. They tried to break our spirits by cutting off the
water and allowing us only one bag of rice a day for 332 officers and
men. . . The Japs forced us to dig trenches alongside the Shanghai
Nanking [Nanjing] railway. The trenches were filled with sharp-pointed
bamboos, whose effectiveness the Japanese tested by throwing in
harmless peasants. Our commanding officer, Colonel Lei Hsiung [Lei
Xiong], once reached the end of his temper, threw down his spade,
and knocked out the nearest guard. There was a 'free for all' before he

was overpowered. When members of our battalion refused to remove
their Chinese Army uniforms many of us were beaten with iron bars.
The only reason that the Japs did not shoot us was because even Wang
Ching-Wei's puppets admired the stand we had made at Shanghai.
Nine of us . . . decided to escape. We crossed the barbed wire, swam
a river, and made for Nanking's Purple Mountain. Farmers hid, fed,
and clothed us, then guerrillas guided us through the Japanese lines to
French Indo China.[13]

Lei Xiong died of illness due to overwork in Japanese captivity at Yuxikou
in 1943. However, in that year Shangguan Zhibiao successfully escaped and
joined a guerrilla unit:

I also fell ill in the spring of the 32nd year because of the hard labour. In
the meantime, my old stabbing wound recurred, so the enemy allowed
me to go to Wuxi on bail for medical treatment. I took this opportunity
to escape from their clutches, and left for southern Anhui and the Taihu
Lake area to participate in the guerrilla work of the Fourth Jiangsu
Security Column in the Jiangsu-Zhejiang-Anhui Border Region until the
victory of the anti-Japanese war when I returned to Shanghai.[14]

On 2 August 1943, the Japanese officially gave control of the Settlement
to Chen Gongbo, Wang Jingwei's mayor of Shanghai. The French
Concession, controlled by the Vichy regime, initially escaped occupation
but the Japanese handed it over to Wang Jingwei in 1943 after the French
relinquished extraterritoriality. After the Italian Armistice on 8 September
1943, the Japanese interned the San Marco Battalion of Italian Marines,
diplomatic staff and civilians; however, the Japanese later freed 2000 Italian
fascists who pledged their loyalty to Mussolini's Italian Social Republic.[15]

A report of another group of escaped prisoners emerged in February
1944, after 50 soldiers from the Eight Hundred reached Chinese lines after
escaping from a Japanese camp. Two other survivors reached safety in
Sichuan Province and announced that 84 troops from the battalion escaped
Japanese captivity at Wuhu in Anhui Province on 14 March 1943, although
33 others had been killed in a fight during the escape.[16]

DEATH IN RABAUL

In 1942, the Japanese transported 1504 Chinese Army prisoners to Rabaul on the island of New Britain in New Guinea who had previously been held in camps at Nanjing and Shanghai.[17] The Chinese soldiers included survivors who had defended Quzhou Airport in Zhejiang Province in June 1942 and guerrillas from the Loyal Righteous National Defence Army which had operated in Jiangsu and Zhejiang provinces under the control of China's spymaster Dai Li.[18] The Chinese prisoners included approximately 50 soldiers from the Eight Hundred including Tang Di, commander of the 3rd Company. The Japanese had also imprisoned Chinese civilians from New Britain and Malaya in the area.

The Japanese established a major naval base at Rabaul which had been their main staging point for operations in the South Pacific. Prisoners of the Japanese in New Britain lived a harsh existence performing slave labour to build infrastructure. Although General Douglas MacArthur's island-hopping campaign bypassed Rabaul in 1943, the isolated Japanese garrison survived on locally produced food as the prisoners continued to suffer.

On 22 August 1945, following the atomic obliteration of Hiroshima and Nagasaki, General Vernon Sturdee, commander of the First Australian Army, received a signal from Japanese commanders on New Britain who desired a ceasefire. After Sturdee accepted the Japanese surrender on board the aircraft carrier HMS *Glory* on 6 September, he intended to land Australian troops at Rabaul to liberate the island and rescue prisoners of war.[19]

After Captain Morris and Lieutenant Hancock disembarked at Rabaul from the destroyer HMAS *Vendetta*, they encountered a town overgrown with jungle as well as a port and airfield that had been destroyed by numerous bombing raids. Although the two Australian naval officers soon rescued the 28 surviving European prisoners, the Japanese still held 5589 Indian, 688 Malayan and 607 Indonesian prisoners in the vicinity.[20] On 10 September, soldiers from the 4th Australian Brigade disembarked from HMAS *Manoora* and *Katoomba* and began fanning out from Rabaul, moving deeper into the jungle. Reinforcements from the 13th Australian Brigade landed five days later to supplement the operation.

As Australian soldiers advanced further into the jungle, they received an

Former Chinese prisoners of war welcome their Australian liberators in New Britain on 17 September 1945. A sign can be seen in the background, declaring 'Welcome victory for our friendly Australian Imperial Forces'. (AWM)

unexpected and warm greeting on 17 September. Chinese soldiers inside a prisoner of war camp had hoisted the Republic of China flag. Eric Thornton, an Australian war correspondent, witnessed a group of Chinese soldiers and a large banner with a declaration: 'The road to victory was success. Welcome victory for our friendly Australian Imperial Forces'.[21] The soldiers wore improvised Chinese uniforms made from Japanese shirts complete with regimental insignia and cloth caps displaying the Star of China.[22]

During their ordeal, 653 Chinese prisoners (377 soldiers and 276 civilians) had died — a staggering fatality rate.[23] All Chinese prisoners of war had endured cruelty at the hands of Japanese and Taiwanese guards while living off a poor diet consisting mostly of rice that had been rejected for Japanese consumption and performing forced labour under brutal conditions with almost no medical care. Approximately fifteen soldiers from the Eight Hundred had died in Japanese captivity in New Britain.

Former Chinese prisoners of war after liberation in their quarters on 17 September 1945. (AWM)

The Australians had previously not known about the presence of Chinese prisoners in New Britain and they liberated 1397 survivors, including 748 soldiers, from camps on the Gazelle Peninsula near Rabaul. The Australians who liberated the Chinese prisoners understood the special significance of the 36 survivors from Sihang as their newspapers had earlier covered the heroic defence of the warehouse. The war correspondent M.C. Warren, who accompanied the Australian troops, accordingly reported that elements of a Chinese 'Lost Army' had been discovered consisting of men from the 'the crack 88th Division which made a suicide stand at Shanghai'.[24]

On 10 October 1945, the Chinese soldiers in Rabaul held a ceremonial parade in their new camp and the men marched under two arches displaying victory banners celebrating the 33rd anniversary of the Republic of China. General Kenneth Eather, commander of the 11th Australian Division, inspected the guard of honour and received a welcome from Colonel Wu Yien, the senior Chinese officer.[25] Afterwards, Captain Gaul set up a wireless

Three veterans of the Eight Hundred Heroes after being liberated by
Australian soldiers in New Britain in 1945. (AWM)

that picked up a signal from Chongqing, China's wartime capital, and the
men heard their first news from home in years.[26] An Australian reporter also
interviewed Colonel Wu:

> I visited the Chinese camp, where Col Woo [Wu] Yien told me that he
> was shipped to Rabaul in a small freighter with 1,500 other Chinese
> troops. During the voyage they were given only one meal of rice a day
> and one pint of water for every eight men. Several died of thirst and
> many others who felt sick were thrown overboard by the Japs. Col Woo
> [Wu] has nothing but praise for the way the Army authorities here have
> treated his troops.[27]

Following the euphoria of liberation, Chinese soldiers identified Japanese
war criminals.[28] In one trial, Sergeant Tozaburo Matsushima, Private
Harimoto Ayizama and seven Japanese civilians were sentenced to death

for murdering 24 Chinese prisoners on 3 March 1943. Captain Liu Weibao testified that Japanese and Taiwanese guards ordered these men to get into a pit, but after the men refused, the guards attacked the group with sticks and rifle butts before opening fire.[29] Another trial sentenced Lance Corporal Tajima and Suseme, a Taiwanese civilian, to death for murdering four Chinese prisoners in April 1943 while Lieutenant Mitsu Tasaka received a life sentence.[30] Chinese soldiers also testified at the trial of General Akira Hirota, the supply depot commander in Rabaul, who oversaw the killing of sick Chinese soldiers.[31] Colonel Wu testified that Hirota had ordered that any prisoner sick for three days would be killed and 30 Chinese prisoners had been shot or beheaded for this reason.[32] In April 1947, the court found Hirota guilty of responsibility for war crimes committed by his subordinates and sentenced him to seven years' imprisonment.[33]

During the war crimes trials, the Chinese soldiers in Rabaul waited to go home. Colonel Wu, after early repatriation failed to occur, visited Australia in October 1945 and lobbied officials in Melbourne and the Chinese Consul in Canberra.[34] In early 1946, the Australian press complained about the long delay in getting the Chinese survivors home. 'The Chinese seem to be the forgotten men of Rabaul,' Max Coleman reported in *The Mail*. 'All the Indonesian, Malay, and Indian prisoners of war liberated at Rabaul by the Australians have gone home and the Japs are getting away at the rate of 20,000 a month, but the Chinese are still here.'[35] J.S.R. Ferguson, the senior YMCA welfare officer in Rabaul and a chaplain to the Chinese soldiers, similarly declared:

> The keen disappointment of the Chinese has been largely overcome by their inexhaustible patience, but their greatest anxiety is due to the very few replies received in answer to the hundreds of letters sent to China during the past seven months. Letters which have arrived have brought such sad and discouraging news that the survivors of this tragic force are more anxious than ever to return home. I feel absolutely confident that if General MacArthur were aware that these men were still languishing here seven months after the Jap surrender, he would immediately arrange for an American ship or, if that were not available, for some Japanese vessel to come to Rabaul immediately and return them to China.[36]

The Australian Government eventually repatriated the Chinese soldiers, including the 36 survivors from Sihang Warehouse including Tang Di who arrived in Shanghai on 24 August 1946.[37]

THE LAST DAYS OF WAR

By 1943 the war in the Pacific had decisively turned against Japan and Chiang Kai-shek opportunistically waited for American industrial might to defeat the invaders. Roosevelt and Churchill, in a positive indication of a just post-war world, treated him as an equal at the Cairo Conference on 25 November 1943 where the leaders demanded Japan's unconditional surrender and declared that Manchuria, Taiwan and the Pescadores islands would be returned to China.

Mao Zedong also waited for America to defeat Japan and attempted to preserve his forces for the seemingly inevitable civil war that would follow the defeat of Japan.[38] The communist insurgency against the Japanese reached its height between 1938 and 1940, after which Mao focused on political expansion and positioning for advantage for his anticipated showdown with Chiang.[39] The Sino-Japanese War had gravely weakened the *Kuomintang*, which presented an opportunity for the communists to infiltrate their forces into China's heartland south of the Yangtze.[40] Furthermore, Japan's devastating 1944 Ichi-Go offensives, its largest campaigns of the war, routed Chiang's armies and overran large areas of Henan, Hunan and Guangxi, which severely weakened the *Kuomintang*'s ability to make a comeback after the war.[41]

On 10 November 1944, Wang Jingwei died while undergoing treatment in a Tokyo hospital for complications resulting from injuries sustained in an assassination attempt. A power struggle broke out among his fellow collaborators as his dying regime initiated secret talks with the *Kuomintang* and the communists.

After World War II finally ended, the American command ship USS *Rocky Mount* arrived in Shanghai on 19 September 1945, heralding the end of the Japanese occupation. The world of Old Shanghai was over and there would be no restoration of the International Settlement or the French Concession. The United States persuaded Britain to abandon extraterritoriality and the Allies renounced their treaty rights during the war, ending western imperialism in China. Shanghai became a unified city under *Kuomintang* rule and as the party regained control its agents killed and arrested traitors and collaborators. The foreign communities also began their exodus from the city and most White Russians immigrated to America and Canada as the Jewish community departed for Hong Kong, America and later Israel.

In October 1945, Chiang Kai-shek, in an attempt to appear reasonable, told Mao Zedong that 'If we can't pull together, then it's World War III.'[42] Despite American efforts led by General George Marshall to mediate between the two sides, the Chinese Civil War commenced in 1946, although there had been fighting since the Japanese surrender. As the war continued Chiang increasingly lost legitimacy and as corruption eroded his government, his vision of China's future seemed unclear.[43]

Shangguan Zhibiao meanwhile returned to Shanghai and made contact with over 100 survivors from the Eight Hundred. He organized the transfer of Xie Jinyuan's grave to a garden on Singapore Road at 'Lone Battalion Barracks'. In 1947 Shangguan convinced the Shanghai Municipal Government to transform the barracks into Jinyuan Park and to rename Jiaozhou Road next to Sihang Warehouse as Jinyuan Road and to name a nearby school Jinyuan National Elementary School. Shangguan also organized the commemoration of his dead commander:

On 24 April every year, I would gather the 800 warriors to honour
General Xie and the heroes fallen in battles to comfort their souls. After
everything was ready, I followed General Sun Yuanliang to serve in the
Third Front. I joined the Southeast Supervisory Group and travelled
across Jiangnan and Northern Jiangsu to restore local order and work
for post-war rehabilitation.[44]

Zhang Boting similarly recalled: 'After the victory of the anti-Japanese war, comrade Shangguan and I got together again and held a grand memorial service for the isolated troop in Shanghai. We then went together to serve in the Third Front in Wuxi.'[45]

The *Kuomintang*'s post-war rule in Shanghai would be a short-term administration. Although Chiang's reformist son Chiang Ching-kuo arrived in the city in 1947 determined to eliminate corruption and hyperinflation, the People's Liberation Army defeated the *Kuomintang* in Manchuria and northern China. Mao's soldiers entered Shanghai in May 1949 as Chiang's shattered forces fled to Taiwan. The city would change forever as a massive social experiment in communism created a new society that obliterated public memory of the Eight Hundred Heroes, even though communist propagandists had been instrumental in creating the legend during the early days of the Sino-Japanese War.

CHAPTER EIGHT
INSPIRATION AND GLORIFICATION

WARTIME PROPAGANDA IN CHINA

After Sun Yat-sen reorganized the *Kuomintang* along Leninist lines in 1923, he founded the Ministry of Propaganda modelled on Soviet experience that emphasized the ideological indoctrination of his Three Principles of the People. The National Revolutionary Army was subsequently indoctrinated with the help of Soviet-trained commissars to ensure the army was politically loyal. During the Eastern Expedition of 1925, propaganda units went in advance of the army to inform the population that the revolutionary soldiers were not warlords but friends of the people. After the Northern Expedition, the *Kuomintang* attempted to centralize and control information through censorship, political training and the distribution of publications.[1] However, such efforts only had limited effectiveness given the new regime's ineffective control over the country and the presence of the Great Powers in the treaty ports.

Foreigners established modern commercial journalism in the Treaty Ports during the 1870s, a development which allowed a remarkably open press that continued into the twentieth century. Shanghai was the centre of foreign reporting and the *North China Daily News*, the oldest British-owned newspaper founded in 1850, personified the mind of the British 'Shanghailanders'.[2]

The *Kuomintang*'s attempts to control the media failed as banned materials were readily available in the Treaty Ports.[3] Despite the bloodshed of the Shanghai Massacre in 1927, communists effectively organized in the city by taking advantage of the Treaty Port system. For example, Agnes Smedley, a journalist based in Shanghai and Comintern agent, founded the *China Forum*, which was legally an American newspaper but was controlled and funded by the Chinese Communist Party.[4] Underground communist propagandists had greater effectiveness than their *Kuomintang* counterparts, as demonstrated by the 'Xi'an Incident' when the 'Young Marshal' Zhang Xueliang, under the influence of propaganda, kidnapped Chiang Kai-shek, which led to the creation of the anti-Japanese United Front.

After the *Kuomintang* established its wartime capital at Chongqing, it reorganized and attempted grassroots activism by despatching propaganda teams into the provinces it still controlled. The party's message glorified the epic retreat from Wuhan in an effort to reassure the civilian population and recruit new soldiers. A propaganda campaign also focused on recent successes, notably the major Chinese victory at Taierzhuang in 1938.[5] A *Kuomintang* slogan intending to persuade people to accept the sacrifices of war declared: 'For the country, for the race, for democracy, for freedom, for oneself, for one's family, for one's descendants'.[6]

The legend of the Eight Hundred Heroes formed a central pillar in the *Kuomintang*'s wartime propaganda. After the commencement of hostilities, the party established the Shanghai Cultural Circles National Salvation Federation to mobilize intellectuals and help them produce propaganda. By September 1937, the Federation had a membership of 121 cultural societies and 5000 people who were mostly from the communist-affiliated national salvation unions. The Federation was a United Front organization with the *Kuomintang* and the Communist Party sharing leadership at the top, but the communists dominated the organization at the grassroots level.[7]

Although the Eight Hundred Heroes were National Revolutionary Army soldiers, the popular mythology concerning their heroic deeds was heavily shaped by communist propaganda. As Japanese forces advanced through Shanghai on 26 October 1937, the Federation's communist intellectuals responded to the imminent Chinese collapse by resolving to create 'more propaganda work in the form of writings'.[8] The new program intended to

A Chinese propaganda image of Xie Jinyuan in *The China Pictorial*.

(Author's Collection)

raise fighting spirit and the Eight Hundred became central to this effort.[9] The Federation's intellectuals immediately elevated the Eight Hundred to legendary status. Three consecutive special issues of *National Salvation Daily* included articles and poems glorifying the 'Lost Battalion' as a defiant symbol of the Chinese spirit that would eventually defeat Japan.[10] During this time Yi Guan composed the poem 'The Resistance Spirit of the Eight Hundred Warriors':

In the spreading shade of dusk,
we pull up the shining national flag.
It represents the unique holiness and purity
of our national uprightness.
Inside our eight hundred lives is hidden
the spirit of China.
We shall win one day.[11]

The communist intellectuals also linked the Eight Hundred to other symbolic events in Chinese history, further enhancing the mythology. For example, they noted that the battalion's breakout into the International Settlement occurred on the anniversary of the death of Huang Xing, the second most important leader of the 1911 Revolution after Sun Yat-sen.[12]

Propagandists produced other heroic accounts of Sihang Warehouse in the immediate aftermath of the battle. The book *The Eight Hundred Heroes Who Shook the World* was published in 1937 less than two months after the events and its title referenced John Reed's classic communist account of the Russian Revolution *Ten Days That Shook the World*. In 1937 Gui Taosheng wrote the highly emotional and popular 'Eight Hundred Heroes Song' and Xia Zhiqiu composed the music, which became a virtual national anthem. The 'Eight Hundred Heroes Song' even became a feature in the upper echelons of the Communist Party and He Shide, who composed the communist 'New Fourth Army Song', sung it for party officials.[13] Xie Jimin in *My Father, General Xie Jinyuan* remarked that the song 'became an immortal song encouraging each Chinese descendant to love his country and rally to resistance against aggression'.[14]

The story of the Eight Hundred was also told in theatre, as the journalist

W.M. Peacock explained in the Australian newspaper *The Age* on 13 May 1939:

> The most stirring and popular of the war-time plays is The Lone
> Battalion . . . The heroine is a Girl Guide who, defying the Japanese
> soldiers, crosses the Soochow [Suzhou] Creek, and presents a huge
> Chinese flag to the doomed men, which they proudly fly — the last
> Chinese banner in Chapei [Zhabei], waving amidst a forest of Rising
> Suns. These plays are performed all over China, and proceeds go to
> China's War Chest.[15]

Propaganda concerning the Eight Hundred struck a chord with the Chinese people. For example, Madam He Xiangning, a member of the *Kuomintang* Central Executive Committee, reportedly wept at accounts of their deeds:

> Each one of you has a revolutionary and sacrificial spirit. Because of
> you, the martyrs will become even greater, the soldiers at the front-
> line will fight more bravely, the Chinese people will become united and
> people in the world will become more just.[16]

After reading about the exploits of the Eight Hundred in a Chinese newspaper, Chen Kewen, a resident of Nanjing, recorded in his diary that he 'was inspired, and moved to tears'.[17] The Eight Hundred became the central feature of propaganda glorying Chinese soldiers as heroic defenders of the nation.[18]

After the fall of Shanghai, communist propagandists created their greatest legacy regarding the Eight Hundred in the temporary capital at Wuhan. Before the war, Shanghai had a vibrant film industry and the city was known as the 'Hollywood of the East'. After the war devastated the city's movie industry, many directors and actors joined the exodus of refugees into the interior and many personnel from the Nationalist Central Studio relocated to Wuhan.[19] The *Kuomintang* wanted patriotic films and, as the party owned two studios through the China Motion Picture Corporation in the territory it still controlled, it had the means to make them.[20] The government founded the All-China Film Circles Wartime Resistance Association in Wuhan on 29 January 1938, which became central to the production of wartime propaganda films and communists played a prominent role. *Kuomintang*-sponsored films made in Wuhan at this time included *Defending Our Land* and *Warm Blood, Loyal Spirit*, but the most influential film produced during this time concerned the Eight Hundred.

Kuomintang officials in Wuhan commissioned a major patriotic movie in early 1938 to tell the story of Sihang Warehouse and three prominent Chinese communists and a fellow traveller made the resultant film — *Eight Hundred Heroes* (1938). Ying Yunwei, a prominent left-wing director who had joined the Association as a 'progressive filmmaker', directed the movie.[21] Yang Hansheng, the screenwriter, had joined the Association as a 'Communist Party member'. The actor Yuan Muzhi played Xie Jinyuan and the actress Chen Bo'er portrayed the Girl Guide Yang Huimin. After the outbreak of war, Yuan Muzhi, a well-known star in Shanghai, fled to Wuhan along with Chen Bo'er. Both had joined the Communist Party in 1937 and had been invited by Zhou Enlai, a prominent communist leader, to come to Mao Zedong's stronghold in Yan'an to establish a film production team. Although Yuan and Chen intended to eventually create a communist film-making organization in Yan'an, in the meantime they starred in *Eight Hundred Heroes*.

Ying Yunwei made a documentary-style movie designed to make its story accessible to the masses.[22] *Eight Hundred Heroes* is a black and white silent film that glorifies the brave defenders but also places much emphasis on Yang Huimin's bravery in delivering the Republic of China flag to Sihang Warehouse.[23] The movie ends with a montage sequence in which news of the heroic battle spreads throughout China and then across the world through newspapers, radios and other mediums as international crowds salute the Republic of China flag in solidarity with the Eight Hundred.

Eight Hundred Heroes contained strong nationalistic themes and was intended to inspire Chinese people to resist the Japanese invasion.[24] The movie found an audience and a foreign journalist reported that it was 'being exhibited throughout China'.[25] Although one film critic dismissed *Eight Hundred Heroes* as 'thoroughly news-like' and 'ultimately uninspiring', most Chinese moviegoers found the movie inspirational.[26] The film's wide release certainly raised awareness of the nation's dire plight.[27] Xie Jimin in *My Father, General Xie Jinyuan* spoke fondly of the movie: 'Its enormous

The Chinese actress Chen Bo'er portraying Yang Huimin alongside Chinese soldiers in the movie *Eight Hundred Heroes* (1938). (Author's Collection)

popularity among soldiers and civilians gained since its premiere in 1938 endured during the whole period of the anti-Japanese war. People were remarkably encouraged, and morale was lifted.'[28]

Yuan Muzhi later travelled to Yan'an where he joined the Yan'an Film Corps, established in September 1938 by the Eighth Route Army Political Department, as did Chen Bo'er where they both became instrumental in establishing the communist film industry.[29] After Mao later founded the People's Republic of China, Yuan continued to be a major figure in communist cinema before his death on 30 January 1978. Chen Bo'er oversaw the North East Film Studio in 1947 and married Yuan Muzhi before dying suddenly on 10 November 1951. Ying Yunwei made films in Maoist China until he was murdered during the Cultural Revolution on 17 January 1967. Yang Hansheng later worked with the legendary Soviet director Sergei Eisenstein during the production of *Ivan the Terrible Part I*

Chen Bo'er as Yang Huimin giving a Girl Guide salute in the movie *Eight Hundred Heroes* (1938). (Author's Collection)

(1944) in Moscow. He fled to Hong Kong in 1948 to escape the *Kuomintang* before returning to Shanghai after 1949.[30] Although Yang Hansheng had to 'apologize' for his earlier collaboration with the *Kuomintang*, he worked for the Communist Party's film industry. Yang was arrested during the Cultural Revolution in 1966, but he was later reinstated as Vice Chairman of the China Federation of Literary and Artistic Circles. He died in Beijing on 7 June 1993.

After the war *Eight Hundred Heroes* became a lost film, but fortunately Daniel Wang, a Hong Kong resident, protected a copy during the Japanese occupation and his daughter Dolores Wang donated it to the Hong Kong Film Archive in 1994, which restored the movie and organized screenings. 'Despite being produced as a silent film due to production limitations,' a spokesman from the Archive declared, 'Eight Hundred Heroes is a spectacular and realistic re-enactment of the epic battle, proving that wartime patriotic propaganda films can also have artistic and aesthetic merits.'[31]

Like most war movies, *Eight Hundred Heroes* contains inaccuracies. The film depicted Yang Huimin swimming across Suzhou Creek when in reality she crossed New Lese Bridge. Her swim was likely intended to depict a psychical aesthetic associated with the Girl Guide movement and she even promoted the film alongside the female swimmer Yang Xiuqiong.[32] However, the association of Yang Huimin with swimming is not wholly inaccurate as she did swim back to the International Settlement after delivering the flag. *Eight Hundred Heroes* also depicted Yang saluting the men and leading them in a procession during the iconic flag-raising ceremony, when the actual ceremony was more of a low-key event. Yang was not entirely happy with the way the film portrayed her actions as it exaggerated her courage.[33]

A second movie about Sihang Warehouse was made in China in 1938. Lu Si directed *Eight Hundred Heroes*, made in Hong Kong at the Beyond Dadi Studio, but this version sadly no longer exists, as Weihong Bao explained:

Although the film is no longer extant, newspaper publicity indicates that it was more narrative driven than its mainland counterpart, mixing romance, comedy, and even Cantonese theme songs in order to appeal to the largest-possible audience. Film reviews criticized some of these elements, which ended up compromising the message to its target audience. Yet the publicity highlighted not the romance but the sensational thrills, heroism, and use of documentary footage. The ads used large type to underscore 'real Shanghai scenery,' that 'the real eight hundred heroes appear on screen,' and the 'human flesh bomb' — a soldier wrapping himself with explosives, jumping from a skyscraper, and killing more than thirty enemies.[34]

The travellers W.H. Auden and Christopher Isherwood visited China in early 1938 and when in Hong Kong they visited Beyond Dadi Studio during the post-production of *Eight Hundred Heroes*, and they provided a highly ethnocentric account of the film:

> At present the studio was producing only war-films. Just now they were at work on the story of Shanghai's 'Doomed Battalion'. It would be called Fight to the Last. We were shown some of the rushes. The war-scenes were brilliant. The producer had an astonishingly subtle feeling for grouping; his weakness lay in the direction of the actors themselves — he had indulged too often the Chinese talent for making faces. All these grimaces of passion, anger, or sorrow, seemed a mere mimicry of the West. One day a director of genius will evolve a style of acting which is more truly national — a style based upon the beauty and dignity of the Chinese face in repose.[35]

The saga of the Eight Hundred inspired the Chinese community in Hong Kong. In January 1938, Shanghai Scout leaders visited the British colony to raise funds for the war effort and the local version of *Eight Hundred Heroes* was screened to thousands of school children.[36] Patriotic Chinese students in Hong Kong created the All-Hong Kong Students' National Salvation and War Relief Association in September 1937 to raise funds for the war effort. Stanley Kwan recalled how the heroic stand at Sihang inspired his fellow students in Hong Kong after they watched a charity performance by the Wuhan Ensemble:

> Their repertoire included songs depicting the sufferings of the people and extolling China's war efforts: 'Defend our Country China', 'March of the Volunteers', 'On the Songhua River', 'Fight Our Way Back to the Northeast' and 'Ode to the Eight Hundred Heroes'. The concert was a rousing success, and as the voices of the singers soared to the tall white ceilings of our school hall so did our spirits. Thunderous applause resounded through the hall after each song. The headmaster, William Kay, was deeply moved and became so sympathetic to the students' cause that, aside from urging the audience to donate as much as they could, he himself presented the manager of the ensemble with a big cheque. It was one of the most emotional moments of my life.[37]

The legend of Sihang Warehouse also inspired the Chinese community in Malaya and Singapore where the artist Liu Kang observed how his colleagues admired the Eight Hundred and incorporated the story in their work.[38] Wang Gungwu in his memoir about growing up in Singapore recalled stories about the Eight Hundred:

> Late in 1938, the Wuhan Choir, already famous among the Chinese overseas, arrived in Malaya to raise funds for the war effort in China. They started with Singapore and were visiting all the states with a sizeable Chinese population. When they eventually turned up in Ipoh the next year, they won the hearts of most local Chinese. The choir's leader was already well known to us. He was the composer of 'The 800 Heroes'.[39]

Wang Gungwu also recalled seeing the film *Eight Hundred Heroes*:

> After 1937, my parents began taking me to cinemas to see patriotic films. I do not remember how many we saw, but one that I saw in 1938 left a very deep impression. This was Babai zhuangshi (The 800 Heroes), a film showing how the opening battle of Shanghai in late 1937 ended in retreat. I joined everyone in the cinema at the end of the film to cheer the heroes who fought bravely before they abandoned the large warehouse that they had been desperately defending. . . I also became more attentive to other war or patriotic films my parents took me to see. None had the same impact as The 800 Heroes, but I did find one of them memorable.[40]

The legend of the Eight Hundred did not just enter consciousness within Chinese communities as westerners also became invested in their story.

ACROSS THE GLOBE

The *Kuomintang* created international propaganda by forming relationships with foreign journalists working in China.[41] The major western wire news agencies all had bureaus in the country including Reuters (British), The

Associated Press (American), Wolf (German) and Havas (French).[42] The *Kuomintang*'s official statistics recorded the presence of over 500 foreign journalists in the country during the war and it made strong efforts to influence their reporting.[43]

In September 1937, Chiang Kai-shek placed Dong Xianguang, an American-trained journalist, in charge of international propaganda.[44] Dong used contacts with western journalists to spread pro-China propaganda and their reports from seemingly neutral observers enhanced credibility.[45] In this way, Archibald Steele, who was close to Dong, became the first journalist to report the 'Rape of Nanking' to the outside world through his graphic account in the *Chicago Daily News*.[46]

Dong Xianguang tirelessly cultivated good relations with foreign reporters by swiftly acting upon their information requests and arranging interviews with high-ranking Chinese officials; his department organized over 300 press conferences between 1 December 1937 and 24 October 1938.[47] The foreign press largely reported the war with a pro-Chinese bias, in part due to Dong's effort. For example, the British journalist Hubert Hessell Tiltman wrote after touring the front:

> There is most emphatically no resemblance whatever discernable between the Chinese army of yesterday and the confident, well-disciplined men whom I saw. They are facing incredible hardships with a courage which deserves the most flattering tribute that a pen can write.[48]

The *Kuomintang* reached audiences outside China through the newspapers published in the Treaty Ports which were integrated into the international press system. In this way, sympathetic reports on the Eight Hundred spread across the globe in near real time, as content that first appeared in newspapers like the *North China Daily News* was swiftly repeated in major overseas newspapers like *The New York Times*. This process was aided by reporters who often simultaneously worked for Treaty Port newspapers and the international press.[49] The influential foreign Treaty Port newspapers also had large readerships among China's elite and its rising bilingual middle class. Furthermore, these newspapers increasingly hired cosmopolitan

Chinese writers who knew how to appeal to western sensibilities when reporting Chinese news.[50] Therefore, it is unsurprising that international sympathy overwhelmingly rested with China, as Zhang Boting, the 88th Division's chief-of-staff, explained:

> The '800 warriors' spared no effort in defending Sihang Warehouse. Their heroic spirit was full of power and earthshaking, not only inspiring people of the country, but also causing a sensation in the whole world through news reports by foreign journalists and people from friendly nations who experienced and witnessed this in the cosmopolitan city of Shanghai. People from friendly nations unanimously placed unlimited respect and sympathy towards the '800 warriors'.[51]

In contrast to Dong Xianguang's efforts, the Japanese in China failed to win over foreign reporters largely because they treated them as enemy spies. After the Marco Polo Bridge incident, American and British journalists in Beijing could not cable their stories out of the city as the Japanese had cut the telegraph wire. The Japanese in Beijing also imprisoned two foreign newspaper editors for demonstrating bias towards the *Kuomintang*.[52] Japanese press conferences often became tense after their spokesmen displayed hostility towards British and American journalists, which only increased sympathetic reporting on China.[53] This hostile relationship became apparent during the defence of Sihang Warehouse in Rear Admiral Tadao Honda's disastrous press conference after his arrogance resulted in the western press labelling him the 'news ogre'.

After the Japanese occupied the Chinese districts of Shanghai, their agents attempted to seize English language newspapers in the mail sent from the still neutral foreign concessions.[54] In 1938, the Japanese prevented Harold Timperley from *The Manchester Guardian* from sending stories from Shanghai after reporting on the 'Rape of Nanking', and their censors banned the distribution of the *Shanghai Evening Post* because of 'very anti-Japanese' articles.[55] Japan's futile attempts to censor foreign reporters further solidified international opinion behind China as the story of Sihang Warehouse reached an ever-increasing audience overseas.

Footage of the actual defence of Sihang Warehouse appeared in the

THE LONE BATTALION

BY SAPAJOU

A cartoon depicting the courage of the Eight Hundred Heroes printed in the *North China Daily News* on 30 October 1937. (Author's Collection)

documentary propaganda film *Ravaged Earth* (1942) and one reviewer commented, 'The heroic resistance of the trapped "Doomed Battalion" of Chinese troops against overwhelming odds is also pictured.'[56] The Eight Hundred created an emotional reaction in western minds and the Wuhan movie *Eight Hundred Heroes* inspired both Chinese and foreign audiences. The film was shown in numerous locations including Hong Kong, the Philippines, Malaya, France, Switzerland and the United States.[57] One American Girl Guide who watched the movie was so moved that she arranged for her troop to exchange letters with Chinese Girl Guides.[58] During China Week held at the Memorial Union in Wisconsin in October 1945, cultural events were organized including Chinese dancing, music, shadow plays, book talks and tea in an attempt to promote understanding of Chinese culture. The activities also included a special screening of *Eight Hundred Heroes*.[59]

After the Fall of Shanghai and the failure of the Nine-Power Treaty conference, the *Kuomintang* reconsidered its wartime diplomacy and prioritized winning American support, and Chiang Kai-shek explained this logic:

> Great Britain is experienced and astute, and hard to lobby for help, and Russia has her own national policy, and our appeal to her for help has failed. But the United States is a democratic country in which public opinion matters, and it is relatively easy to activate her chivalrous spirit; moreover, President Roosevelt is ambitious to resolve the Far Eastern question thoroughly and comprehensively. If public opinion is sympathetic and Congress is supportive, then President Roosevelt will achieve his goals.[60]

The American press had a largely positive view of Chiang since the 1930s and photographs of him regularly featured on the front pages of newspapers and magazines.[61] Henry Luce, the son of a missionary working in China, founded Time Inc., the first global media empire which published *Time, Fortune, Life* and *Sports Illustrated*. Luce left China in 1912 shortly before the 'Warlord Era' and returned in 1932 during the *Kuomintang*'s 'Nanjing Decade' where he formed strong connections with powerful individuals in the new government including the Christian convert T.V. Soong, Chiang's brother-in-law and finance minister.[62] Luce hoped to inspire China into becoming a Christian nation modelled on the American example and believed the country had 'embarked upon a vast reformation — partly inspired by the Christian gospel'.[63] After Chiang converted to Christianity at the urging of his American-educated wife Soong Mei-ling, Luce perceived the event as evidence of his vision coming true.[64] The power couple seemingly embodied American hopes for China and Chiang appeared on *Time* magazine covers ten times.[65]

Although the United States could not provide direct military assistance due to the Neutrality Act, the government allowed China to purchase small-calibre weapons and other goods. In 1938, the *Kuomintang* used loan credits from the Sino-American Silver-Gold Exchange Agreement to purchase $48 million worth of armaments and the following year both countries signed the Tung Oil Loan Agreement worth $25 million that China used to purchase vehicles and improve the Burma Road.[66]

In September 1937, a Gallup poll indicated that only 43 per cent of Americans sympathized with China over Japan and that 55 per cent supported neither side. The determined Chinese resistance in Shanghai, the 'Rape of Nanking' and the sinking of the gunboat USS *Panay* in the Yangtze by Japanese aircraft on 12 December shifted American public opinion. By February 1938, 59 per cent of Americans sympathized with China and 36 per cent supported arms shipments to China.[67] A 1939 Gallup poll indicated that 74 per cent of Americans sympathized with the Chinese cause and by 7 September 1941, 70 per cent of the public supported halting Japanese military expansion even at the risk of war.[68] These sentiments represented a shift in public perception that resulted in part from the efforts of a Chinese Girl Guide who electrified American crowds.

YANG HUIMIN ABROAD

The *Kuomintang*, through the Chinese Scouting Association, promoted Yang Huimin as a model heroine to inspire other Girl Guides and she became a spokesperson for the Chinese war effort after Soong Mei-ling presented her with an award for valour. Yang toured war-ravaged China as part of her continued service with the Shanghai Wartime Service Scouts to raise morale and in doing so she became an icon, appearing on magazine covers alongside film stars.[69]

Dong Xianguang, head of the *Kuomintang*'s international propaganda, sponsored Yang Huimin to attend the World Youth Congress in America, to take place at Vassar College in New York State in August 1938, and she would travel there via Singapore and Britain. In July, the *North China Daily News* reported that the Chinese delegation to the Congress would comprise fifteen people including Yang who 'braved great personal danger' to present a flag to the Eight Hundred.[70] Later that month Yang received a strong reception in Malaya where the press portrayed her as a model exemplar of Chinese womanhood.[71] When she arrived in London, *The Guardian* portrayed Yang as a free-spirited and adventurous young woman who in 'childhood mingled with foreign children and grew up into a "wild girl" in the eyes of her Chinese neighbours' before pointing out that she 'was the first Chinese girl in Chinkiang [Zhenjiang] who could swim and ride a bicycle'.[72] The newspaper also reported a mostly inaccurate account of Yang's actions at Sihang Warehouse as mythology came to dominate the narrative:

> The Generalissimo, Chiang Kai-shek, decided to send the order for retreat, and one of the three chosen to take the order was Girl Guide Yang Hui-min. She carried the Chinese flag to indicate their intention and bore the order across that perilous 100 yards. The warehouse was evacuated, 300 of the battalion escaped uninjured, and all the wounded were safely carried to the International Settlement. Miss Yang stayed to the end to help the wounded.[73]

Chiang did not entrust the retreat order to Yang as Zhang Boting, the 88th Division's chief-of-staff, gave the order to Xie Jinyuan over the telephone, and nor did she stay to help the wounded until the end. Yang herself rarely exaggerated to reporters and since she did not speak English, it is also possible that her interpreters misrepresented her words or that *Kuomintang* propaganda officials provided the dubious information to the western press.

Yang Huimin attended the White House-sponsored World Youth Congress where she met Eleanor Roosevelt. During the proceedings, she delivered a message of peace and global friendship, highlighting that Chinese Scouts attended to Chinese and Japanese wounded, but she asked delegates to consider an oil embargo against Japan. Yang also recounted the pride she felt after the Chinese flag was raised over Sihang Warehouse.[74]

After the Congress, Yang travelled to New York City where the journalist Julia McCarthy interviewed her on 15 August 1938:

> A 100-pound projectile that routed twelve Japanese soldiers last Nov. 12 in the Nantao [Nanshi] district of Shanghai whizzed into New York yesterday. Her name is Miss Yang Hui-ming and she is 21. She did it all with a simple gesture of which her ancestors Goddess of Mercy would be proud. "I was saving refugees that day", explains modern Miss Yang between chopstick bites at lunch in the Port Arthur Restaurant with other Chinese delegates to the Second World Youth Congress. "With several, other girl guides, I encountered these Japanese soldiers. They drew pistols on us. I asked them to wait a minute. I threw open

the doors of a truck. In it, we had the refugees. Among them were a number of Japanese wounded. They put away their guns when they saw their own people inside."[75]

McCarthy incorrectly reported that Yang carried the retreat order and was with the soldiers during the breakout before continuing:

Fashion, social life and matrimony are things courageous Miss Yang doesn't think about. 'Dress? Give me a uniform. Love? I love my world peace. Chinese women the younger ones want no personal life today. The time is not ripe yet for anything but working for a united front for China.' . . . 'It is a long time since I have been in touch with my family,' says Miss Yang, fingering the government's decoration for valor attached to the shoulder of her long blue cotton Chinese dress.[76]

By the end of August, Yang's story had been recreated in an American radio play for *March of Time* and the actress Joan Tetzel, in an interview in *Life* magazine, shared her experience of playing the famous Girl Guide:

It was not so much the dialect that was hard, it was feeling the same thrill and terror of the Chinese girl, thinking the way she was thinking — being taken out of the self that I had been all my life. I only hope I was able to put all that into my voice as fully as I felt it.[77]

On 6 September 1938, a reporter for the *St. Louis Globe-Democrat* interviewed Yang Huimin and referred to her as the 'Joan of Arc of China':

Over a couple of bowls of bird's nest soup in a Mott street restaurant, Hui-Min recalled she was doing relief work with Boy Scouts and Girl Guides in Shanghai when her big moment came. . . Besides the red sweater, blue serge dress and purple scarf she was wearing, she traveled all the way to America via Europe with only one other costume in her knapsack. The Chinese Consul had one of his oddest assignments taking her around New York stores and helping her to buy everything from evening gowns to whatnots.[78]

The story repeated the legend that she had carried the retreat order and also claimed that she made five more trips to Sihang to deliver supplies to the Eight Hundred when she actually visited the warehouse only once.

In September 1938, the Detroit's Girl Guides welcomed Yang to their city, and she was also a guest on NBC's popular national radio show *Ripley's Believe It or Not*. The host Bob Ripley referred to Yang as the 'most amazing Chinese girl I ever have seen' and she learned enough English to say on air: 'I have seen many horrible things in war. I came to America to attend the World Youth Congress. I work for peace throughout the world.'[79] On 30 September, Yang addressed a crowd at a high school in Akron, Ohio accompanied by Peng Luo-Shan, a fellow Chinese delegate to the World Youth Congress and general secretary of the refugee relief commission in Wuhan Province. A journalist, who referred to Yang as 'the Chinese Joan of Arc', covered the event:

> Miss Yang, wearing a high-collared, mandarin-styled frock, strode eagerly toward the audience when she rose to speak, her lips pressed grimly together and her eyes blazing. She poured out her speech in the musical rising and falling cadences of the mandarin dialect, pausing from time to time to permit Peng to translate her remarks to the audience. But so expressive were her gestures, her hands, her features, and her eyes, one could almost follow her thought without waiting for Peng's translation.[80]

On 5 October, Yang and Peng spoke at a YWCA auditorium in Cincinnati where they were joined by Dr Lin, Assistant Secretary of Sun Yat-sen University in Guangzhou who also attended the World Youth Congress. Dr Lin predicated that Japan would soon be financially ruined as its gold supply was almost exhausted. Yang described the conditions that Chinese people endured in the war zones and Peng explained that the traditionally peace-loving Chinese people were now willing to fight and die for their country. The trio afterwards went to the Shanghai Inn restaurant, owned by Charlie Yu, head of the local Chinatown, where they dined with the town's mayor James Stewart.[81] Yang and Peng gave another talk at the Indiana War Memorial auditorium five days later sponsored by the

China Aid Council of Indianapolis where she spoke of 'indiscriminate bombings' by Japanese planes. Peng explained that the 'suffering of the Chinese people in the present war has demonstrated the national unity and solidarity of our race in its most beautiful form'.[82] After the talk the organizers held an afternoon reception for them at the Bamboo Inn Chinese restaurant.

As their American tour continued, Yang and Peng appeared in South Bend, Indiana at the Masonic Temple and at the First Presbyterian Church on 14 October 1938. Yang called for a boycott of Japanese goods but emphasized that she did not hate the Japanese people who had been forced into the war by militaristic leaders.[83] A reporter interviewed Yang three days later in St Louis, Missouri:

> Understanding English only slightly and able to speak it even less, Miss Yang's statements were interpreted by her companion, Peng. . . When interviewed in the Park Plaza Hotel, Miss Yang was wearing a long, pale blue Chinese dress, with short sleeves and high collar and a skirt reaching to her insteps. She has dark, bobbed hair. She frequently laughed, and gestured with her arms. . . 'I had to be smuggled out of Shanghai,' she said through her interpreter, 'because the Japanese had placed a price on my head.'[84]

Although Yang and Peng's grassroots activism successfully connected with American people, their busy schedule took a toll on their physical and mental health. While in Wisconsin during October, they cancelled talks after both suffered breakdowns caused by the strain of the lecture circuit.[85] They also cancelled appearances at a Wisconsin high school due to continued illness.[86] However, Yang and Peng recovered and spoke in Des Moines, Iowa on 25 October. 'In the best sense of the word,' one reporter declared, 'these young people are propagandists. No idle theorists about a future war, these young people! They have seen war, heard it, smelled its uncleanness, felt and tasted it.'[87] Yang again called for a boycott on Japanese goods and stressed that she cared for Chinese and Japanese wounded in hospitals. Donald Grant, a local journalist, attended Yang's next appearance at a YWCA youth forum the following day:

The heroine of the fall of Shanghai flailed her thin arms as she spoke in Chinese. . . The high excitement in her voice burst through the careful English of her interpreter as she gesticulated at her audience, trying to make her 250 hearers feel the patriotic fervor that burned within her frail body. 'China never will be conquered,' she shouted in the strange tongue of her native land. . . 'Like 15 million other Chinese refugees,' she said, 'I am homeless. I do not know what became of my parents, my brothers or my sisters. The only thing left for me is my country.' As the Chinese girl began her talk, she paced up and down in her long, sleeveless gown, visibly agitated by the events of the day.[88]

Yang and Peng addressed a crowd at the First Presbyterian Church the same day where they asserted that the Japanese occupation of China was skeletal as the invaders had not conquered the vast interior.[89]

On 1 November, Dorothy Edwards, a local Girl Guide director, announced that Yang Huimin would be greeted at Salt Lake City by a delegation of Girl Guides after arriving on the Denver Rio Grande Western railroad.[90] *The Salt Lake Tribune* reported that the anticipated event would take place at the First Methodist Church in five days:

The coming of Miss Yang Hui-min touring member of the Girl Guides' organization of China is anxiously awaited by the people of Utah whose prayers and sympathies are with her and her country in their efforts to repel greedy invaders and preserve the land which has belonged to the Chinese from time immemorial.[91]

After Dorothy Edwards and her Girl Guides greeted Yang and Peng, they were taken on a sightseeing trip of Salt Lake City before having dinner with the local Chinese community. *The Salt Lake Tribune* also covered their speaking event:

Miss Yang in a dramatic address delivered in her own language and punctuated with impressive gestures told through an interpreter . . . of her experiences as a Chinese girl guide and war horrors visited upon Chinese women and children. 'We never ceased being puzzled as to why the Japanese killed our civilians' said Miss Yang 'But even our children are glad to do their part. More than 250,000 of our youth are now in active service at base hospitals in refugee camps and wherever they can help.'[92]

On 12 November, Yang Huimin again recounted her story of delivering the flag to the Eight Hundred while in California, and one journalist described her as 'the toast of Los Angeles' Chinatown'.[93] As Yang's American odyssey came to an end, in a clear indication that she had achieved her mission of rallying the American public to China's cause, one reporter equated her struggle with the American Revolution:

But it is mostly, mass heroism, due to the team method of modern fighting such exploits as that of Yang Hui-ming, foolhardy, perhaps, but inspiring nevertheless, are few and far between. But they indicate a patriotism that is as real and prevalent as when the fourteen-year-old sons of the American colonists grabbed muskets and accompanied their sires to the battlefields of the Revolution.[94]

Yang returned to London in February 1939 on her journey home to China and by this time stories of her exploits included increasingly sensational tales of daring and espionage, as a British journalist reported: 'Time and again she has slipped into Japanese territory and come back with the news of troop movements.'[95] The press repeated these espionage claims in March and one reporter claimed that 'as a spy, her information saved thousands of Chinese soldiers'.[96] The accounts of Yang's exploits as a spy became even stranger in April when reporters began referring to her as 'China's Mata Hari', adding a sensual angle to her legend when previously she had been portrayed as a stoic Girl Guide.[97]

After returning to China, Yang was injured in a car accident in Chengdu and reports emerged in October 1939 that she was recovering in hospital.[98] By this time World War II had erupted in Europe and the ongoing Sino-Japanese War became increasingly sidelined as westerners fixated on Hitler's conquests. Although the United Aid to China Fund used Yang's story in advertisements in British newspapers in 1942 and the international press mentioned her on occasion, the story of the brave Girl Guide carrying a flag to the Eight Hundred was yesterday's news.[99]

There is another reason Yang Huimin disappeared from Chinese propaganda. The actress Hu Die apparently disliked Yang after she refused to help her move 30 suitcases containing valuables. After Hu Die became the mistress of China's spymaster Dai Li, the actress got her revenge after police arrested Yang in 1942 on suspicion of being a communist and a Japanese agent. After Dai Li died in a plane crash in 1946, the *Kuomintang* released Yang from prison after four years of captivity, but her reputation had been damaged as character assassinations continued in the press and public opinion considered her a criminal.[100] Although the stories about Yang's espionage exploits were fiction, she had become a victim of intrigue.

After World War II the western world barely remembered Yang Huimin as Sihang Warehouse receded from memory. However, after 1949 the exiled *Kuomintang* in Taiwan brought with them a powerful cultural legacy that would help them transform the island as they reorganized following their comprehensive defeat — memory of the Eight Hundred Heroes.

CHAPTER NINE
LEGACY IN EXILE

MEMORY IN TAIWAN

The surviving remnants of the *Kuomintang*, defeated by Mao Zedong during the Chinese Civil War, fled the mainland to the island province of Taiwan in disgrace while their western allies largely despised them for poor governance and rampant corruption. This perception was reinforced by effective communist propaganda that persuaded many influential westerners in China that Mao's peasant guerrillas were benevolent reformers unlike the bureaucratic functionaries of Stalinist terror in the Soviet Union. For example, the United States Army Observation Group, known as the Dixie Mission, established official relations with the Communist Party in Yan'an. The mission reported that Mao's guerrilla army would make a useful ally because his administration was more effective and less corrupt than the *Kuomintang*. President Roosevelt sent Vice President Henry Wallace to China in 1944 and his mission concluded that the communists were agrarian democrats and the State Department called for a change of policy to favour them. At the same time Mao's stronghold in Yan'an became 'The Camelot of China' to American journalists disillusioned with Chiang Kai-shek.[1]

In 1937 westerners were captivated by the Eight Hundred Heroes, viewing them as brave soldiers fighting the Japanese with a vision of a modern democratic China. After Pearl Harbour, China and the western

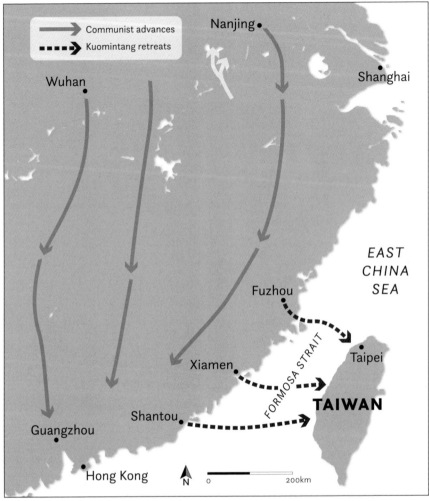

The final phase of the Chinese Civil War, 1949.

democracies became wartime allies and the Eight Hundred helped forge this alliance in the popular mind. However, after World War II the legend stopped appearing in media as the need for anti-Japanese wartime propaganda no longer existed. Furthermore, the western world looked down on the *Kuomintang* following its defeat in 1949 and the story of the Eight Hundred no longer had meaning. The west no longer cared about Sihang Warehouse which rapidly vanished from its collective memory, but the opposite occurred in Taiwan.

Chiang Kai-shek dreamed of a triumphant comeback and perceived Taiwan as a staging ground for an invasion of the mainland. The Republic of China, despite only ruling Taiwan, considered itself the legitimate government of the entire country and was recognized as such by the United Nations. The growing Cold War tensions and the Korean War (1950–53) resulted in Chiang again receiving American military aid as Taiwan became an ally in a proxy war against communist China. Chiang rebuilt his military power and President Eisenhower formally incorporated Taiwan into the western defence perimeter protected by the US Seventh Fleet. In 1963, Taiwan fielded 600,000 soldiers, the largest army in the world in proportion to population.[2]

The *Kuomintang*'s reforms in Taiwan were also political, resulting from genuine reflection about what had caused poor governance and corruption on the mainland. Chiang returned to Sun Yat-sen's Leninist principles of the 1920s by creating a network of party cells in the government, military and society. In July 1950, he replaced the Central Executive Committee with the Central Reform Committee and established an Advisory Committee of old party leaders. Chiang's efforts largely abolished factional interests, allowing the party to centralize control and making his influence greater than ever.[3] The party's administration became largely free from corruption, relative to its recent mainland experience.[4] The GNP increased by an average of 6.3 per cent between 1953 and 1961, and this rapid economic growth became known as the 'Taiwan Miracle'. During the 1970s the island became the second fastest growing economy in Asia after Japan. Taiwan became a successful alternative model to the People's Republic, demonstrating a non-communist path to modernization. *Kuomintang* rule in Taiwan continued to be authoritarian and the population lived under martial law, with military control over the judiciary, and the society experienced extensive surveillance. During martial law, authorities imprisoned or executed 140,000 people as suspected communists during Taiwan's 'White Terror', but this repression was not as brutal as Maoist communism on the mainland.[5]

In Taiwan, the *Kuomintang* kept the memory of the Eight Hundred alive in the consciousness of the population and the story continued to be part of a patriotic Chinese identity.[6] In Taiwanese schools the story of their heroism and sacrifice was taught to children as an example of martyrdom in service of the nation.[7] In particular, the Girl Guide Yang Huimin's courage in delivering the Republic of China flag to Sihang Warehouse was emphasized in textbooks.[8]

During the Chinese Civil War, *Kuomintang* officers disillusioned by defeat and corruption looked back on the first two years of the Sino-Japanese War as an imagined heroic age before the party disgraced itself.[9] In this way, as the *Kuomintang* reformed itself in Taiwan, the Eight Hundred became part of an idealized past when unblemished national heroes had fought the Japanese before the corruption of the 1940s eroded its prestige. If such greatness once existed, then surely by following their example such glory would come again.

The memory of Sihang Warehouse in Taiwan became firmly established with the publication of texts written by key surviving members of the Eight Hundred who fled to the island in 1949. Zhang Boting, the 88th Division's chief-of-staff, served as deputy commander of the Taiwan Division after World War II. The Military Law Bureau later tried him for corruption in 1963, which diminished his reputation, but his 'Summary of the Songhu Battle' was published in Taiwan and provided a valuable account of the Eight Hundred as he had coordinated the battle from outside the warehouse. Zhang was hit by a car and later died in a Taipei hospital from internal injuries on 17 March 1985.

After the Chinese Civil War, Yang Huimin fled to Taiwan where she married Professor Zhu Chongming, an academic at National Taiwan University, in 1948 and they had two sons, Zhu Fugui and Zhu Fuhong.[10] Yang worked at the Taipei Women's Teachers College, a private senior high school for girls, and later at the Chinese Culture University. Although Yang actively participated in and promoted scouting activities, the experience of spending four years in a *Kuomintang* prison left her disillusioned with politics and her former celebrity status. After rebuilding her life on the island, she lived anonymously under the assumed name Yang Xixian and didn't speak about her past. However, she later had a change of heart and wrote an account of her exploits titled *The Eight Hundred Heroes and I* (1970). Yang's book contains much mythology and, as Kristin Mulready-Stone concluded, it 'has an extreme tendency toward self-aggrandizement' and 'includes accounts of her own heroism that defy belief'.[11] For example, Yang Huimin claimed that she led a group of Girl Guides who stormed into the office of Major-General Alexander Telfer-Smollett, commander of British forces, to demand help in order to transport supplies to the Eight Hundred.[12]

In August 1947, Shangguan Zhibiao, the executive officer, served as the military chief in Tainan County, Taiwan. Shangguan later died on 27 September 1967, but he had earlier reflected upon how he wanted to be remembered:

> I think the innocent and humble compatriots and colleagues in Taiwan will definitely give a state funeral with respect to the death of this great soldier, Shangguan Zhibiao! If a 'state funeral' is not limited to official status, then we should do it for him. Such a loyal and patriotic soldier as Shangguan Zhibiao should really be given a state funeral for permanent memorial.[13]

Zhang Boting remembered his comrade and reflected: 'Since the death of comrade Shangguan Zhibiao, the years have passed in a flash. I mourn for his death infinitely!'[14] Later his son Shangguan Baicheng, who served in the Air Force, wrote *The Eight Hundred Heroes and the Diary of Xie Jinyuan* (1976), which contains numerous accounts of survivors and the diary Xie wrote in internment. Zhang assisted Shangguan in this endeavour:

> Shangguan Baicheng released all historical records pertaining to 'eight hundred heroes' and asked me to write a preface for the book of the same name that he compiled by using those materials and collecting records and narrations from each officer. Personally, I consider it a precious book containing firsthand information despite its contents appearing a little disorganized.[15]

Zhang also emphasized the contemporary political significance of the book as it 'can serve as a textbook for the education of our nationals and the spirit of cultivation in troops' in preparation for the 'commencement of counterattack against the mainland'.[16]

Notable examples of other books published in Taiwan during this time include Yu Ruihai's *The Eight Hundred Heroes* (1976), Lu Hanhun's *The Eight*

Hundred Heroes (1976) and Yao Xiaotian's *The Patron Saint of Shanghai: The Biography of Xie Jinyuan* (1982). These Taiwanese accounts contain useful information on the Eight Hundred wrapped inside heavily propagandized mythology and must be read with caution and also because of imperfect memory as Zhang Boting acknowledged: 'as thirty-nine years has lapsed, some memories have been either erased or blurred'.[17] In a typical example of myth-making, Shangguan Zhibiao declared in *The Eight Hundred Heroes and the Diary of Xie Jinyuan*:

> Despite our disadvantageous situation arising from enemy siege on three sides, all officers and soldiers of the battalion entrusted with the mission at the critical juncture resolved to win or to die, and share the same fate with the warehouse so that the righteousness of the Chinese nation would be upheld and the spirit of the revolutionary soldiers be manifested.[18]

Zhang Boting similarly declared in his preface to the book: 'The renowned heroic story of eight hundred heroes occurring in China's modern history manifests the essence of the allegiant and brave soul of our National Revolutionary Army and the tenacity and awe-inspiring righteousness of the Chinese nation.'[19]

The *Kuomintang* continued to patronise the memory of the Eight Hundred and the government released a series of six commemorative stamps on 3 September 1975, which depicted famous *Kuomintang* martyrs from the Sino-Japanese War including Xie Jinyuan.[20] The Eight Hundred would receive a far more grandiose tribute the following year with the release of the third film to be made about Sihang Warehouse, bringing their story back to the forefront of popular consciousness.

RETURN TO THE SCREEN

Taiwan entered a difficult decade during the 1970s. The United Nations recognized the People's Republic as the sole government of China on 25 October 1971, a move which expelled the Republic of China from the international organization.[21] President Nixon's 1972 visit to mainland

China further eroded Mao's isolation and the improved Sino-American relationship led to the establishment of full diplomatic relations in 1979. Earlier in 1972, Japan broke diplomatic relations with Taipei in favour of Beijing, rekindling strong anti-Japanese feelings in Taiwan. The *Kuomintang* had not felt this isolated since the opening days of the Sino-Japanese War. On 5 April 1975, Chiang Kai-shek died from acute renal failure, following a heart attack and pneumonia, and Taiwan entered a new and uncertain era with increased calls for democratic reform. Taiwan's economic success continued but came at a high price as social tensions existed in the factories manufacturing goods for western markets and pollution became a major problem.[22] As Taiwan experienced international isolation while coping with social and economic problems, the legend of the Eight Hundred was retold on cinema screens in service of a new social need.

In October 1972, Mei Changling became head of the Central Motion Picture Corporation, a film studio established by the *Kuomintang* in 1954 that dominated Taiwan's movie industry through a state-owned monopoly.[23] 'At that time,' the production manager Hsiao Yeh recalled, 'senior posts such as chief managers and above were always given to people with military or intelligence backgrounds. And we made our films according to policies from above.'[24]

Mei Changling, born in Henan Province in 1924, had fled to Taiwan in 1949 and later produced *Storms Over the Yangtze River* (1969), an anti-Japanese movie that became a box office hit.[25] After taking charge of the Central Motion Picture Corporation, he wanted to make a new type of film which reflected the *Kuomintang*'s earlier wartime movies and in doing so established the *Kangri* (Resist Japan) genre.[26] The first of these films was *Everlasting Glory* (1976) directed by Ting Shan-hsi. The movie, filmed in 1974, was a biopic about General Zhang Zhizhong, a martyr who died fighting the Japanese on 16 May 1940 — the highest-ranking *Kuomintang* officer killed during the war. Another example is Liu Chia-chang's *Victory* (1976) that concerned a family's struggle under the brutal Japanese occupation with a strong theme on the need to resist and make sacrifices for the country. Chang Tseng-tse's *Heroes of the Eastern Skies* (1977) depicted outnumbered Chinese aces fighting Japanese aircraft in 1937, focusing on the action at Shanghai and Nanjing. Liu Chia-chang also directed *A Teacher of Great Soldiers* (1978), the story of a young female teacher who sacrificed her life to save her students from being conscripted by the Japanese.

The war movies produced by Mei Changling, as Zhang Yingjin explained, 'attempted to retrieve the memory of "victories" so as to fortify a defense mechanism vis-à-vis the present-day political setbacks'.[27] The anti-Japanese genre was also a government policy of revenge against contemporary Japan for breaking diplomatic relations with Taipei.[28] The most notable film produced by the Central Motion Picture Corporation of this type was *Eight Hundred Heroes* (1976), directed by Ting Shan-hsi who had earlier made *Everlasting Glory*. Ting shot *Eight Hundred Heroes* over the winter of 1975–76 and his budget of 30 million Taiwanese dollars, financed by the National Defence Ministry, was large for a Chinese movie. The *Kuomintang* was heavily involved in the film's production because Taiwanese cinema, as Chiu Chi-ming explained, is not just a 'cultural activity but also part of the state apparatus for constructing national identity and maintaining the political hegemony of the Nationalist Party'.[29]

Eight Hundred Heroes starts at the beginning of hostilities in Shanghai in August 1937 with a deadly Japanese air raid, with no mention of 'Bloody Saturday' when the Chinese Air Force accidentally bombed the International Settlement. The film depicted brave Chinese soldiers resisting a Japanese amphibious landing, eventually being pushed back and culminating in a scene in which a Chinese officer shoots himself as enemy troops enter his command bunker. The movie also portrayed Operation Iron Fist, the failed conventional offensive to drive the Japanese marine garrison from the city, as a reimagined costly but effective commando-style raid on a Japanese headquarters by underground fighters — a scaling down most likely resulting from budget limitations. Xie Jinyuan and his family are depicted as the commander struggles between his duty as a soldier and his desire as a father. Yang Huimin selflessly helps refugees in the Settlement and cares for them in a camp. As the Chinese retreat from Zhabei begins, the film's central narrative unfolds as Xie is ordered to defend Sihang Warehouse to the death.

The Eight Hundred are depicted as a courageous and unified body of soldiers, completely willing to sacrifice their lives without a second thought or hope of survival — a one-dimensional representation without moments

The Eight Hundred Heroes defending Sihang Warehouse as depicted in *Eight Hundred Heroes* (1976). (Author's Collection)

of overt fear or doubt. The suicide attack of Chen Shusheng jumping from the warehouse is glorified and inspires two other soldiers to also jump from the roof with explosives in a dramatic but disturbing sacrifice that saves the others by stopping a Japanese armoured car attack. A heavy emphasis is placed on the flag-raising ceremony as the men form a human pyramid to keep it flying while being strafed by a Japanese plane. Many are killed and wounded as emotional crowds watch from the Settlement in a clear indication that the men were prepared to die for their symbolic mission of demonstrating Chinese determination to resist. In reality the flag-raising ceremony was a more of a low-key event. The film also contains a stirring montage scene during a Japanese attack as the 'Song of the Eight Hundred Heroes' is heard.

Eight Hundred Heroes focuses on Xie Jinyuan, played by Ko Chun-hsiung, and his determination to defend the warehouse for as long as possible before dying. After the order to retreat arrives, Xie is torn between his previous acceptance of death in battle with its eternal glory and duty to obey the order despite the shame of living. A phone call from his wife Ling Weicheng and the advice of an officer convinces him to retreat as instructed. The

A pivotal scene in *Eight Hundred Heroes* (1976) after Yang Huimin (portrayed by Brigitte Lin) presents the Republic of China flag to Xie Jinyuan (portrayed by Ko Chun-hsiung). (Author's Collection)

film also devotes much screen time to Yang Huimin, played by Brigitte Lin. After Yang crosses New Lese Bridge, she starts a shouting conversation with Chinese soldiers who tell her that 800 soldiers are defending the warehouse. She subsequently breaks the news that there are still soldiers fighting in Shanghai to the rest of the city that quickly spreads. Yang in reality did not herald the legend of the Eight Hundred as wounded soldiers evacuated from the warehouse were the source of the famous number. The next night she swims across Suzhou Creek to deliver the flag after convincing the Chamber of Commerce to donate supplies. In fact she crossed the bridge to deliver the flag but did swim back.

In the movie the Japanese are largely a faceless horde with scenes of despicable warmongers planning conquest and arrogant officers briefing the press within the Settlement. The film places little emphasis on foreign journalists covering the story, but a strong focus is given to Chinese onlookers

A movie poster of the film *Eight Hundred Heroes* (1976). (Author's Collection)

being moved into patriotism with shouts of 'Long Live China', a likely expression of the international isolation felt in Taiwan at the time.

The film ends with the dramatic breakout as the men hurl themselves across the bridge to safety under intense fire from Japanese soldiers and an enemy patrol boat. The actual breakout was less bloody and there was no Japanese patrol boat present. The movie depicted sympathetic British soldiers watching the breakout as Major-General Alexander Telfer-Smollett shouts encouragement. The survivors form a column and march away with Xie on horseback as his family watch on in pride while the 'Song of the Eight Hundred Heroes' is played as if the men would fight again another day. In reality, the exhausted survivors were disarmed by the British and trucked into internment and Xie was never reunited with his family. The film makes no mention of internment and Xie's assassination by four of his own soldiers.

Eight Hundred Heroes was well-received in Taiwan and won high acclaim from critics and was popular with audiences.[30] The movie was Taiwan's official entry to the Academy Awards under the category of Foreign Film. At the 1976 Asia Film Festival, it won the Best Dramatic Feature award, Brigitte Lin won the Best Actress award and Hsu Feng, who played Xie's wife Ling Weicheng, won the Special Actor award. Ko Chun-hsiung also won a Golden Horse Award for his portrayal of Xie. The movie was shown in schools and to local communities as part of a state policy to promote nationalism, but it was also entertainment designed to distract the populace from social problems on the island. Teachers and students were also encouraged to bring their families to screenings and the government hoped it would persuade young men to join the army. Zhang Boting remarked, 'The war drama film recently produced by the Central Motion Picture Corporation evokes our endless memories.'[31] General Gu Zhutong, deputy commander of the Third War Zone during the Battle of Shanghai, had earlier given a speech in a pre-shooting ceremony during the film's production on how the film could assist the reconquest of the mainland:

> After the victory of the War of Resistance against Japanese Aggression, unfortunately, rampant banditry pervaded across the country, scourging our seven hundred million compatriots. I eagerly hope that the shooting

of the film Eight Hundred Heroes will transplant the high enthusiasm
and morale and the tenacious fighting spirit from that time to our current
base in Taiwan and Penghu so that the great cause of counterattack can
be completed strictly in compliance with the teachings of our deceased
leader [Chiang Kai-shek] as soon as possible.[32]

Although the *Eight Hundred Heroes* did well in Taiwan and Asia, the film did
not find a meaningful audience in the western world, and it failed to reignite
general interest in Sihang Warehouse across the globe. However, a British
film critic did write a positive review in 1978:

First and foremost, *Eight Hundred Heroes* is a splendidly mounted
and excitingly made war film, and can be enjoyed as such by general
Western audiences with little or no knowledge of the historical events
concerned. Secondly (and for the Taiwanese especially), it is a strident
piece of Nationalist propaganda with a customarily virulent anti-
Japanese bias; students of political history may also care to regard the
Japanese as a metaphor for Mainland Communist China. Thirdly, it is a
study of heroism — straightforward, uncluttered, and viewed through
the filter of the Chinese family structure.[33]

The reviewer continued:

The film's major failing is the absence of any attempt to sketch the
political ramifications of the period, a particularly confused time when
the Chinese were scarcely in control of their own destiny. Shanghai
was policed and carved up by various foreign powers (like Beijing
earlier), and most of this information is taken as read rather than
enlarged upon. . . Despite this, however, and despite the sometimes
cloying nationalism . . . *Eight Hundred Heroes* wins on sheer energy
and verve.[34]

Yang Huimin visited the film set and spent time with Brigitte Lin and
watching the film helped her come to terms with the traumatic events of her
past and she enjoyed life more afterwards. However, she sustained serious

Yang Huimin meets the Taiwanese actress Brigitte Lin on the film set of *Eight Hundred Heroes* (1976). (Author's Collection)

injuries in a car accident on 28 October 1977, resulting in partial paralysis on the left side of her body. After suffering a stroke in February 1992, Yang Huimin died at Taipei Veterans General Hospital on 9 March 1992, aged 77 years.

DEMOCRACY AND PROTEST

Sun Yat-sen's Three Principles of the People — Nationalism, Democracy and People's Livelihood — continued to be *Kuomintang* ideology on Taiwan. Within this vision, there was a three-stage plan to establish constitutional government in China: a period of military rule followed by political tutelage under a one-party state to educate the masses followed by genuine democracy with citizens enjoying full electoral rights. Although the *Kuomintang* failed to achieve Sun's vision during its rule on the mainland before 1949, the party did oversee a slow transition to democracy in Taiwan.

In 1951, Chiang Kai-shek established a system of local elections and later allowed elections to the National Assembly and Legislative Yuan in 1969. These experiences started the gradual democratization of Taiwan which accelerated after Chiang Ching-kuo succeeded his father and became president on 20 May 1978, a position he held until his death on 13 January 1988. One-party rule ended after the centre-left Democratic Progressive Party, founded in 1986, became an opposition party and martial law ceased in 1987. Lee Teng-hui, the next president, continued democratic reforms as the political progress became entrenched within civil society. Chen Shui-bian of the Democratic Progressive Party served as Taiwan's first non-*Kuomintang* president between 2000 and 2008. The Democratic Progressive Party formed the largest party in the Legislative Yuan in 2002 following elections, although a *Kuomintang* coalition with the People First Party and the New Party allowed the older party to retain control.

The Eight Hundred Heroes remained a powerful cultural force in democratic Taiwan and their legacy has been invoked by both the *Kuomintang* and the Democratic Progressive Party. Ma Ying-jeou from the *Kuomintang* became president on 20 May 2008, after winning the presidential election. In a New Year's Day speech in 2011, commemorating the 100th anniversary of the Republic of China, President Ma mentioned the Eight Hundred:

My fellow countrymen, all of us in today's Taiwan have together experienced the growth and transformation of this land. We possess collective memories and experiences. We all experienced the thrill as our baseball teams achieved international glory, we all felt the indignation as we lost our seat in the United Nations, and we have all shed tears of pride upon seeing our national flag hoisted at international events. Yes, that blue, white and red flag symbolizing Heaven, Sun and Earth unites us, inspires us, and moves us. It gave the Eight Hundred Heroes the strength to fight valiantly in defending Sihang Warehouse in Shanghai back in 1937. That flag is a collective memory we have all had since we were young, and is a rallying point for our patriotism.[35]

As Taiwan is a democracy, its citizens question politicians invoking history and an editorial in the *Taipei Times* criticized President Ma's appropriation of the Eight Hundred and their relevance to Taiwan, where questions of Chinese identity and a desire for formal independence from the mainland are highly divisive political and cultural issues:

Ma said he feels deeply moved by the Eight Hundred Heroes who took part in the Defense of Sihang Warehouse in China in 1937, but for the people of Taiwan, that is really just another piece of some other country's military history and is about as relevant to Taiwan as the 300 Spartans who fought the Battle of Thermopylae against the Persian Empire. Would Taiwanese who know this piece of history suddenly identify with Greece and propose that Taiwan is part of Greece?[36]

Of course, other segments of public opinion strongly identify with China. In the same year the *Taipei Times* interviewed Yang Yu-mei, known as 'the national flag girl', who owns a Republic of China merchandise shop in Greater Kaohsiung. Yang's father, a veteran, taught her to be patriotic and loyal to the *Kuomintang*. She also worked for the party during election campaigns where she is well-known for her energy and wearing clothing displaying the flag. The interviewer noted her connection to the Eight Hundred:

Yang's heroine, not surprisingly, is girl scout Yang Hui-min, who delivered an ROC [Republic of China] flag to soldiers defending a warehouse under Japanese siege in Shanghai in 1937. In 2005, after discovering in a flea market an out-of-print book titled *The Eight Hundred Heroes and I* written by Yang Hui-min, the excited Yang Yu-mei made the book the 'treasure of the store.' Afterwards, relatives and friends began to call her 'the modern Yang Hui-min.' Yang Yu-mei said that because both she and Yang Hui-min bear the surname 'Yang,' they could trace their ancestry back to Zhenjiang, Jiangsu Province, China. She added that because both of them love the ROC flag, she is proud to be called 'the modern Yang Hui-min.'[37]

In 2014, a Taiwanese newspaper declared that 'teenage students are all familiar with the heroic story of Col. Xie Jinyuan and the Eight Hundred Heroes who defended the warehouse and fought against Japanese troops'.[38] President Ma again honoured the Eight Hundred at an official event commemorating the 70th anniversary of the end of the Sino-Japanese War held at the National Dr Sun Yat-sen Memorial Hall on 3 July 2015. During the ceremony, he presented a Republic of China flag to Zhu Fugui, the son of Yang Huimin. On the same day, a Taiwanese newspaper published an interview with Yang's other son Zhu Fuhong:

[Zhu Fuhong] described his mother as a woman with extraordinary courage. 'Who would care about life or death when the country was going through such an ordeal?' Chu [Zhu] asked, citing his mother's remarks while recalling her volunteering to make the delivery after learning that the soldiers wanted a national flag to declare their determination to guard their land. Yang once recalled that seeing the warehouse surrounded by Japanese flags during the siege made her feel it would be a great glory to hoist a Republic of China flag on top of the warehouse.[39]

Tsai Ing-wen became leader of the Democratic Progressive Party in 2008, becoming the first female leader to head a major party in Taiwan. The 2016 election propelled the party into power for the first time after winning a majority of seats in the Legislative Yuan and Tsai Ing-wen won the presidential election. Under President Tsai's leadership, the Eight Hundred became the focus of protest and dissent as unhappy citizens utilized their legacy in defiance of her plans to cut pensions and retirement benefits for around 333,000 public sector workers, including civil servants and teachers as well as 63,000 retired military officers.

On 21 February 2017, around 1500 veterans staged a mass demonstration in Taipei at the Legislative Yuan.[40] The veterans waved flags and sung songs while moving in solidarity around the building. Wu Chi-liang, a retired general and now Deputy Secretary General of the Veterans Association of the Republic of China, acted as a spokesman for the demonstrators: 'The troops are the first ones the government calls to deal with whatever problems it has and the first to get screwed when it has nothing better to do.'[41] Wu Chi-liang also accused the government of lacking empathy: 'If government is indeed facing serious financial crisis, why doesn't the president herself, the premier, ministers and lawmakers voluntarily give up half their monthly salaries first?'[42] Wu Shih-huai, Deputy Head of the Military Academy Alumni Association, announced to the media: 'Now all of a sudden the government has made up its reform proposals, all without consulting with us. How can we accept that?'[43]

The protesters vowed to demonstrate outside the Legislative Yuan every day for the next month and they referred to themselves as the '800 Heroes Defending Their Rights'. Wu Ting-yu, a Democratic Progressive Party Legislator, denounced the veterans and accused them of childlike behaviour which sullied the reputation of the real Eight Hundred.[44] Wang Ding-yu, another Democratic Progressive Party Legislator, labelled the protest 'absurd' before accusing the veterans of being too close to the People's Republic, as retired Taiwanese officers often visited the mainland to promote peaceful reunification:

The 800 Heroes sacrificed themselves for the survival of the nation, whereas those honorless retired generals want to sacrifice the nation's finances to line their own pockets. . . Those people who went to China to play golf with People's Liberation Army officers . . . did an injustice to their comrades in uniform and Taiwanese taxpayers. Their shamelessness knows no bounds.[45]

Peng Ming-min, a former Democratic Progressive Party presidential adviser, also questioned the veterans' patriotism:

> Following several decades of brainwashing focused on 'recovering the mainland,' Taiwanese have been expecting their soldiers to conquer China and kill its leaders. In contrast, these soldiers are living in comfort and enjoying a carefree lifestyle. Should we be happy about that, or ashamed? Many generals have joined the demonstrations against pension reform in front of the Legislative Yuan, referring to themselves as the '800 Heroes' and treating legislators pushing for reform as the enemy. If the Chinese officers who they once called their brothers launched an attack on Taiwan, would these 'heroes' treat them as friend or foe?[46]

Those expressing opinions against the protesters were not exclusively from the Democratic Progressive Party and a plurality of views can be identified. For example, Professor Chi Chun-chieh from National Dong Hwa University supported the government's reforms despite a personal interest in the status quo:

> I am a public-school teacher and I will retire within the next 10 years. Regardless of which version of the pension reform act is passed, my pension is certain to shrink. Despite this, I give my full support to the ongoing effort to reform a pension system that violates the principle of intergenerational justice. . . It is an indisputable fact that if the pension system is not reformed, it would create insurmountable fiscal problems before long.[47]

Chi Chun-chieh also mocked the veterans' 'illustrious name' and added: 'Look at these so-called "800 Heroes" and the violence that occurred outside the Legislative Yuan: They are doing a pretty good job of vilifying themselves, and they still have the stomach to tell other people not to vilify them.'[48]

Invoking the Eight Hundred can feel foreign for those with Taiwanese identity and memories of the *Kuomintang*'s 'White Terror' on the island remain strong. For example, the government crushed an uprising on

28 February 1957 resulting in 5000 to 28,000 deaths, a critical date for the Taiwanese independence movement that remembers the massacre as the '228 Incident'. Chen Ping-hsun, an academic at National Chengchi University, noted how the glorification of the Eight Hundred can obscure Taiwanese history, including the '228 Incident':

> There has long been a lack of films or TV shows that view war from a Taiwanese perspective. War movies by the Central Motion Pictures Co are all about the Nationalist army. One such film is *Eight Hundred Heroes* from 1975. . . . The industry has not invested in Taiwanese war stories because of the KMT's [*Kuomintang's*] White Terror, which forced an erasure of history and wiped out any traces of the 228 Incident and the following March Massacre. Fortunately, the nation has now democratized and this part of history is gradually being remembered.[49]

In June 2017, the government passed the pension reform bill, which fuelled additional anger.[50] The '800 Heroes' reacted by throwing eggs and shoes at President Tsai, forcing her to cancel a visit to a temple, and they later blocked the entrance of a stadium, which delayed the opening ceremony of the World University Games.[51] On 3 September, authorities expected the '800 Heroes' to protest outside the National Revolutionary Martyrs' Shrine in Taipei while President Tsai made an appearance for Armed Forces Day; however, 30,000 protesters surprisingly appeared at railway stations and halls in fourteen cities and counties across Taiwan.[52]

The protests continued and around 1000 veterans gathered outside the Executive Yuan on 13 November, demanding the government negotiate with them, and by this time members of the '800 Heroes' had camped outside the building for 266 days.[53] After the government ignored their demand, they stopped traffic for two hours until the government announced it would include them in negotiations.[54] Tensions escalated on 27 February, after members of the '800 Heroes' and other protest groups broke into the Legislative Yuan and, after police forced them from the building, they continued protesting outside. 'The government has betrayed our trust and broken its promise to us,' Wu Shih-huai declared, 'but now the Executive Yuan is about to pass the draft proposal and there has been no communication at all.' The nature of the protests had also changed as they also clashed with the pro-independence group 908 Taiwan Republic Campaign as identity politics became just as important as the pension issue.[55]

During the protest at the Legislative Yuan, Miao Te-shen, a 62-year-old retired colonel and member of the '800 Heroes', fell from a building and landed head first. He was taken to hospital in a coma but died on 5 March after his family removed him from life support. Miao was also secretary-general of Blue Sky Action Alliance, a hard-line pro-unification group diametrically opposed to the Democratic Progressive Party. Luo Jui-ta, chief executive of the '800 Heroes', declared: 'It would be a great insult to colonel Miao to say it was all about pensions for him.'[56] Wu Shih-huai similarly stressed that they were no longer just focused on pensions but also on opposing Taiwanese independence and the vilification of military personnel.[57]

At the end of March, the government announced that its pension reforms would take effect on 1 July, without negotiating with the '800 Heroes'. The legislation would reduce the monthly minimum pension for retired military personnel and set a ten-year timeframe for abolishing the 18 per cent preferential interest rate on their savings accounts.[58] As anger boiled, the '800 Heroes' organized 2000 veterans who protested outside the Legislative Yuan, and some of them assaulted journalists and police. At least 21 journalists and 84 police officers sustained injuries during the violence and protesters even assaulted journalists from CTiTV, a station strongly opposed to President Tsai and sympathetic to their cause.[59] An editorial in *Taipei Times* condemned the protesters:

> At a time when there is a national consensus that pension cuts are a bitter, but necessary medicine required to salvage the cash-strapped pension programs, all of the 800 Heroes' demands come down to one simple, but impossible request: no cuts.[60]

The editorial concluded that the protesters had resorted to violence to attract attention as their movement had disappeared from media coverage.

On 1 July the pension reforms took effect and although the '800 Heroes' lost their struggle, the group became a registered association in June and planned marches with the *Kuomintang* to support the armed forces and oppose Taiwanese independence. In June 2019, the '800 Heroes for the Republic of China Association' commissioned a book that documented their 485 days of protest.[61]

The Eight Hundred Heroes have been part of the social fabric in Taiwan since the *Kuomintang* fled to the island in 1949, although the meaning of their story has changed as well as the social functions their legacy performs, but not all citizens identify with them, especially for those advocating independence. Although the *Kuomintang* perceives itself as the guardian of the Eight Hundred's memory, it does not have a monopoly on their legend and the heroes have made a surprising comeback, defying the odds, inside the People's Republic of China.

CHAPTER TEN
MEMORY AFTER REVOLUTION

FORGETTING AND REMEMBERING

After the communist victory during the Civil War in 1949, Mao Zedong's new China placed little importance on commemorating the Sino-Japanese War. This may seem strange as communist soldiers had fought the Japanese alongside the *Kuomintang* during the United Front. This development in part came about because the Sino-Japanese War's conclusion did not bring peace. The civil war resumed, and China accordingly lacked the triumphalism that other Allied nations experienced in 1945. When peace returned to China in 1949, the dominant narrative explaining recent history focused on the Chinese Communist Party's victory over the *Kuomintang*, not the defeat of Japan. In this environment acknowledging the *Kuomintang*'s contribution to victory against Japan became politically impossible as it would contradict the narrative that attributed victory over Japan exclusively to the communists.[1]

Although Maoist propaganda glorified the People's Liberation Army, communist officials were actually suspicious of their own veterans who had social bonds outside party control, which constituted a threat to the revolution.[2] The new society even lacked formal veteran organizations, a national day for veterans or streets named after them. Communist military heroes could also vanish from memory.[3] For example, General Peng Dehuai led the 'Hundred Regiments Campaign' in 1940, a notable Chinese victory against Japanese forces, but after he opposed Mao's disastrous Great Leap Forward (1958–62), which caused enormous famine in rural areas, he largely disappeared from official accounts of the war.[4] The Sino-Japanese War largely vanished from public space in China with a noticeable absence of memorials, museums and war literature.[5]

As Mao's China did little to commemorate communist veterans of the Sino-Japanese War, *Kuomintang* veterans unsurprisingly had almost no public space to remember their sacrifices and the Eight Hundred Heroes accordingly vanished from collective memory.[6] Historians during this time presented China's victory over Japan as entirely resulting from communist mobilization of the peasants while the *Kuomintang* surrendered huge portions of territory with little resistance and schemed to restore capitalism and semi-feudalism.[7] In 1954, an official party statement noted that Chiang Kai-shek only announced resistance to Japan 'under nationwide pressure of the people' but in actuality he 'adopted the reactionary policy of passivity'.[8] The communists did not condemn all *Kuomintang* veterans, who could as individuals rehabilitate themselves in the new society, but their wartime contribution was not publicly acknowledged. After the revolution, former *Kuomintang* soldiers lived in fear of being denounced as 'enemies of the people', which intensified during the Cultural Revolution (1966–76).

After President Nixon's visit to China in 1972, Sino-Japanese relations improved, which created a new motive to suppress memories of the war in the interests of not harming the new economic ties with Japan.[9] The party during this time encouraged Chinese historians to focus on communist heroes of the war and avoid Japanese atrocities such as the 'Rape of Nanking'.[10] Chinese youth were not taught about Japanese atrocities in school and stories concerning them survived in private within families and small groups.[11]

During the Deng Xiaoping era (1977–92), the party downplayed class identity under its policy of state capitalism and a new Chinese nationalism took its place which reinterpreted the Sino-Japanese War. In the early 1980s tensions also arose in the Sino-Japanese relationship over political and trade disputes, opening more space in national memory to remember the war.

Historians now educated people about Japanese atrocities and the barbarity of their occupation was depicted in new movies, television shows, books and museum exhibits. The Memorial Hall for the Victims of the Nanjing Massacre opened in 1984 and the Nanjing Massacre Museum published victim stories as part of the new patriotic education.[12]

As memory of the war expanded, the party allowed a more sympathetic portrayal of the *Kuomintang*, and its veterans accordingly ended their silence and wrote their memoirs. Biographies of *Kuomintang* commanders were also published during the 1980s.[13] This rehabilitation was not unchallenged and many Chinese historians continued depicting the *Kuomintang* as counter-revolutionaries who passively resisted the Japanese.[14] Hu Qiaomu, a senior party politician and historian, declared in an editorial in the *People's Daily* on 7 August 1987:

> We completely acknowledge the wartime contribution of the Nationalist government's army's patriotic generals, but before the war, Chiang Kai-shek's government was carrying out the mistaken policy of a partial war of resistance (that is, just the military, without the people). From 1939 onward, it carried out a . . . War of Resistance, pursuing a reactionary policy that was anti-communist, anti-people, to the point that its military nearly lost all of its fighting strength.[15]

Nevertheless, the Central Party History Commission established the correct party line the following year as Wang Pei, one of the contributors, explained:

> In the war of resistance there were two battle fronts. One was the Kuomintang government's military taking on frontal battles; one was the CCP [Chinese Communist Party] led Eighth Route Army and New Fourth Army and other people's military units in the liberated zone behind enemy lines. These two battle fronts were mutually dependent, co-ordinated in making war, and embodied the spirit of the KMT [*Kuomintang*] and CCP co-operating to resist Japan. Of course, KMT controlled units adhered to many incorrect lines.[16]

As the internal party debate continued on how far the *Kuomintang* could be rehabilitated, the Eight Hundred made a comeback. *The August 13 Songhu Battle: Personal Recollections from the War of Resistance Against Japan by Former Nationalist Commanders* was published in Beijing in 1987. The book included wartime accounts including Yang Ruifu's 'Account of the Lone Unit's Four Days of Battle', Zhang Boting's 'Summary of the Songhu Battle' and Sun Yuanliang's 'Xie Jinyuan and the 800 Heroes'. The principal accounts of the Eight Hundred were now available in the mainland and the party facilitated this rehabilitation by highlighting that Mao Zedong had labelled the Eight Hundred 'models of national revolution' on 12 October 1938.[17]

During the 1990s, the new nationalism and narrative of the Sino-Japanese War continued and the State Education Commission instructed teachers to educate their students in 'historical lessons, and not to forget imperialist invasion and Chinese people's heroic resistance'.[18] In the twenty-first century, the Eight Hundred benefitted from this development as the 60th anniversary of victory allowed the story of Sihang Warehouse to be told at the national level for the first time, as Lu Pan observed:

> Media coverage of the battle at Sihang Warehouse and the life of the veterans who fought there have been rare and only began to emerge in 2005 on the 60th anniversary of China's victory over Japan in WWII. Chinese media outlets such as the Beijing TV Station, Shanghai Xin Min Evening News made reports and a feature documentary about the few soldiers of the 800 heroes who were still alive.[19]

The official commemoration for the 60th anniversary also included special China Telecom cards and one featured Xie Jinyuan and Sihang Warehouse.[20] In the following year, the Central Propaganda Ministry, Party History Research Office and Xinhua News Agency initiated a Sino-Japanese War-themed propaganda campaign which included commemoration of the *Kuomintang*'s resistance and included outreach to Taiwan.[21] The party also approved a history textbook which praised the Eight Hundred:

> Xie Jinyuan, a regimental commander, received orders to command 800 soldiers in defense [of] Sihang Warehouse in order to protect the main force to withdraw. . . In the middle of the intense fighting, a girl student

named Yang Huimin, risking her own life, ferried across the Suzhou
River from the public concession, and carried a national flag to the top
of Sihang Warehouse. The sight of the national flag fluttering at the top
of the warehouse gave people limitless courage and strength to fight.[22]

In 2014, the Ministry of Civil Affairs made a list of 300 national martyrs
which included Xie Jinyuan.[23] In the following year, to commentate the
70th anniversary of victory, Chinese museums hosted special exhibitions
that included content on the Eight Hundred.[24]

The increasingly pro-*Kuomintang* narrative in the mainland also formed
part of a new policy aimed at rapprochement between the two parties
and peaceful reunification with Taiwan.[25] Mainland commemoration of
the Eight Hundred served this goal and was apparent in President Hu
Jintao's speech to commemorate the 60th anniversary on 3 September
2005, in which he specifically mentioned Sihang Warehouse when
praising 'the 800 heroes' who 'were outstanding representatives of the
Chinese people in defying the brute force and fighting against the enemy
heroically'.[26] In a similar speech ten years later, President Xi Jinping also
invoked the Eight Hundred during the 70th anniversary in Beijing on
2 September 2015:

Heroes are born from times of great misfortune. During China's 14-year
struggle against the aggression of Japanese militarists, and especially
during its 8-year all-out War of Resistance, the peoples of China, united
as one, stood together to resist foreign aggression and save themselves
from annihilation. Bound by a common purpose, they moved the world
with their epic deeds. Many heroes emerged from their struggle . . .
[including] the KMT [*Kuomintang*] Army's 'Eight Hundred Heroes.'[27]

In Shanghai memory is a localised affair and public opinion in what had
once been the most cosmopolitan metropolis in Asia had never been fully
indoctrinated by Mao's revolution, as fond memories of westerners remained
alive in the city. During the Korean War, the party detected widespread
misgivings over China's involvement and confusion over why America
was suddenly an enemy.[28] Party officials also noted that workers 'still do

not feel much hatred towards the United States'.[29] Citizens in Shanghai unsurprisingly later charted their own course when commemorating the Sino-Japanese War and honouring *Kuomintang* veterans.

The rehabilitation of the Eight Hundred in Shanghai began in the 1980s when the grave of Xie Jinyuan, which had been vandalized during the Cultural Revolution, was transferred to the Wanguo Public Museum in the city in 1983 to rest beside other Chinese heroes.[30] The Shanghai Jin Yuan Middle School also constructed a memorial statue of Xie.[31] Professor Yu Qiuyu, former Chancellor of Shanghai Theatre Academy, recalled, 'I studied at a junior secondary school dedicated to national hero General Xie Jinyuan.'[32]

In the twenty-first century, the Eight Hundred's legacy benefitted from party officials who encouraged efforts to highlight local history during 'patriotic education', and high-school history textbooks were accordingly written for different regions in which national history was supplemented with local examples.[33] Under this policy a textbook compiled specifically for Shanghai students in 2010 included the Eight Hundred:

'The Eight Hundred Brave Men,' bathed in blood, bravely fought against the Japanese Army day and night, repelled more than ten Japanese attacks, eliminated over 200 Japanese soldiers, and left behind moving, heroic achievements.[34]

Xie Jimin, son of Xie Jinyuan, became the most prolific advocate of the Eight Hundred in Shanghai. After the Chinese Revolution, Xie Jinyuan's wife Ling Weicheng remained on the mainland with their children.[35] Xie Jimin wrote *My Father, General Xie Jinyuan: Eight Hundred Heroes Fighting in Blood* (2010) and *Xie Jinyuan's Anti-Japanese Diary: Interpretation by Xie Jimin* (2015). Xie Jimin honoured his father in his preface to the diary:

On 26 October when more than 500,000 troops commenced westward retreat, the Regimental Commander Xie Jinyuan led 'eight hundred heroes' (an exaggerated number) by order to defend Sihang Warehouse on the north bank of Suzhou Creek. They resolved to take the final field as their own graves. This year marks the 70th anniversary of the victory of the Chinese People's Anti-Japanese War and the World Anti-Fascist War, at the moment of which publishing this book underscores its immeasurable historical significance.[36]

In 2015, Shanghai Opera House commemorated the 70th anniversary of victory with a symphony orchestra and chorus performance of a new Eight Hundred Heroes song composed by Gan Lin, and a program for the event declared:

> The work depicts the well-known Shanghai Sihang Warehouse
> defending battle in the war, deploying various forms of this genre,
> e.g. the instrumental music, chorus for mixed voices and for children,
> vocal solo and ensemble to give a full expression to Chinese people's
> patriotism and determination to fight a life-and-death battle with the
> invading enemy.[37]

In the same year Li Xinran announced in the *Shanghai Daily*:

> I've also heard that local authorities and artists are working on a new
> comic book version of 'Sihang Warehouse and the Eight Hundred
> Heroes,' a well-known story set in Shanghai during the War of
> Resistance Against Japanese Aggression. I first encountered this story
> in an early edition of *Children's Pictorial* when I was four or five.[38]

The graphic novel *Eight Hundred Heroes* by Li Gang and Wang Yufeng was published in Shanghai in 2015. The book contains stunning black and white illustrations, and the introduction contained a vivid preview of the story to follow:

> The painter with patriotism-infused brushstrokes portrays a group
> of national heroes featuring a squad leader who tactfully terminated
> enemies with grenades concealed in a bunker, a soldier who sacrificed
> his own life to dynamite an enemy tank with grenades tied around his
> waist, a Girl Guide who came to Sihang Warehouse to deliver a national
> flag from the opposite side of Suzhou Creek at the risk of her life, and

all walks of life that fully supported the Eight Hundred Heroes, none
of which fail to arouse our deepest feelings. At the pinnacle of the
precipice Xie Jinyuan seemingly still stands, as high as mountains and
as long as rivers our hero's nobility remains.[39]

The book provides an exciting account of the Chinese withdrawal from
Zhabei and the Eight Hundred's stand inside Sihang Warehouse, and Yang
Huimin's arrival with the flag is the novel's central emotional moment.[40]
News of the event reached Mao Zedong who praised the actions of the
Eight Hundred as models of revolution for their 'heroic resistance' and
'sacrifice of life for our country'.[41] The novel ends with an illustration of
contemporary People's Liberation Army soldiers, the inheritors of the Eight
Hundred's revolutionary legacy, and words to complete the communist
appropriation of the legend:

The isolated soldiers were not alone, with their admirable deeds
widely renowned and nationwide support earned, helping the
Chinese nation forge a stronger bond. China would not perish, a firm
conviction embraced by the Eight Hundred Heroes. China is bound
to prosper, a strong desire cherished by all the sons and daughters of
the Chinese nation.[42]

Another novel aimed at children, Guo Mengmeng's *Anti-Japanese Heroes
Story Series: Xie Jinyuan* was also published in 2015. The book is another
fictionalized account of the Eight Hundred and it reminded readers,
'Despite his departure from this world for good, our anti-Japanese hero
Xie Jinyuan's patriotism will remain in the mind of future generations
eternally.'[43] The book is also a communist appropriation of the legend as
it highlighted Mao's praise of the Eight Hundred as 'models of national
revolution' and further stated:

After the founding of the People's Republic of China, the Shanghai
Municipal People's Government commended Xie Jinyuan's glorious
deeds of 'engaging in resistance against Japanese aggression and
sacrificing life for the country' and moved his grave to the 'celebrity

grave area' in the Wanguo Public Mausoleum, allowing later generations to visit, pay respect, remember and commemorate.[44]

The Guangdong Museum of Art displayed a special exhibition in 2017 showcasing several hundred Guangdong items on loan from over 40 museums in China. Wang Haiying covered the exhibition for the *Shenzhen Daily* and noted Hu Yichuan's print 'Eight Hundred Heroes' that 'not only accurately depicts the fighting soldiers but also emphasizes their bravery via the painting's simplified forms'.[45] In 2019, Shanghai staged many revolutionary activities during the People's Republic's 70th anniversary and the Shanghai Centre Theatre staged shows depicting wartime stories including a stage recreation of the Eight Hundred fighting the Japanese.[46] In Shanghai, Sihang Warehouse as the site of the actual battle became the epicentre for remembering the Eight Hundred.

RESTORATION OF SIHANG WAREHOUSE

After 1949 Sihang continued to function as a warehouse and a small business later became established in the building with little public awareness of the location's importance. Shanghai city officials formally declared the site a memorial of the Sino-Japanese War in 1985.[47] Shanghai Bailian Group, the warehouse owner, built a memorial display room in 1995 which it expanded in 2002. The group also donated numerous items to the site's museum such as paintings, calligraphy, coins, books and other objects including the diary of Xie Jinyuan.[48] However, the building was dilapidated, as Lu Pan observed in 2012:

> Flows of various commercial activities have pushed the site of memory into visual and mental oblivion. The only space that can remind visitors of its war history is an exhibition room no larger than 100 square meters. . . [and] this semi-official commemorative space is only open to the public for a few hours on Friday afternoons. As a result, many Chinese do not recognize or are not aware of its historical significance. Visitors are also of small number.[49]

Given the lack of public space at Sihang dedicated to public memory, a local committee lobbied for a new museum in the warehouse; however, the building continued to be rundown as the architect Marta Kubacki observed in 2014:

> The building, which once strengthened the identity of the Chinese people at a critical point in their history, is now in disrepair and soon to be assimilated into a more modern and gentrified vision of the new Zhabei District. Sihang warehouse is an integral part of Shanghai's collective cultural memory and, arguably, a part of Shanghai's identity.[50]

Plans to renovate Sihang commenced in 2013 as part of a wide development plan for the Zhabei district.[51] Significant progress occurred after city officials announced on 15 July 2014 that the warehouse, as an important symbol, would be restored and the surrounding area along Suzhou Creek would become a memorial square. Lai Hsiao-yeh, director of the Taiwan Affairs Office in Zhabei, also announced plans to repair the bronze statue of Xie Jinyuan and restore the wall to display the original bullet holes and shell craters.[52] The architect Tang Yu'en oversaw the restoration and he envisaged removing extensions that were not part of the original structure and restoring the battle damage. The new complex would also feature a prominent museum featuring paintings, sculptures and a multimedia show.[53]

After being closed for one year during the renovations, Sihang Warehouse reopened to the public on 3 August 2015. The museum opened ten days later and Xie Jimin, now aged 78, observed artefacts at an exhibition during the grand opening, as the *Shanghai Daily* reported:

> Exhibits that most impressed Xie Jimin included a monument featuring a letter written by his father before leaving home for battle and a video clip showing how the colonel encouraged his soldiers. 'The letter showed my father's complicated feelings, as he had to shoulder his responsibility as a soldier while feeling guilty about leaving his family,' said Xie. 'It was a "death order" and he showed great courage.'[54]

The renovated warehouse attracted locals to the site immediately after its

A bust of Xie Jinyuan dedicated to his memory inside the entrance of Sihang Warehouse. (Wikipedia)

reopening. 'Stories of these heroes have faded over time, especially among the young,' Shanghai resident Lin Yankun told a reporter. 'I plan to educate my kids on Sihang heroes so they too can feel proud to be Chinese.'[55] Pictures of the Eight Hundred by the American photographer Hyland Lyon taken immediately after their breakout into the International Settlement were also displayed at an exhibition inside the warehouse.[56] The Sihang Warehouse Battle Memorial became a popular site as the *Shanghai Daily* reported two years later:

> The battle is 're-enacted' through audio effects and 3D holographic projection. Visitors can stand among bronze statues of soldiers and listen to Colonel Xie Jinyuan talking. They can also experience the sensations of 'stout resistance' and 'raging flames' outside the warehouse. The memorial periodically will hold 'interactive plays,' with middle school children re-enacting some of the historical events.[57]

An aerial view of the restored Sihang Warehouse and New Lese Bridge taken in 2020. (Contributor: Imaginechina Limited/Alamy Stock Photo)

The memorial space in front of the restored Sihang Warehouse taken in 2020. The preserved battle damage is clearly visible on the building's west wall.
(Contributor: Imaginechina Limited/Alamy Stock Photo)

On 4 January 2018, city officials added six Shanghai historical landmarks into the 20th Century Chinese Architectural Heritage List, including Sihang Warehouse.[58] The site, like the Alamo in Texas, became sacred space and a place of pilgrimage in which Chinese people could honour the memory of the Eight Hundred, but not all visitors would display respect.

THE SIHANG FOUR

On 8 August 2017, four young Chinese men — all university students and collectors of Japanese military memorabilia — posted photographs of themselves on social media standing in front of Sihang Warehouse wearing Imperial Japanese Army uniforms, which had been taken five days earlier. 'There are so many people around the Sihang Cangku in the evening,' one of the men remarked. 'So taking a photo is like stealing a manhole cover — we finished it in several seconds.'[59] A netizen named 'Shangdizhiying_5zn' (God's Eagle) saw the image and felt 'a gust of undeniable anger' and reposted it on the social media site Weibo, hoping that authorities would punish the men. 'Now some people don't feel grateful,' the netizen explained. 'Instead, they wear the enemy's uniforms and take photos at the site where the martyrs shed their blood and write mocking captions. To me, such behavior is no different from peeing and pooing over the martyrs' remains.'[60]

After the pictures went viral, they provoked a furious backlash on Chinese social media and major newspapers reported the story. A spokesman from the Sihang Warehouse Memorial Museum condemned the 'Sihang Four' for their 'impudent blasphemy'.[61] The warehouse owners similarly denounced the men's 'shameless and profane behaviour'.[62] The incident became a national story resulting in an enormous amount of commentary. 'My grandfather was one of the soldiers in that battle and he died,' one Weibo user declared. 'Those who sacrificed their lives for the country and the people should never be forgotten or insulted, especially at the same place where they died.'[63]

Earlier on 5 August, two Chinese tourists had been arrested in Berlin after posing for photographs in front of the German Federal Parliament while giving Nazi salutes — an offence under the law which prohibits hate speech.[64] The police charged the tourists with 'using symbols of illegal organizations', but they were soon released after posting bail.[65] Chinese commentators immediately linked the 'Sihang Four' to the recent event in Berlin, resulting in a wider public debate about adopting German-style laws, and one Chinese netizen announced: 'Isn't there anyone to intervene? In Germany, the government intervenes, why doesn't China?'[66] As these incidents attracted more attention, Li Yang from the *China Daily* reported:

> The Nazi salute by the two Chinese tourists and the Japanese army uniforms that the four youths in Shanghai put on have been nailed to the shameful pole of history. The crimes the Nazis and Japanese forces committed against humanity will continue to remind us to never let down our guard against fascism and its symbols.[67]

The *Qianjiang Evening News*, another mainland newspaper, made a similar case:

> Not long ago, photos emerged of a few young good-for-nothings posing as invading Japanese military officers in uniform at the Sihang Warehouse War Memorial, a sacred site of the war of resistance. . . Trampling on history means trampling on national dignity and it is a second insult to the whole nation.[68]

As the story gained further traction, Chinese professionals chimed into the debate. Professor He Jianmin from Shanghai University advocated that China should have laws forbidding behaviour that betrays national dignity and patriotism at special sites.[69] 'Such things don't happen by chance,' Da Zhigang, another academic, noted. 'It reveals problems in our young people's view of history. While criticizing these people, we should also reflect on how young people are educated about history.'[70]

On 24 August, the Chinese media reported that the 'Sihang Four' and the fifth student who took the infamous photo had turned themselves in to the police who detained three of them for violating public security laws and released the other two with a warning as they were under eighteen. The police stated that the five youths had expressed regret and they wrote letters of apology for hurting the feelings of the Chinese people.[71]

The story of the 'Sihang Four' seemed to be over until 21 February 2018, when a photograph of two men in Japanese Army uniforms taken at the martyrs' memorial site in Purple Mountain, Nanjing went viral, triggering another social media incident after 'Shangdizhiying_5zn' spotted the imagine and reposted it on Weibo.[72] Police swiftly announced they were investigating the incident and vowed to severely punish the men.[73] The Chinese media linked this act to the infamous 'Sihang Four', rekindling demands for such acts to be vigorously punished.[74] Zhang Jianjun, curator of the Nanjing Massacre Memorial Hall, called for stronger punishment of such behaviour: 'The scars of a nation cannot be made fun of. The country should make laws to forbid such behaviour. We live in a peaceful era, but we dare not and will not forget history.'[75]

One week later police detained the two men as the media storm continued, but under existing laws they could only be detained for fifteen days, which caused Wang Yilong, a 95-year-old survivor of the Nanjing Massacre, to declare: 'A mere 15-day detention is not a serious enough penalty for them.'[76] Chen Deshou, an 87-year-old survivor of the massacre, similarly announced: 'My family members were killed in the massacre. It is really necessary to give a harsher punishment to people like those two men, rather than merely giving them a few days of detention.'[77]

As public calls for stronger punishment grew, Ren Tanzhen, president of the Nanjing Lawyers Association, advocated new harsher laws to deal with such incidents.[78] Wu Xianbin, curator of the Nanjing Folk Anti-Japanese War Museum, similarly called for the establishment of new legislation to combat 'fascist speech and conduct'.[79] In a slightly different vein, Ling Xi, vice-curator of the Nanjing Memorial Hall, advocated greater understanding to help young people 'evaluate history correctly'.[80] On 10 March, the *China Daily* reported that over 30 political advisers from art, culture and entertainment spheres had called for a law to protect China's national dignity and He Yun'ao, a history professor at Nanjing University, advocated new laws to 'to punish those who publicly promote fascism or Japanese militarism, or who insult revolutionary martyrs and national heroes', an idea backed by martial arts superstar Jackie Chan.[81]

Given the outrage directed at the 'Sihang Four', it would seem that the Eight Hundred Heroes are firmly established and safe in the People's

Republic of China; however, this is not the case as demonstrated by one of the most controversial Chinese movies of all time.

THE CANCELLED PREMIERE

On 14 September 2017, Chinese director Guan Hu announced that his latest movie *The Eight Hundred* would soon begin filming in Suzhou, Jiangsu Province. Guan Hu, who had been working on the project since 2010, wanted to make a film to help the younger generation understand the soldiers' sacrifice.[82] He envisaged a world-class Chinese blockbuster but also wanted the film to reach international audiences unfamiliar with China's wartime experience. Guan accordingly hired Hollywood stunt coordinator and second unit director Glenn Boswell who had worked on *The Matrix*, *Titanic* and *The Thin Red Line* to help film the battle scenes as well as Tim Crosbie, the visual effects supervisor from *The Lord of the Rings* trilogy. Professor Zhang Yiwu from Beijing University noted the intended film heralded a shift in how *Kuomintang* veterans were being depicted: 'The heroes are no longer just Communist Party members. The timing has been expanded as well. The change is a good indication of progress in the Chinese movie industry.'[83] Guan's use of western cinematic expertise marked a departure from traditional Chinese film-making, as Xu Fan announced in *China Daily*: 'In the past, the revolutionary stories or military movies hardly used non-Chinese mainland filmmakers, let alone foreigners.'[84]

The Eight Hundred, produced by the Huayi Brothers Media Corporation, took almost a decade to make and the original script written by Hu Kun was officially approved in 2013.[85] The movie, the first Chinese film shot entirely with IMAX cameras, had an enormous budget of over US$80 million and its massive sets that recreated the epic grandeur of Old Shanghai took eighteen months to construct.[86] On 8 June 2019, tickets went on sale for the premiere that would take place at the 22nd Shanghai International Film Festival over 15–24 June, followed by the general release in Chinese cinemas on 5 July.[87] However, the day before the premiere, festival organizers announced that the event had been cancelled due to 'technical reasons'.[88]

The Chinese Red Culture Research Association five days earlier had hosted an academic conference and participants disapproved of *The Eight*

Hundred for its positive depiction of the *Kuomintang*. 'The Eight Hundred goes to great lengths to highlight the Republic of China flag,' Si Manan, an attendee, remarked. 'Irrespective of what historical background the movie was based on, such overt portrayal [of the flag] is terrifying.'[89] Guo Songmin, another participant, similarly disapproved of the flag: 'If we do that, whether it's intentional or not, we will hurt the feelings of Chinese people, especially those old soldiers who risked life and limb to build modern China.'[90] The secretary general of the Association also asserted:

> It is a reversal of history and misleads the audience. If left unchecked, it will certainly deprive the entire Communist party of its historical basis. Once the party's leadership is lost, the Chinese nation is bound to fall into the deep, miserable abyss of colonized and semi-colonized countries.[91]

The participants agreed that it would be inappropriate to release the movie during the People's Republic's 70th anniversary.

The general release of *The Eight Hundred* was also cancelled, causing the Huayi Brothers Media Corporation's shares to drop by 8 per cent on the Shenzhen Stock Exchange.[92] The decision caused online outrage and one netizen noted that Sihang Warehouse 'boosted the Chinese people's confidence and passion in countering the Japanese', before continuing:

> What's the problem of making a movie based on that? What's the problem of exalting the sacrificial spirit [of the soldiers]? For the leftist Maoists, if you like, you can make your own movies. No one will object to that. For the showing of the Flag of the Republic of China, anyone with general understanding of history knows that the persistent standing of the flag led to the rousing scene at the warehouse. What's the problem of highlighting the flag? Will you be satisfied if history is distorted by showing the Five-starred Red Flag instead?[93]

Another online commentator remarked: 'Nationalist soldiers constituted the main forces fighting the Japanese. This is fact. *The Eight Hundred* is a good movie. I hope it can be released.'[94] A Weibo user also complained about the cancellation: 'Why was this? Because the eight hundred brave fellows who fought the Japanese were from the Nationalist armies, not the Communists?'[95]

The cancellation made international news, as Steven Lee Myers reported in *The New York Times* that 'the cancellation came amid a broadening political crackdown on cultural works that are not sufficiently in tune with the ideology of China's leader, Xi Jinping'.[96] Myers also noted how the cancellation indicated a shift in the official party line:

> In fact, the battalion's actions have been lauded previously by the Communist government, which in 2015 turned the warehouse building, located on the Suzhou River in Shanghai's center, into a memorial museum. The state television network, CCTV, lionized the battle when the museum opened. Under Mr. Xi, it seems, political winds have since shifted.[97]

Conservative communists are uncomfortable with the *Kuomintang*'s rehabilitation, fearing that an opening up of public debate will allow criticism of the party, and this fear is evident in a *Global Times* editorial:

> Nowadays, a morbid nostalgia for the Republic of China has emerged among a few Internet communities and a small number of intellectuals. . . KMT [*Kuomintang*] rule in the mainland was a mess. Its national governance failed to reach the grass roots and smash the separatist warlord regimes. Moreover, KMT was subject to Western powers. British warships were still sailing in the rivers of the Chinese mainland in the 1940s. China as a gigantic country was unable to resist the aggression of a small island nation like Japan. The KMT regime is held responsible for the humiliation that China suffered from the Japanese invasion.[98]

The irony of the cancellation and the party's discomfort with the film is that communist propagandists were largely responsible for creating the legend of the Eight Hundred during the wartime United Front. The Wuhan version, *Eight Hundred Heroes* (1938), was made by prominent communist film-makers who later founded the party's movie industry in Yan'an and their depiction contained the original patriotic flag-raising ceremony which became the template for the later films.

A movie poster of the film *The Eight Hundred* (2020). (Author's Collection)

The cancellation did not constitute a ban and *The Eight Hundred* was released the following year on 21 August 2020. The movie did experience cuts and the final version was thirteen minutes shorter than the original, although it is unclear what content was removed. The film critic Steve Rose speculated in *The Guardian* that the depiction of the Republic of China flag had been scaled down: 'As for the troublesome flag, it is usually seen from a distance, and is conspicuously missing its white sun symbol.'[99] Despite the reduced seating capacity resulting from the ongoing COVID-19 pandemic, *The Eight Hundred* became the highest-grossing movie in the world in 2020, taking over US$472 million at the international box office.

The Eight Hundred is a spectacular film with exceptionally well-crafted battle scenes and an incredible recreation of the International Settlement with bars, nightclubs and bright neon lights. The foreign concessions are populated with carefree and initially detached foreigners and Chinese residents, contrasted with war-ravaged Zhabei. 'Over there is heaven,' a Chinese officer in Sihang Warehouse declares while pointing at the brightly lit Settlement at night. 'Here is hell,' he says, pointing at the warehouse. The contrast between the two parallel universes separated by Suzhou Creek is expertly conveyed.

The Eight Hundred followed the conventions of the previous Wuhan (1938) and Taiwanese (1976) movies and contains the same inaccuracies. Yang Huimin swims across the creek to deliver the flag and the flag-raising ceremony is anything but low key as the men willingly sacrifice themselves to keep it upright while being strafed by a Japanese plane. The soldiers eventually escape from the warehouse and rush across the bridge without any explanation of their internment or Xie Jinyuan's later assassination by four of his own men. Despite the transfer of these conventions from the previous films, *The Eight Hundred* is a vastly different movie with an entirely different tone without the one-dimensional heroics and propaganda of the other versions. The film offers a more intelligent and complex human story by focusing on a sub-group of stragglers, not from the 88th Division, who by twists of fate end up inside Sihang Warehouse. These men are not willing participants, but they gradually become invested in the events occurring around them after becoming aware that the outside world is perceiving them as heroes.

The Eight Hundred begins as soldiers from the Hubei Security Corps arrive in Shanghai as reinforcements, only to find a ruined city, and they are quickly dispersed by Japanese troops. As the *Kuomintang*'s National Revolutionary Army is retreating and shooting deserters, some of the Hubei men along with other stragglers are escorted to the warehouse by Captain Lei Xiong and his Machine Gun Company, the last of the Eight Hundred to assemble at the fortress. The group — which includes thirteen-year-old Xiao Hubei, an old soldier Yang Guai, another soldier Lao Tie and military accountant Old Abacus — are isolated as deserters as Xie decides what to do with them while his men prepare to defend the warehouse.

On day one the first Japanese assault fails after its men are annihilated, but the Japanese retaliate with a historically inaccurate gas attack and the toxic cloud crosses Suzhou Creek into the Settlement. The stragglers are given a chance of redemption by shooting Japanese prisoners and some do. At night three of them attempt to escape through a waterway and, after spotting Japanese troops entering the warehouse the same way, they alert the defenders to the threat as watchers across the creek praise their actions. On day two foreign journalists and other onlookers watch a determined Japanese attack and enemy sappers almost succeed in blowing a hole into the wall until Chen Shusheng jumps to his death and inspires others to become suicide bombers. On day three the men raise the flag provided by Yang Huimin, which remains upright and visible in a sea of Japanese flags despite a deadly enemy air attack. At night the men watch a shadow puppet show that links their story to ancient tales of heroism. On day four Xie talks to his opponent Colonel Isao Konoe under a flag of truce and he remains defiant, causing the Japanese officer to lose face. A *Kuomintang* official sneaks into the warehouse and orders Xie to retreat, convincing him not to seek martyrdom in death. At night the Eight Hundred storm across the bridge and enter the pantheon of legendary Chinese heroes. In the morning a beautiful white horse, which is earlier found in the warehouse and seen running wild numerous times, escapes the ruins as a symbol of hope. The film ends with a shot of the warehouse today against the backdrop of Shanghai's high rises and a moving adaptation of the Irish folk song 'Londonderry Air' is heard during the end credits.

Xie Jinyuan and Yang Huimin are not the focus of *The Eight Hundred*, unlike the previous films, as the narrative is principally seen through the eyes of the stragglers who are given a chance at redemption and mostly stay behind as a suicidal rearguard to allow the Eight Hundred to escape. The film also focuses on Chinese characters inside the Settlement who are increasingly moved by the spectacle taking place across Suzhou Creek and are inspired to take action in various ways. A university professor, Zhang, watches the events from his apartment and later shoots at the Japanese with a shotgun as the Eight Hundred run across the bridge. A Chinese journalist, Fang Xingwen, a self-serving individual disinterested in the outcome of the war, enters the warehouse and documents the soldiers' plight until the end. A Chinese gangster, Daozi, is killed by a Japanese sniper after running across the bridge carrying a telephone cable which allows the Eight Hundred to communicate with the outside world. A casino owner, Rong, the epitome of 1930s 'Shanghai Decadence', donates her supply of morphine to the wounded soldiers.

The Eight Hundred also differs from the earlier Taiwanese version in its depiction of westerners inside the Settlement by focusing on the journalists covering the battle, not the British and American soldiers guarding their concessions. Little screen time is given to the British soldiers guarding the bridge and there is no portrayal of Major-General Alexander Telfer-Smollett, although during the breakout one British soldier yells at the Japanese before opening fire to cover the Chinese breakout. Western journalists cover the events with great interest, including from a Goodyear blimp giving them a perfect view of the battle, symbolizing that the world is watching, and they become increasingly sympathetic to the Chinese cause.

The Eight Hundred received much praise in international film reviews. A reviewer in *Sino-Cinema* noted the film's surreal qualities:

> Guan & Co.'s most striking innovation — and an apt comment on the whole craziness of war — is to underline how events were played out in full view of civilians and foreign media in the international concessions on the south bank of Suzhou creek, where the city's night life continued pretty much as normal.[100]

Empire magazine declared that 'everywhere you turn there is fantastic filmmaking, flitting between grand sweep (a set-piece involving supplies being run across a river) and quieter moments'.[101] A reviewer for *Asian Movie Pulse* concluded:

> And while there's never any doubt that the film is designed to glorify China's past, it simply can't be written off as mere propaganda. . . Perhaps it's because Guan centers his story around rural bumpkins, ineffective academics, petty crooks. . . Yes, they mostly turn into heroes, but they ground the film in a more difficult reality than we usually see from this type of state-sponsored storytelling.[102]

The Eight Hundred in general electrified Chinese moviegoers who rated the film highly on the movie website Douban, as Yilin Chen reported in *Caixin Global*:

> The most-liked review on Douban reads, 'After the movie ended, the entire theater was silent. It seemed like all the viewers were still immersed in the tragic atmosphere and couldn't bring themselves back to real life.' Others said that the film's patriotic message and majestic scenes . . . lifted their morale in the wake of the pandemic and recent floods across southern China.[103]

Chinese audiences were moved by the film, as the journalist Ai Pang observed: 'As the lights turned back on in the theater, the entire audience . . . continued to sit motionless in their seats, even long after the screen went dark. They were so shocked and moved by the movie they had just seen.'[104] Online Chinese reviews also expressed emotional responses, as one moviegoer expressed:

> It allows me to see things that are overlooked in history. The film gave delicate portrayals of various characters who just want to be reunited with their families. They laid down their lives for the country, and that touches the audience. I feel that the contemporary Chinese communists can give recognition to the Japanese-fighting Nationalists.[105]

The Eight Hundred resulted in a boom of visitors at Sihang Warehouse and museum staff noted thousands of them arriving since the film's release, forcing them to limit visitors.[106] 'During the summer peak season, we usually receive 1,000 to 2,000 visitors a day,' Jiang Shanyong, the deputy director of the memorial, noted. 'But since the movie's release, the daily number has reached full capacity at 2,500.'[107] A large number of flowers also started to be left at the warehouse in a sign of remembrance.[108] After Wang Zhe, a Shanghai resident, watched the movie, he brought his ten-year-old son to the warehouse: 'It's my son's idea. He said he wanted to present flowers to honor the heroes. It's important for him to understand our past and thus cherish our present.'[109] Qu Ziyu, another child, told a reporter at the warehouse that the movie 'made me feel like I was in history' and his friend Zong Xuehao announced his desire to become a soldier 'to defend my homeland'.[110] The journalist Cao Siqi observed visitors at the warehouse, as reported in *Global Times*:

> Three days after I watched the Chinese war epic *The Eight Hundred* in Beijing, I was so eager to visit the old building where the battle took place that I booked a ticket for Shanghai. It was a rainy Saturday, but the heavy downpours did nothing to dampen the enthusiasm of hundreds of fans like me who had come to see what the Sihang Warehouse looks like.[111]

Cao Siqi observed flowers and People's Republic flags that had been placed on the lawn, before adding:

> I saw several primary students come and offer milk tea and candies as their tribute. Police officers nearby had to take them away as they were not an 'appropriate gift.' I was dumbfounded, but also touched by their innocent and pure reverence.[112]

Western audiences had a harder time connecting with the movie given a lack of understanding of historical background and cultural significance. For example, Michael Ordoña in the *Los Angeles Times* remarked: 'American audiences will largely be wondering what is going on as Chinese troops

A Chinese child places a People's Republic of China flag at Sihang Warehouse in 2020 as a token of respect towards the Eight Hundred Heroes.
(Contributor: Imaginechina Limited/Alamy Stock Photo)

in German helmets . . . hold their ground between Japanese hordes and noncombatants in Shanghai's "international concessions".'[113] Maggie Lee in *Variety* similarly declared:

> For those with little knowledge of the Sino-Japanese War, the bombardment of facts, action and characters in the 147-minute film can be too much to take in at one go. But the spirit of the mission, like that of 'The Alamo,' should be easy for any audience to root for.[114]

A reviewer for the *Economist* concluded it 'is an unusual Chinese film for its depiction of Nationalist soldiers as heroes' who are 'typically portrayed as villains and stooges on Chinese screens'.[115] Westerners were nevertheless moved by the film, as Brian MacNamara expressed in his review:

> To be perfectly honest there were a few times throughout this film that I found myself in tears, including one part where someone

sacrifices themselves to save everyone, or the students that get in over their heads, or that moment you knew was coming but it still hit hard. What makes it all the harder to watch is knowing that the defence of the Warehouse didn't do what it was meant to do as none of the European powers intervened. There are moments in the film that have weight just by being there. The moment someone mentions Nanjing [heralding the later massacre], you could feel the tension in the room as that name hit everyone.[116]

Audiences in the People's Republic could interpret *The Eight Hundred* through a hard-line nationalistic prism. For example, Ai Pang's review contrasted the heroes with recent protests in Hong Kong and the democracy and self-determination activist Agnes Chow:

Most of them [the Eight Hundred] were only 16 to 18, much younger than Hong Kong secessionist Agnes Chow, yet they did everything they could, including giving up their very lives, for the survival of the people and their country. . . Secessionists like Chow need to go to the cinema to see what Japan did to their grandparents decades ago. Hopefully, they may actually learn something from the movie if their blood still carries a bit of sense of being Chinese.[117]

Cao Siqi's review also became nationalistic:

Indeed, the life we have now was made possible by the blood of millions of martyrs. The strong, wealthy country we live in is built on the courage to denounce militarism and invasion. This strong will is still precious for us now as we face the US' reckless provocations and blatant slander, telling us that we should work and fight harder.[118]

Perceptions of ultra-nationalism turned some western audiences off, including a British reviewer in *The Times* who perceived the film as 'so wildly jingoistic that it even includes a postscript praising the Communist Party'.[119] Sonny Lo Shiu Hing noted the film's darker side in *Macau Business*: 'The strong showing of *The Eight Hundred* may not be fully understood by some China observers outside the PRC [People's Republic of China], for its popularity underscores the rise of assertive Chinese nationalism in the entire PRC.'[120] Nevertheless, Lo also acknowledged that the movie contained a 'soft but hidden appeal to Taipei' concerning peaceful reunification with Taiwan.[121]

The Eight Hundred and the legacy of the actual defenders of Sihang Warehouse can be appropriated in the name of aggressive nationalism or alternatively for understanding and a desire to peacefully resolve Chinese political questions. As the People's Republic is at the crossroads, China's political direction ultimately remains unclear, but the Eight Hundred Heroes will continue to be invoked no matter which way the zeitgeist goes.

EPILOGUE

The overwhelmingly intense fighting caused worldwide sensation and our Chinese soldiers impressed people around the world. With regard to its scale and nature, the defence of Sihang Warehouse, despite being a skirmish in the major battle, possessed widespread influence and remarkable significance. It highlighted our Chinese nation's spirit of 'allowing no affront', earned international sympathy, and lifted morale at home, which imperceptibly laid a solid foundation for the final victory and sounded the death knell for the Japanese militarist invaders.

General Gu Zhutong
— Deputy Commander of the Third War Zone in Shanghai

JUNGLE GRAVES OF LOST HEROES

After the Chinese survivors of Japanese captivity in Rabaul departed New Britain in 1946, they left behind a monument they built after liberation to commemorate their dead which displayed an inscription, 'Memorial to the Fallen Chinese Cantonese People'.[1] After its construction, the Australian Army, the Chinese Army and the local Chinese community attended a ceremony in which offerings of food, candles and flowers were given. The repatriated Chinese also left behind their dead.

In 1946, the Australian War Graves Services, in consultation with

Reinterred graves with new markings belonging to some of the 377 Chinese prisoners of war that died in Rabaul, New Britain during Japanese captivity. (AWM)

The monument built by former Chinese prisoners of war to commemorate their 377 comrades who died during Japanese captivity in Rabaul. (AWM)

The monument built by former Chinese prisoners of war to commemorate their 377 comrades who died during Japanese captivity in Rabaul. An inscription is visible in English and Chinese. (AWM)

Colonel Wu Yien, the senior Chinese officer, exhumed the remains of all 377 Chinese soldiers in New Britain before reburying them in the Rabaul War Cemetery, next to the British Empire War Cemetery at Bita Paka.[2] The Australian Army maintained this cemetery and the Chinese graves until this responsibility transferred to the Imperial War Graves Commission. Although the Commission's charter did not allow funds to be spent on maintaining graves for non-British Empire soldiers, it offered to conduct this work if the Chinese Government repaid the costs.[3] In April 1947, the Chinese Foreign Ministry forwarded this offer to the Ministry of Defence, and the Chinese Consulate in Australia considered the proposal. By 1948, no decision had been made as the ongoing civil war between Chiang Kai-shek's *Kuomintang* and Mao Zedong's communists prevented a resolution of the issue. In January, the Australian Legation in China again raised the question with the Foreign Ministry and Chinese officials considered building a permanent cemetery. Chinese diplomats in Canberra also contemplated exhuming all graves, cremating the remains and transporting the ashes to China. In the end no action was taken and on 1 October 1949 Mao proclaimed the People's Republic of China as the remnants of the defeated *Kuomintang* retreated to Taiwan. Beijing and Taipei had no interest in Chinese war graves in Rabaul, which were now maintained by the local Chinese community.[4]

In April 1964, R. Levi, Chairman of the Kokopo Town Advisory Council, and Father English from the Roman Catholic Mission raised the future of the Chinese graves with W.J. Chalmers, Director General of the Australian War Graves Commission. Chalmers declared that the Commission would 'not do anything about the marking of the graves of about four hundred Chinese'.[5] Chalmers also incorrectly asserted that the graves belonged to Chinese civilians. The Australian press reported 'stories around Rabaul' that 'the Chinese were Nationalist Chinese troops, captured by the Japanese and brought to Rabaul as slave labour'.[6] The graves, now the subject of rumour and folklore, receded further from memory and the jungle eventually consumed the resting places of the forgotten Chinese soldiers.

In December 2008, over four decades later, the Taiwanese *United Daily News* reported that an Australian pilot had discovered tombs of Chinese soldiers in Rabaul, including members of the Eight Hundred Heroes.[7] The pilot had contacted the Chinese embassy in Papua New Guinea, but officials displayed no interest in the graves. However, after a Chinese netizen in Beijing reposted the media report on the internet, the story went viral on the mainland and within a fortnight 100,000 people had signed an online petition demanding their government repatriate the remains to China for reburial. The public reaction forced Beijing and Taipei to act, as neither government wanted to be seen disrespecting the defenders of Sihang Warehouse.[8]

On 9 January 2009, *Taipei Times* reported that Taiwan's representative office in Papua New Guinea had located the graves of Chinese soldiers. Lee Tsung-fen, from the Ministry of Foreign Affairs, confirmed that the Ministry of National Defense would send officials to Rabaul to identify the graves and consider transporting the remains to Taiwan after consultation with relatives of the fallen.[9] After the taskforce investigated the cemetery, the ministry despatched another mission in February to restore the graves and conduct a memorial service. The mission returned home the following month with a tablet symbolizing the spirits of the soldiers who died in Papua New Guinea that was placed in the National Revolutionary Martyrs' Shrine in Taipei.[10]

The mainland Foreign Ministry also sent officials to Rabaul to inspect the graves. In March 2009, the ministry announced that the remains would return to China and the *Xinhua News Agency* reported:

> The Chinese embassy in Papua New Guinea is looking for and identifying remains of the dead soldiers, but the Foreign Ministry refused to provide more details as to when their bodies will be sent back to China. 'China has attached great importance to the treatment of the remains of these Chinese soldiers and will have the issue settled without delay,' said Foreign Ministry spokesman Qin Gang at a routine press briefing. Qin said China will hold a grand memorial ceremony when the remains return.[11]

In October 2009, the Chinese Government repaired the cemetery with the blessing of local land owners, and Zheng Kang, a counsellor from the Chinese Embassy, conducted a ceremony at the site with local officials, as the *Papua New Guinea Post* reported:

> A few Chinese businessmen were present to witness the event; the owners of the site killed a pig for lunch and performing the traditional ritual of breaking tabu, then exchanged the traditional currency, as a formal recognition that their ancestral spirits will approve the transaction.[12]

Despite the intent to repatriate the graves, the remains of the soldiers stayed in Rabaul and in April 2015 Ambassador Li Ruiyou visited the cemetery during commemorations marking the 70th anniversary of victory against Japan.[13] A Foreign Ministry press release noted that prisoners held on New Britain included members of the Eight Hundred who alongside other captives 'were abused and tortured, some of them died and were buried here'.[14] In August, another delegation held a memorial ceremony in which

Gu Chaoxi, China's Vice Minister of Civil Affairs, declared that the soldiers buried in the cemetery were martyrs and a source of national pride who the Chinese people would remember forever.[15]

THE LAST HEROES

Sun Yuanliang, commander of the 88th Division who ordered Xie Jinyuan and the Eight Hundred Heroes to defend Sihang Warehouse, later helped defend Nanjing. During the 1944 Ichi-Go offensives, Japanese forces approached to within 200 miles of the wartime capital Chongqing and Sun's 29th Army stopped them at the town of Dushan in Guangxi Province. He later fought the communists during the Chinese Civil War before fleeing to Taiwan with the remnants of the *Kuomintang*. Sun retired from the military and lived a quiet life on the island, possibly because he had fallen out of favour with Chiang Kai-shek.[16] He later reflected on the outbreak of the Sino-Japanese War:

> When we implemented the scorched earth policy in the beginning of the War of Resistance, we encouraged the population to move inland and disperse. But we did not make any appropriate arrangements for our loyal compatriots, we extended no helping hand to refugees with no place to go; we just let them scatter like rats, to survive or die. This probably was the beginning of us losing the trust of the people in the mainland.[17]

Sun Yuanliang died on 25 May 2007 aged 103 years. Before he died his reputation as a patriotic general had been restored in the People's Republic of China.

In 2005, Guo Xingfa, an 89-year-old veteran of the Eight Hundred and resident of Baoshan District, remembered the battle:

> A bullet hit the ground, and suddenly, it sprang up into one of my legs. Another bullet went flying past my scalp so close that I even felt its heat. Just imagine if it had followed a lower route through my forehead. I would have been dead for decades now.[18]

General Sun Yuanliang, commander of the 88th Division. (Author's Collection)

Guo Xingfa stayed in touch with Xie Jinyuan's family. 'I maintained contact with the colonel's wife and son until the 1980s,' he reflected. 'I have deep love for them and miss them.' The commander's son Xie Jimin expressed: 'Guo Xingfa retained the dignity of Chinese people while facing enemies, and made great contribution to our final victory.'[19]

Guo Xingfa returned to Sihang Warehouse on 13 August 2005, where he had an emotional reunion with Zhou Fuqi, another Eight Hundred survivor from Hubei Province who also remained on the mainland after 1949.[20] Both former soldiers, in a highly publicized event with strong media presence, knelt in front of the statue of Xie Jinyuan as they paid their respects to their former commander. Zhou Fuqi pointed at a wartime photo of Sihang Warehouse and told the story of his experiences.

Yang Yangzheng, a 91-year-old veteran of the Eight Hundred from Chongqing, returned to Sihang Warehouse for the first time since the battle on 4 July 2005.[21] He had travelled on a train with several family members on a journey sponsored by a Shanghai newspaper. Yang lost his left eye during the battle and in old age he lost sight in his right eye. 'Please don't call me a hero,' Yang insisted during the trip. 'I simply did what a soldier should do — obey orders and defend my country.'[22] Yang touched the statue of Xie Jinyuan and broke down in tears when touching paper on which a soldier had written an oath during the battle.

Yang Yangzheng had endured Japanese captivity in a camp in Baoshan District and later carried coal as a slave labourer at another camp in Anhui Province until he escaped: 'We managed to escape and join the Chinese troops a month after we reached the coal mine. I walked to Chongqing in 1944.'[23] Peter Harmsen later interviewed Yang:

> I was taken to his modest home on the outskirts of Chongqing by a local city government official who had arranged the visit. Despite his advanced age, he was a big man, and you could imagine he must have been a fearsome fighter in his youth. He had been in one of the iconic battles of the Anti-Japanese War, but he had never bragged about it. Some of his closest neighbors had no idea that they lived next to an actual hero. But the veneration that you could immediately feel among the neighbors once they realized Yang's past was proof that

the war remains an important fact for many Chinese. [24]

Yang Yangzheng died of illness in Chongqing on 16 December 2010. During his final trip to Sihang Warehouse, he reflected: 'But I am gratified that the sacrifices made long ago have not been forgotten and the devotion to our country has been kept alive.'[25]

Another veteran, Yang Genkui, born in 1921 in Sichuan, became the last known Eight Hundred veteran on the mainland after revealing his past while visiting Jianchuan Museum, and his story became a major news event.[26] During the Maoist years, Yang Genkui attempted to conceal his former status as a *Kuomintang* soldier but rumours spread and he experienced persecution. He later enquired with local officials to see if he could obtain a veteran pension or medical care. The officials replied, 'Go to Taiwan to ask the Kuomintang for benefits.'[27] News of this poor treatment caused online outrage across China and sympathetic journalists defended Yang Genkui while being careful not to overtly criticize the Communist Party.[28] Yang Genkui, reflecting on his life, declared, 'We are not afraid of death, we are afraid of being forgotten.'[29]

SIGNIFICANCE

The Battle of Shanghai, as Peter Harmsen noted, 'was full of smaller, dramatic stories of heroism and sacrifice' but 'none more exciting and moving than the struggle of the 800 heroes at Sihang Warehouse'.[30] During the battle the world held its breath in a way that was not equalled until the *Admiral Graf Spee* sailed into Montevideo, Uruguay on 14 December 1939 and the international media became fixated on the German warship's fate.

The day before the Eight Hundred escaped from Sihang Warehouse, an American journalist declared, 'The heroic stand of the little band has fired all China with patriotic pride unlike anything else that has happened since the war broke out.'[31] The day after their breakout into the International Settlement, an Australian reporter similarly announced: 'The epic of the "Doomed Battalion," is symptomatic of the awakening in China of a desperate patriotism in no sense inferior to the spirit which animates the invading force.'[32] The Eight Hundred succeeded in their symbolic mission

An iconic photograph of Xie Jinyuan on horseback. (Author's Collection)

of demonstrating Chinese determination to resist, as Kristin Mulready-Stone explained:

> The lone battalion's four-day resistance had no hope of bringing a
> Chinese victory in the Battle of Shanghai; instead, it made clear to the

people of Shanghai and beyond that the Chinese army was not done
fighting. . . Yet for the people of Shanghai, Xie Jinyuan was the living
embodiment of China's determination to be victorious in the larger war.[33]

The successful last stand secured a propaganda victory that restored Chinese
morale and won western sympathy to the *Kuomintang* cause. 'Despite the
enormous price,' Zhang Boting, the 88th Division's chief-of-staff, reflected,
the 'three-month bloody, morale-lifting fighting encouraged people and
laid a solid foundation for the victory of the long-term resistance against
aggression'.[34] Zhang added: 'The ensuing tragic but heroic desperate
defence [at Sihang Warehouse] with backup unavailable astonished the
whole world.'[35]

The Eight Hundred Heroes can correctly be considered modern
China's equivalent of the 300 Spartans at Thermopylae, the American
'Lost Battalion' in the Argonne Forest and the Texans at the Alamo. Sihang
Warehouse can also be seen as a sacrificial rebirth similar to the Easter
Rising in Ireland. Unlike these other famous last stands, Xie Jinyuan and
his soldiers evaded the enemy and escaped their predicament with relatively
minor casualties. Despite initially assuming they would fight to the death,
a fate they stoically accepted, Chiang Kai-Shek and the Chinese High
Command wisely realized during the battle that international sympathy had
shifted solidly behind China; therefore, the defenders of Sihang Warehouse
had achieved their mission. Chiang and his wife Soong Mei-ling understood
western sensibilities and realized that world opinion wanted the Eight
Hundred to live. The legend did not require the men to all die gloriously
and they were permitted to escape and some survived into old age.

Xie Jinyuan and his men fought against a superior Japanese force and
prevailed, but their legacy also survived against the odds. The legend of
the Eight Hundred largely became a forgotten story across the world after
the Chinese Civil War with the exception of Taiwan and overseas Chinese
communities, which is unsurprising given Mao Zedong's complete victory
in mainland China. After 1949 the communist revolution obliterated public
memory of the 'Lost Battalion' for the vast majority of Chinese people. At
the same time the western world's inaccurate perception of the *Kuomintang* as
irredeemably corrupt and hopelessly incompetent banished its admiration

of the Eight Hundred, evident until the end of World War II, into oblivion.

Localized commemoration of Sihang Warehouse in Taiwan and the Chinese diaspora seemed to be the fate of Xie Jinyuan and his men. After all, not all legends survive in popular imagination. The American 'Lost Battalion' of World War I achieved mythic dimensions during the 1920s and 1930s, but the soldiers who fought in the Argonne Forest are almost completely forgotten in the United States today. On the other hand, the legend of the Alamo is alive and well and has never been in doubt.

The Eight Hundred Heroes' comeback has been an extraordinary journey, especially in the People's Republic of China where the men are now publicly praised as patriots who fought bravely against an invader alongside a rehabilitated and more mature representation of the *Kuomintang*'s Sino-Japanese War veterans. Despite the objections of hardliners in the Chinese Communist Party, the film *The Eight Hundred* received an overdue cinema release and electrified audiences across the world, becoming the biggest movie of 2020, and westerners are rediscovering the legend through this blockbuster. The Eight Hundred Heroes' place in the world pantheon of epic last stands is now assured, although the meaning of the legend will continue to change in response to the social needs of people, just as great myths always do.

BIBLIOGRAPHY

CHINESE LANGUAGE BOOKS

Guo Mengmeng, *Anti-Japanese Heroes Story Series: Xie Jinyuan*, Unity Press, China, 2015

Li Gang and Wang Yufeng, *Eight Hundred Heroes*, Shanghai Education Publishing House, Shanghai, 2015

Shangguan Baicheng, ed., *The Eight Hundred Heroes and the Diary of Xie Jinyuan*, Taipei, 1976:
— Gu Zhutong, 'The Chinese Nation's Spirit of "Allowing no Affront"'
— Shangguan Zhibiao, 'Records of Defence of Sihang Warehouse'
— Sun Yuanliang, 'A Moment in a Billion Years'
— Zhang Boting, 'Preface'
— Zhang Boting, 'Tribute to Comrade Shangguan Zhibiao'

The August 13 Songhu Battle: Personal Recollections from the War of Resistance Against Japan by Former Nationalist Commanders, Chinese Literature and History Press, Beijing, 2015:
— Chen Desong, 'The Isolated Soldiers Desperately Fighting for the Country in Sihang Warehouse'
— Sun Yuanliang, 'Xie Jinyuan and the 800 Heroes'
— Yang Ruifu, 'Account of the Lone Unit's Four Days of Battle'
— Zhang Boting, 'Summary of the Songhu Battle'

Xie Jimin, *My Father, General Xie Jinyuan: Eight Hundred Heroes Fighting in Blood*, Unity Press, China, 2010

Xie Jimin, *Xie Jinyuan's Anti-Japanese Diary: Interpretation by Xie Jimin*, Shanghai Far East, Shanghai, 2015

Yao Xiaotian, *The Patron Saint of Shanghai: The Biography of Xie Jinyuan*, Taipei, 1982

NEWSPAPERS AND MAGAZINES

'5 Punished Over Japanese Uniforms Outrage', in *Shanghai Daily*, 24 August 2017

'6 More City Sites Put on List of Landmarks', in *Shanghai Daily*, 4 January 2018

'17 Chinese Flee Nanking. Sole Survivors of "Lone Battalion" Escape Jap Camp', in *The Journal Times* (Wisconsin), 13 December 1942

'17 Chinese Flee Prison Camp, in *The New York Times*, 13 December 1942

'70th Anniversary of Songhu Battle Against Japan in Shanghai' in China Daily, 13 August 2007, https://bbs.chinadaily.com.cn/forum. php?mod=viewthread&tid=575355

'76 years ago today, April 24, 1941, the rate of eight hundred. The bloody Anti Japanese hero Xie Jinyuan assassination traitors', in *Best China News*, 24 April 2017, http://www.bestchinanews.com/History/11025.html

'A Chinese Girl Guide', *The Guardian* (London), 30 July 1938

'A Chinese Heroine', in *Reno Gazette-Journal* (Nevada), 14 November 1938

'A Letter From Shanghai — By a Shanghai Englishman', in *Japan News-Week*, 28 September 1940

'A New Spirit', in *Times Herald* (New York), 21 August 1941

'A Second "Doomed Battalion"', in *North China Daily News*, 20 May 1938

'Advertisement' in *The Guardian* (London), 16 October 1942

Ai Pang, 'Director Guan Hu's War Epic an Ode to Patriotic Soldiers and the Great Chinese People', in *Global Times*, 16 August 2020, https://www. globaltimes.cn/content/1197890.shtml

'All Chapei in Flames! Shanghai Captured!, in *The Dunn County News* (Wisconsin), 25 November 1937

'An Exhibition of Legends', in *China Daily (USA)*, 22 August 2015, http://usa. chinadaily.com.cn/culture/2015-08/22/content_21669670.htm

'Anniversary Observed in Internment Camp', in *North China Daily News*, 27 October 1939

'Anniversary Precautions Show Results as Day Passes Calmly', in *North China Daily News*, 11 October 1940

'Artillery's Blast Precede Battalion's Withdrawal', in *North China Daily News*, 1 November 1937

Arundel, Keane, '200 in Chinese Alamo Hold Off 40,000 Japs', in *Daily News*, 29 October 1937

'Australia Refuses to Mark Chinese Graves', in *The Canberra Times*, 4 April 1964

'Away From the Settlement', in *The Sydney Morning Herald*, 10 November 1937

'Battalion in Chapei Flies Chinese Flag', in *North China Daily News*, 30 October 1937

'British Soldiers' Funeral', in *Western Argus* (Kalgoorlie), 9 November 1937

'Brussels Conference in New Peace Move', in *The Boston Globe*, 4 November 1937

Cang Wei, 'Historic Battlefield Disrespect Slammed', in *China Daily (Hong Kong Edition)*, 23 February 2018

Cao Chen, 'Outrage Grows Over Nanjing Selfies', in *China Daily (US Edition)*, 27 February 2018

Cao Siqi, 'War Epic "The Eight Hundred" Prompts Spike in Visits to Site', in *Global Times*, 9 September 2020, https://www.globaltimes.cn/content/1200335.shtml

Chen Ping-hsun, 'Films and TV Must Tell Taiwanese War Stories', in *Taipei Times*, 25 March 2017, https://www.taipeitimes.com/News/editorials/archives/2017/03/25/2003667422

Chen Yu-fu and Chin, Jonathan, 'Veterans Protest Pension Reform Plans', in *Liberty Times Net*, 22 February 2017, https://news.ltn.com.tw/news/focus/breakingnews/1982557

Chi Chun-chieh, 'Protesters Have No Ground to Stand On', in *Taipei Times*, 29 April 2017, http://www.taipeitimes.com/News/editorials/archives/2017/04/29/2003669607

'China Ends 6th Year of War with Victories in Field on Home Front', in *The Indianapolis News*, 5 July 1943

'China Heroine Toast of LA', in *The Ogden Standard-Examiner* (Utah), 13 November 1938

'China Holds Memorial Ceremony in PNG for Martyrs in Anti-Japanese War', in *Xinhua News Agency*, 24 August 2015

'China Suicide Squad Leaves Post of Peril', in *The Times-News* (North Carolina), 30 October 1937

'China, Taiwan Press', *BBC Monitoring Asia Pacific* (London), 24 August 2017

'China To Bring Back Remains of its Soldiers from Papua New Guinea', in *Xinhua News Agency*, 24 March 2009

'China Watchlist for 22 February', in *BBC Monitoring Asia Pacific* (London), 22 February 2018

'China Youth Here Condemn Jap Acts', in *The Indianapolis Star*, 10 October 1938

'China's Joan of Arc £50,000 on Her Head', in *Mount Barker and Denmark Record* (Albany), 27 February 1939

'China's Mata Hari Has No Fear of $250,000 Reward', in *The Times* (Indiana), 7 April 1939

'Chinese Delegates Say Cause Strong', in *The Lincoln Star* (Nebraska), 27 October 1938

'Chinese Fight to Finish', in *The New York Times*, 28 October 1937

'Chinese Girl Tells of Daring Trips', in *St. Louis Globe-Democrat* (Missouri), 6 September 1938

'Chinese Ill; Substitute to Speak Here', in *Wisconsin State Journal*, 21 October 1938

'Chinese "Lost Army" Found', in *The Daily News* (Perth), 18 September 1945

'Chinese Men Honored', in *San Antonio Express* (Texas), 21 September 1975

'Chinese Plead For Help', in *The Akron Beacon Journal* (Ohio), 30 September 1938

'Chinese President's Speech on War Victory Commemoration', in *Xinhua News Agency*, 3 September 2005

'Chinese Shed Inscrutability as They Identify Rabaul Japs', in *The Daily News* (Perth), 4 December 1945

'Chinese Still Hold Death Post', *Chronicle* (Adelaide), 4 November 1937

'Chinese Student Asks Aid for China', in *Wisconsin State Journal*, 23 October 1938

'Chinese Troops Among Japs on Gazelle Peninsula', *The Canberra Times*, 19 September 1945

'Chinese Youth Leaders Will Receive a Cordial Welcome', in *The Salt Lake Tribune*, 5 November 1938

'Chungking and "Lone Battalion"', in *North China Daily News*, 21 August 1939

'Chungking Deplores Murder', in *North China Daily News*, 26 April 1941

'Chungking Protest Against Internment Camp Fray', in *North China Daily News*, 21 September 1940

'Conditions in Camp Revert to Normal', in *North China Herald*, 2 October 1940

'Dash to British Post', in *The Observer* (London), 31 October 1937

'Death Penalties for Execution of War Prisoners', in *The Canberra Times*, 24 April 1946

'Dialling Data', *Harrisburg Telegraph* (Pennsylvania), 24 September 1938

'"Doomed" Battalion Kept Fighting Japs', in *The Courier-Mail* (Brisbane), 31 July 1943

'"Doomed Battalion" Nearby', in *News* (Adelaide), 10 February 1938

'"Doomed Battalion" Now Athletic', in *North China Daily News*, 25 October 1938

'"Doomed Battalion" Riot', in *North-China Herald*, 17 August 1938

'Doomed Chinese Refuse U.S. Aid', in *The Boston Globe*, 28 October 1937

'Doomed Remnants. Chinese Still Holding Sections of Kiangyin Forts', in *The Mercury* (Hobart), 3 December 1937

'Double Ten Day Fervor Humiliates History', in *Global Times*, 10 October 2014, https://www.globaltimes.cn/content/885475.shtml

'Editorial: Meaningful Protest and Futile Rage', in *Taipei Times*, 27 April 2018, https://www.taipeitimes.com/News/editorials/archives/2018/04/27/2003692063

'Epic Chinese Heroism. "Suicide Legion" Will Not Surrender', in *The Age* (Melbourne), 30 October 1937

'Epic Stand by Chinese', in *The Argus* (Melbourne), 29 October 1937

'Evening Post on "Lost Battalion"', in *Manchuria Daily News*, 20 August 1938

'Evidence Against Japs for Cruelty Towards Chinese in Rabaul', in *The Canberra Times*, 22 March 1947

'Famous Chinese Division Wiped Out', in *The Tribune* (Philippines), 5 February 1938

Fan Meijing, 'Soldier Recalls Resistance to Japan', in *Shanghai Daily*, 11 August 2005, https://archive.shine.cn/news2007/20050811/118022

'Fierce Fight for Capture of Bank Godowns', in *North China Daily News*, 31 October 1937

'Financial Ruin of Japan is Predicted by Chinese Speaker Delegates to Youth Conference', in *The Cincinnati Enquirer* (Ohio), 6 October 1938

'Forecasts Final Defeat of Japan in Guerrilla War', in *The St. Louis Star and Times* (Missouri), 17 October 1938

'Forgotten Army of Chinese Located in Camp on Rabaul', *The Age* (Melbourne), 19 September 1945

'Former Country Club Hides Dark Past', in *Shanghai Daily*, 3 August 2015

'Fortress Abandoned. Doomed Battalion Ordered to Withdraw', in *Newcastle Morning Herald and Miners' Advocate*, 1 November 1937

Frater, Patrick and Davis, Rebecca, 'Shanghai Film Festival Abruptly Pulls Opening Film "The Eight Hundred", in *Variety*, 14 June 2019, https://variety.com/2019/film/news/shanghai-film-festival-pulls-opening-film-the-eight-hundred-huayi-bros-1203243335/

Freer, Ian, 'The Eight Hundred Review', in *Empire*, 18 September 2020, https://www.empireonline.com/movies/reviews/the-eight-hundred/

'General Sun Yun-liang', in *The Times* (London), 18 June 2007

'Generalissimo Observes 53rd Birthday Quietly', in *North China Daily News*, 28 October 1939

'Girls to Greet Chinese Visitor', in *Salt Lake Telegram*, 1 November 1938

Gong Qian, 'Never Forget the Great Achievement of Our Heroes During WWII', in *Global Times*, 3 September 2020, https://www.globaltimes.cn/content/1199747.shtml

'Hankow Hit by Bombs. Attack Marks Anniversary of Japanese Shanghai Offensive', in *The Honolulu Advertiser*, 13 August 1938

'Happy Chinese in Rabaul Did Not Want Swing Music', in *The Argus* (Melbourne), 12 October 1945

'Heroic Chapei Defenders Sold to Invaders', in *The Workers Star* (Perth), 26 November 1937

'Hostility Shown By Japanese', in *The Northern Herald* (Cairns), 6 November 1937

'Humane Conduct of British Troops', in *The Guardian* (London), 29 October 1937

'"I'm Still Mayor." Chinese Version of Old Job', in *The Horsham Times* (Victoria), 25 January 1938

'Injured Internees Taken to Hospital', in *North China Daily News*, 22 September 1940

'Inmate Disappears from Lone Battalion Camp', in *North China Daily News*, 22 February 1939

'Internee Wounded While Escaping', in *North China Daily News*, 8 October 1940

'Internment Camp Inquiry Ordered by Chungking', in *North China Daily News*, 20 September 1940

'Internment Camp Settlement', in *North China Herald*, 2 October 1940

'Internment Camp Situation Calm', in *North China Daily News*, 9 October 1940

'Jap Commander Faces Atrocity Trial Against Chinese at Rabaul', in *The Canberra Times*, 21 March 1947

'Jap General Sentenced Gaol for Seven Years', in *The Sydney Morning Herald*, 4 April 1947

'Japan and China', in *Western Star and Roma Advertiser* (Toowoomba), 6 November 1937

'Japan's Grip' in *The Northern Herald* (Cairns), 27 November 1937

'Japanese Brutality in Shanghai', in *The Sydney Morning Herald*, 29 October 1937

'Japanese Cross Soochow Creek', in *The Sydney Morning Herald*, 29 October 1937

'Japanese Mop Up in Chapei', in *North China Daily News*, 2 November 1937

'Japanese Renew Drive to Encircle Shanghai', in *Hartford Courant* (Connecticut), 1 November 1937

'Japanese Send Wreaths. British Soldiers Buried', in *The Albury Banner and Wodonga Express*, 5 November 1937

'Japs Go Home But Chinese Must Wait', in *The Mail* (Adelaide), 6 April 1946

'Kaohsiung Lady Makes Name for Self Selling Flags', in *Taipei Times*, 10 February 2011, https://www.taipeitimes.com/News/taiwan/archives/2011/02/10/2003495535

Kor Kian Beng, 'China Shines Spotlight on WWII Heroes: Push Comes as Nation Prepares to Mark 70th Anniversary of Victory over Japan', in *The Straits Times* (Singapore), 14 August 2015

'Last-Ditch Defenders Are Target', in *The Tribune* (Philippines), 11 November 1937

'Last Rites for "Lone Commander"', in *North China Daily News*, 3 May 1941

Lee, Maggie, '"The Eight Hundred" Review: Blockbuster Chinese War Epic Delivers Imax-Scale Spectacle', in *Variety*, 26 August 2020, https://variety.com/2020/film/reviews/the-eight-hundred-review-ba-bai-the-800-1234747527/

Lehrbas, Lloyd, 'Runs Gauntlet of Jap Gunfire', in *The La Crosse Tribune* (Wisconsin), 31 October 1937

'Lest We Forget the Sacrifice of Battle Heroes', in *Shanghai Daily*, 2 September 2020, http://www.shanghai.gov.cn/shanghai/n46669/n48081/n48088/u22ai130004.html

Li Qian, 'Historical Monuments to Nation-Building', in *Shanghai Daily*, 25 June 2019

Li Xinran, 'Cartoon Industry More Than Mere Child's Play', in *Shanghai Daily*, 30 July 2015

Li Yang, 'Symbols of Fascism Have No Place in Our Society', in *China Daily: European Weekly* (London), 18 August 2017

Life (Magazine), 28 August 1938

'Life of Adventure Readies Kansas City "Ranger" for Job', in *The Kansas City Star*, 27 December 1942

Lin Chia-nan, 'Military Retirees Demand Pension Talks, in *Taipei Times*, 14 November 2017, http://www.taipeitimes.com/News/taiwan/archives/2017/11/14/2003682225

Lin, Sean, 'Amendments to Set Lower Limit on Military Pensions', in *Taipei Times*, 13 April 2018, https://www.taipeitimes.com/News/front/archives/2018/04/13/2003691215

Lo, Sonny Shiu Hing, 'Opinion — The Soft Politics of a Mainland film: Cross-Border Implications of "The Eight Hundred" in 1937 Shanghai', in *Macau Business*, 5 September 2020, https://www.macaubusiness.com/opinion-the-soft-politics-of-mainland-film-cross-border-implications-of-the-eight-hundred-in-1937-shanghai/

'"Lone Battalion" Angers Japanese', in *North China Daily News*, 16 August 1939

'"Lone Battalion" Head Claims Privileges', in *North China Daily News*, 18 August 1939

'Lone Battalion Incident', in *North China Daily News*, 7 January 1939

'Lone Battalion Men Escape in Fog', in *North China Daily News*, 2 April 1939

'Lone Battalion Murder Trial', in *North China Daily News*, 22 June 1941

'Lone Battalion of China Holds Fete', in *Dayton Daily News*, 2 January 1941

'"Lone Battalion" Remembered', in *North China Daily News*, 2 November 1937

'Lone Battalion Still Hold on To Their Posts', in *North China Daily News*, 29 October 1937

'"Lone Battalion" Support', in *North China Daily News*, 14 March 1939

'"Lone Battalion" to Start Factory', in *North China Daily News*, 17 January 1940

'Lone Battalion's Leader Encoffined', in *North China Daily News*, 26 April 1941

'Lost Battalion Doomed', in *The Michigan Daily*, 30 October 1937

'Lost Battalion Escapes. 200 of its Members Die', in *Honolulu Star-Bulletin*, 30 October 1937

'"Lost Battalion" Fights on. International Settlement Watches Gallant Defence', in *The Sydney Morning Herald*, 30 October 1937

'"Lost Battalion" Men Promoted', in *The New York Times*, 2 November 1937

'"Lost Battalion" Runs Gauntlet to Withdraw to International Zone', in *The Post-Crescent* (Wisconsin), 30 October 1937

'"Lost Battalion" Saved in Shanghai: Will Be Interned', in *The New York Times*, 31 October 1937

'Lost Battalion to Take Refuge in Foreign Area', in *Evening Star* (Washington, DC), 30 October 1937

Lowa, Sharon, 'Chinese Remember War Dead in East New Britain', in *Papua New Guinea Post*, 10 April 2015

Madame Chiang Kai-shek, 'Heroes Thank British', in *The Daily Telegraph* (Sydney), 2 November 1937

Madame Chiang Kai-shek, 'Stand of the "Death Brigade" Seen Inspiring to China', in *Asbury Park Press* (New Jersey), 30 October 1937

'Mass Tribute Paid to Col. Hsieh', in *North China Daily News*, 28 April 1941

Maxon, Ann, 'Police Thwart Legislature Break-in by Protesters', in *Taipei Times*, 28 February 2018, https://www.taipeitimes.com/News/front/archives/2018/02/28/2003688396

Maxon, Ann, 'Returning Pensions Tops Gou's List', in *Taipei Times*,

21 June 2019, https://www.taipeitimes.com/News/taiwan/
archives/2019/06/21/2003717318

Maxon, Ann, 'Veteran Injured in Legislative Protest Last Week Dies', in *Taipei Times*, 7 March 2018, https://www.taipeitimes.com/News/taiwan/
archives/2018/03/07/2003688830

McCarthy, Julia, 'Chinese Girl Hero Scorns Dress, Love', in *Daily News* (New York), 16 August 1938

'Memorial Meeting for Col. Hsieh', in *North China Daily News*, 1 May 1941

'Memorial Meeting for Late Col. Hsieh', in *North China Daily News*, 3 May 1941

'Missionary to China Writes of Experiences', in *The News and Observer* (North Carolina), 28 March 1938

'Mob Trouble Near Internment Camp', in *North China Daily News*, 13 February 1940

'Mr. Wang Ching-wei is Denounced', in *North China Daily News*, 4 January 1939

'Murder of Chinese Evidence of Survivor', in *The Age* (Melbourne), 11 April 1946

Myers, Steven Lee, 'Patriotic Movie Apparently Falls Afoul of China's Censors', in *The New York Times*, 27 June 2019

Ng, Florence, 'I Let Fate Determine My Future — We Drew Lots for University Places', *South China Morning Post* (Hong Kong), 11 August 2001

'No Camp in Wuhan Area', in *Manchuria Daily News*, 19 August 1938

'Not Ended, Say Chinese', in *North China Daily News*, 20 December 1938

'One-Armed Fighter', in *The Economist* (London), 19 September 2020

'One Mutineer Saved', in *The Morning Call* (New Jersey), 1 November 1941

Ordoña, Michael, 'Review: Chinese Soldiers Face Overwhelming Odds in Historical War Blockbuster 'Eight Hundred', in *Los Angeles Times*, 16 September 2020, https://www.latimes.com/entertainment-arts/
movies/story/2020-09-16/review-chinas-eight-hundred-heroes-face-
overwhelming-odds-historical-war-blockbuster

Orere, Barney, 'War Cemetery to be Revived', in *Papua New Guinea Post*, 13 October 2009

'Patriotism Prompts Girl Guide to Bravery in 1937 Shanghai Battle', in *Central News Agency*, 3 July 2015, https://www.taiwannews.com.tw/en/
news/2764884

Peacock, W.M., 'Chinese Art in War-Time', in *The Age* (Melbourne), 13 May 1939

Peng Ming-min, 'The Decline of Taiwan's Military', in *Taipei Times*, 5 March 2017, http://www.taipeitimes.com/News/editorials/
archives/2017/03/05/2003666149

'Photos of "Japanese Soldiers" Posing at Chinese War Memorial Site Spark Anger Online: Four Young Men Pose in Second World War Military Attire at Memorial in Shanghai', in *South China Morning Post* (Hong Kong), 10 Aug 2017

'Price on Head But She Return to China', in *Republican and Herald* (Pennsylvania), 6 March 1939

'Program Set for China Week', in *Wisconsin State Journal*, 3 October 1945

Qi Xijia, 'War of the Warehouse', in *Global Times*, 17 August 2015, https://www.globaltimes.cn/content/937493.shtml

'Remnant of 88th Division', in *The New York Times*, 29 October 1937

'Riot of Internees Averted by Guards', in *North China Daily News*, 14 September 1940

'Roll up! Roll up! A Festival of the Classic and New', in *Shanghai Daily*, 8 June 2019

'Rollman Observer of Conflict in China Describes Horrors', in *Laurel Outlook* (Montana), February 1939

Rose, Steve, 'The Eight Hundred: how China's Blockbusters Became a New Political Battleground', in *The Guardian*, 18 September 2020, https://www.theguardian.com/film/2020/sep/18/the-eight-hundred-how-chinas-blockbusters-became-a-new-political-battleground

'Settlement Looms in Camp Dispute', in *North China Daily News*, 9 September 1938

'Sihang Warehouse in Shanghai to Be Memorial of War of Resistance Against Japanese Aggression', in *National Policy Foundation*, 15 July 2014, http://www.taiwannpfnews.org.tw/english/page.aspx?type=article&mnum=112&anum=14754

'Sobs, "China Is Not Lost"', in *The Des Moines Register* (Iowa), 26 October 1938

'Son's Pride in Tribute to Leader of the "800 Heroes"', in *Shanghai Daily*, 14 August 2015

Su Yung-yao, Lee Hsin-fang and Jonathan Chin, 'President, Premier Condemn Violence', in *Taipei Times*, 27 April 2018, http://www.taipeitimes.com/News/front/archives/2018/04/27/2003692072

'Suicide Battalion Interned For Duration', in *The Northern Herald* (Cairns), 6 November 1937

'Suicide Troops Retreat; Marines Escape Death', in *The San Francisco Examiner*, 31 October 1937

'Survivors of 1937 Battle Reach China', in *The Honolulu Advertiser*, 10 February 1944

'Taiwan President Wants to Make Coming Years "Golden Decade"', in *BBC Monitoring Asia Pacific*, London, 1 January 2011

'Technology Enhances Other Museum Sites in the District', in *Shanghai Daily*, 25 July 2017

'The "Doomed Battalion". 377 Escaped Alive', in *Western Argus* (Kalgoorlie), 9 November 1937

'The Eight Hundred', in *The Times* (London), 18 September 2020

'The Enemy We Face', in *The Anniston Star* (Alabama), 25 August 1943

'The Liberty Times Editorial: Stop Fabricating Taiwan's History', in *Taipei Times*, 7 January 2011, http://www.taipeitimes.com/News/editorials/archives/2011/01/07/2003492859

'The Sihang Warehouse Turns into Hot Tourist Spot Following Success of War Epic "The Eight Hundred"', in *Global Times*, 25 August 2020, https://www.

globaltimes.cn/content/1198864.shtml

'The War in China', in *The Advertiser* (Adelaide), 2 November 1937

'There Are Some Things We Should Not Joke About', in *South China Morning Post* (Hong Kong), 14 August 2017

'Tsai vs Taiwan's Veterans: The Cage Fight That Wasn't', in *South China Morning Post* (Hong Kong), 4 September 2017

'Unprecedented Violence, Possible China Link as Anti-Pension Reform Protesters Storm Taiwan's Legislature', in *Sentinel*, 27 April 2018, https://sentinel.tw/violence-prc-link-pension/

'Untitled', in *Japan Chronicle*, 22 September 1940

'Untitled', in *North China Daily News*, 20 July 1938

'Untitled', in *North China Daily News*, 14 January 1940

'Untitled', in *North China Daily News*, 13 October 1940

'Untitled', in *North China Daily News*, 4 November 1940

'Untitled', in *North China Daily News*, 4 January 1941

'Untitled', in *North China Daily News*, 28 April 1941

'Veterans Begin Month Long Pension Protest', in *China Post* (Taipei), 22 February 2017

Wang Haiying, 'Pioneer of Modernity: A Centennial Retrospective of Guangdong Fine Arts', in *Shenzhen Daily*, 22 August 2017

Wang Kaihao, 'Proposed Law Aims to Curb Insulting of Heroes, War Victims', in *China Daily (Hong Kong Edition)*, 10 March 2018

'War Hero Returns to Shanghai', in *Shanghai Daily*, 5 July 2005, http://www.shanghai.gov.cn/shanghai/node26466/node27003/u22ai70423.html

'War in China: Never Anything Greater!', in *Time*, 8 November 1937

'War Memorabilia Donated to Warehouse Museum', in *Shanghai Daily*, 21 July 2015, www.shanghai.gov.cn/shanghai/node27118/node27818/u22ai80461.html

'War's Victims Tell of China', in *The South Bend Tribune* (Indiana), 16 October 1938

'WWII Graves Located', in *Taipei Times*, 9 January 2009, http://www.taipeitimes.com/News/taiwan/archives/2009/01/09/2003433296\

Xu Fan, 'Heroes Coming', in *China Daily* (Hong Kong), 14 September 2017

Xu Ming, 'Chinese Netizens Urge Govt to Criminalize Japanese Military Uniform Cosplay', in *Global Times*, 24 August 2017, https://www.globaltimes.cn/content/1063010.shtml

Yau, Elaine, 'Chinese War Movie The Eight Hundred a Hit with Film-Goers, but Critics Say it is Sensationalist and Distorts History', in *South China Morning Post* (Hong Kong), 27 August 2020, https://www.scmp.com/lifestyle/entertainment/article/3099027/chinese-war-movie-eight-hundred-hit-film-goers-critics-say

Yau, Elaine, 'Why the First Chinese Imax War Film The Eight Hundred was Pulled from Shanghai Film Festival', in *South China Morning Post* (Hong Kong), 8 June 2019

Yilin Chen, 'Trending in China: War Film or Farce? Blockbuster Triggers Debate Over Historical Accuracy', in *Caixin Global*, 25 August 2020, https://www.caixinglobal.com/2020-08-25/trending-in-china-war-film-or-farce-blockbuster-triggers-debate-over-historical-accuracy-101596922.html

'Young Chinese Here Tonight', in *The Des Moines Register* (Iowa), 25 October 1938

'Young Chinese War Workers Describe Horrors of Battle', in *The Salt Lake Tribune*, 7 November 1938

Yu Sen-lun, 'Standing Against the Tide', in *Taipei Times*, 17 June 2001, https://www.taipeitimes.com/News/feat/archives/2001/06/17/0000090445

Yu, Verna, 'Epic Chinese War Film Premiere Cancelled in Apparent Censorship', in *The Guardian*, 28 June 2019, https://www.theguardian.com/world/2019/jun/27/chinese-war-film-the-eight-hundred-premiere-cancelled-in-apparent-censorship

Zhou Wenting, '4 Men Criticized For "Insulting" War Heroes', *China Daily (US Edition)*, 10 August 2017

MONOGRAPHS AND PAPERS

Chiu Chi-Ming, *Taiwanese Cinema and National Identity Before and After 1989*, Doctorate Thesis, University of Wales, 2005

Gregor, A. James and Chang, Maria Hsia, *The Republic of China and U.S. Policy: A Study in Human Rights*, Ethics and Public Policy Center, Washington DC, 1983

Guo, Frances (Xiao-Feng), *China's Nationalism and Its Quest for Soft Power Through Cinema*, Doctoral Thesis, University of Technology, Sydney, 2013

Harmsen, Peter, *Fighting the Last War: The 1937 Battle of Shanghai Through the Prism of WWI*, Paper Presented at The Impact of World War One on China's Modern History, Vienna, 2014

Jacobs, Benjamin, *When the River of History Disappears: The Past in China's Patriotic Education Campaign*, Honors Thesis, Wesleyan University, 2014

Johnson, Matthew David, *International and Wartime Origins of the Propaganda State: The Motion Picture in China, 1897–1955*, Dissertation, University of California, San Diego, 2008

Kubacki, Marta, *On the Precipice of Change*, Thesis (Master of Architecture), University of Waterloo, Ontario, 2014

Li You, *The Military Versus the Press: Japanese Military Controls Over One U.S. Journalist, John B. Powell, in Shanghai During the Sino-Japanese War, 1937–1941*, Thesis Dissertation, University of Missouri, 2008

Rodriguez, Robyn L., *Journey to the East: The German Military Mission in China, 1927–1938*, Thesis (Doctor of Philosophy), The Ohio State University, 2011

Russel, Matthew William, *From Imperial Soldier to Communist General: The Early Career of Zhu De and his Influence on the Formation of the Chinese Red Army*, Dissertation, The George Washington University, 2009

Stein, Michael Robert, *The Chinese Combat Film Since 1949: Variants of*

'Regulation', 'Reform' and 'Renewal', Doctorate Thesis, Murdoch University, 2005

Vu, Linh Dam, *The Sovereignty of the War Dead: Martyrs, Memorials, and the Makings of Modern China, 1912–1949*, Thesis (Doctor of Philosophy), University of California, Berkeley, 2017

JOURNAL ARTICLES

Blackburn, Kevin, and Ern, Daniel Chew Ju, 'Dalforce at the Fall of Singapore in 1942: An Overseas Chinese Heroic Legend', in *Journal of Chinese Overseas*, Volume 1, Issue 2 (November 2005)

Carlson, Evan F., 'Marines as an Aid to Diplomacy in China', in *Marine Corps Gazette*, Volume 20, Issue 1 (February 1936)

Cartledge, Paul, 'What Have the Spartans Done For Us?: Sparta's Contribution to Western Civilization', in *Greece & Rome*, Volume 51, Number 2 (2004)

Cole, Parks M., 'China's "New Remembering" of the Anti-Japanese War of Resistance, 1937–1945', in *The China Quarterly*, Issue 180 (June 2007)

Crouch, Gregory, 'The Shanghai Gambit', in *World War II*, Leesburg, Volume 28, Issue 1 (May/June 2013)

Diamant, Neil J., 'Conspicuous Silence: Veterans and the Depoliticization of War Memory in China', in *Modern Asian Studies (Special Issue)*, Volume 45, Issue 2 (March 2011)

Dickson, Bruce J., 'The Lessons of Defeat: The Reorganization of the Kuomintang on Taiwan, 1950–52', in *The China Quarterly*, Number 133 (March 1993)

Froeschle, Ferd, 'Shanghai 50 Years Ago', in *Leatherneck*, Volume 70, Issue 11 (November 1987)

Geller, Jay Howard, 'The Role of Military Administration in German-Occupied Belgium, 1940–1944', *The Journal of Military History*, Volume 63, Issue 1 (January 1999)

Glass, Sheppard, 'Some aspects of Formosa's Economic Growth', in *The China Quarterly*, Number 15 (July–September 1963)

Gordon, David M., 'The China-Japan War, 1931–1945', in *The Journal of Military History*, Lexington, Volume 70, Issue 1 (January 2006)

Guttman, Jon, 'Other Lost Battalions', in *World War II*, Leesburg, Volume 26, Issue 4 (Nov/Dec 2011)

Hamada, Tomoko, 'Constructing a National Memory: A Comparative Analysis of Middle-School History Textbooks from Japan and the PRC', in *American Asian Review*, Volume 21, Issue 4 (Winter 2003)

Hogan, Patrick Colm, 'The Sacrificial Emplotment of National Identity: Pádraic Pearse and the 1916 Easter Uprising', in *Journal of Comparative Research in Anthropology and Sociology*, Volume 5, Issue 1 (Summer 2014)

Howard, Joshua H., 'Music for a National Defense: Making Martial Music During the Anti-Japanese War', in *Cross-Currents: East Asian History and Culture Review*, E-Journal Number 13 (December 2014)

Jespersen, Christopher T., 'Western Influences and Images of China: The

Persistent Efforts to Engage and Change China', in *Journal of Third World Studies*, Volume 14, Issue 2 (Fall 1997)

Kallgren, Joyce, 'Nationalist China's Armed Forces', in *The China Quarterly*, Volume 15 (July–September 1963)

Lary, Diana, 'Drowned Earth: The Strategic Breaching of the Yellow River Dyke, 1938', in *War in History*, Volume 8, Issue 2 (2001)

Lu Pan, 'The Invisible Turn to the Future: Commemorative Culture in Contemporary Shanghai', in *Culture Unbound*, Volume 4, Issue 3 (2012)

Mitter, Rana, 'Classifying Citizens in Nationalist China during World War II, 1937–1941', in *Modern Asian Studies (Special Issue)*, Cambridge, Volume 45, Issue 2 (March 2011)

Mitter, Rana and Moore, Aaron William, 'China in World War II, 1937–1945: Experience, Memory, and Legacy', in *Modern Asian Studies (Special Issue)*, Volume 45, Issue 2 (March 2011)

Moore, Aaron William, 'The Problem of Changing Language Communities: Veterans and Memory Writing in China, Taiwan, and Japan', in *Modern Asian Studies (Special Issue)*, Volume 45, Issue 2 (March 2011)

Murray, Jeffrey, '"Christ, Our Leonidas": Dracontius' Reception of the Battle of Thermopylae', in *Greece & Rome*, Volume 63, Issue 1 (2016)

Niderost, Eric, 'Chinese Alamo: Last Stand at Sihang Warehouse', in *Military Heritage Magazine*, Volume 9, Number 3 (December 2007)

Niderost, Eric, 'The Lost Leathernecks', in *World War II*, Volume 20, Issue 7 (November 2005)

Polk, Cara Saylor, 'Belgium's Benevolent Occupier', *World War II*, Volume 19, Issue 10 (March 2005)

Rayns, Tony, 'Labyrinth of Chances', in *Sight and Sound*, Volume 11, Issue 7 (July 2001)

Reilly, James, 'Remember History, Not Hatred: Collective Remembrance of China's War of Resistance to Japan', in *Modern Asian Studies, (Special Issue)*, Volume 45, Issue 2 (March 2011)

Rothwell, Richard B., 'Shanghai Emergency', in *Marine Corps Gazette*, Volume 56, Issue 11 (November 1972)

Sacca, John Wands, 'Like Strangers in a Foreign Land: Chinese Officers Prepared at American Military Colleges, 1904–37', in *The Journal of Military History*, Lexington, Volume 70, Issue 3 (July 2006)

Showalter, Dennis, 'Bring In the Germans', in *MHQ: The Quarterly Journal of Military History*, New York, Volume 28, Issue 1 (Autumn 2015)

Smith, C. Rodney, 'Military Lessons from the Chinese-Japanese War', in *Marine Corps Gazette*, Volume 24, Issue 1 (March 1940)

Thompson, Frank, 'Reprinting the Legend: The Alamo on Film', in *Film & History*, Volume 36, Issue 1 (2006)

Tillman, Margaret Mih, 'Engendering Children of the Resistance: Models for Gender and Scouting in China, 1919–1937', in *Cross-Currents: East Asian History and Culture Review*, E-Journal No. 13 (December 2014)

Trundle, Matthew, 'Greek Historical Influence on Early Roman History', in

Antichthon, Journal of the Australian Society for Classical Studies, Volume 51 (2017)

Vu, Linh D., 'Bones of Contention: China's World War II Military Graves in India, Burma, and Papua New Guinea', in *Journal of Chinese Military History*, Volume 8, Issue I (May 2019)

Wasserstein, Bernard, 'Collaborators and Renegades in Occupied Shanghai', in *History Today*, Volume 48, Issue 9 (September 1998)

Worthing, Peter, 'The Road Through Whampoa: The Early Career of He Yingqin', in *The Journal of Military History*, Lexington, Volume 69, Issue 4 (October 2005)

BOOKS

Auden, W.H. and Isherwood, Christopher, *Journey to a War*, Faber and Faber, 1939

Bao Weihong, *Fiery Cinema: The Emergence of an Affective Medium in China, 1915–1945*, University of Minnesota Press, 2015

Bergere, Marie-Claire, *Sun Yat-sen*, Stanford University Press, Stanford, 1998

Brear, Holly Beachley, *Inherit the Alamo: Myth and Ritual at an American Shrine*, University of Texas Press (Illustrated Edition), Austin, 1995

Brinkley, Alan, *The Publisher: Henry Luce and His American Century*, Knopf Doubleday (Kindle Edition), New York, 2010

Carradice, Phil, *The Shanghai Massacre: China's White Terror, 1927*, Pen and Sword, South Yorkshire, 2018

Clark, George B. *Treading Softly: U.S. Marines in China, 1819–1949*, Greenwood Publishing Group, 2001

Crozier, Brian, *The Man Who Lost China*, Angus and Robertson, London, 1976

Earnshaw, Graham, *Tales of Old Shanghai: The Glorious Past of China's Greatest City*, Earnshaw Books, Hong Kong, 2012

Fairbank, John K. and Teng, Ssu-yu, *China's Response to the West: A Documentary Survey, 1839–1923*, Harvard University Press, Cambridge, 1982

Fenby, Jonathan, *Generalissimo: Chiang Kai-shek and the China He Lost*, Simon & Schuster, London, 2003

Fenby, Jonathan, *The Penguin History of Modern China*, Penguin Books, Great Britain, 2008

Four Months of War: A Pen and Picture Record of the Hostilities between Japan and China in and around Shanghai. From August 9th till December 20th, 1937, North China Daily News, Shanghai, 1937

French, Paul, *Bloody Saturday: Shanghai's Darkest Day*, Penguin Random House Australia (Kindle Edition), 2017

Fu, Poshek, *Passivity, Resistance, and Collaboration: Intellectual Choices in Occupied Shanghai, 1937–1945*, Stanford University Press, Stanford, 1993

Gang Lin and Weixu Wu, 'Chinese National Identity under Reconstruction', in Lowell Dittmer, ed., *Taiwan and China: Fitful Embrace*, University of California Press, Oakland, 2017

Grescoe, Taras, *Shanghai Grand: Forbidden Love and International Intrigue on the Eve of the Second World War*, Pan Macmillan (Kindle Edition), 2016

Harmsen, Peter, *Shanghai 1937: Stalingrad on the Yangtze*, Casemate Publishers (Kindle Edition), United States of America, 2013

Japan's War in China: Complete Day-to-Day Record of the First Six Months of the Conflict, China Weekly Review Press, Shanghai, 1938

Jobs, Richard Ivan and Pomfret, David M., eds., *Transnational Histories of Youth in the Twentieth Century*, Macmillan (Kindle Edition), London, 2015

Jowett, Philip, *Soldiers of the White Sun: The Chinese Army at War, 1931–1949*, Schiffer, Hong Kong, 2011

Jubin Hu, *Projecting A Nation: Chinese National Cinema Before 1949*, Hong Kong University Press, Hong Kong, 2003

Kua, Paul, *Scouting in Hong Kong, 1910–2010*, Scout Association of Hong Kong, Hong Kong, 2011

Kwan, Stanley S.K., *The Dragon and the Crown: Hong Kong Memoirs*, Hong Kong University Press, Hong Kong, 2009

Lai, Benjamin, *Shanghai and Nanjing 1937: Massacre on the Yangtze*, Osprey Publishing, Hong Kong, 2017

Lan, Shi-chi Mike, '"Crime" of Interpreting Taiwanese Interpreters as War Criminals of World War II', in Takeda, Kayoko and Baigorri-Jalon, Jesus, eds., *New Insights in the History of Interpreting*, John Benjamins Publishing Company, Amsterdam, 2016

Laplander, Robert. *Finding the Lost Battalion: Beyond the Rumors, Myths and Legends of Americas Famous WW1 Epic*, Lulu Press (Kindle Edition), Waterford, 2016

Lary, Diana, *The Chinese People at War: Human Suffering and Social Transformation, 1937–1945*, Cambridge University Press, New York, 2010

Leitz, Christian, *Nazi Foreign Policy, 1933–1941: The Road to Global War*, Routledge, London, 2004

Long, Gavin Merrick, *Australia in the War of 1939–1945. Series 1 — Army, Volume VII — The Final Campaigns*, Australian War Memorial, Canberra, 1963

Mackinnon, Stephen R., *China Reporting: An Oral History of American Journalism in the 1930s and 1940s*, University of California Press, Berkeley, 1987

Macri, Franco David, *Clash of Empires in South China: The Allied Nations' Proxy War With Japan, 1935–1941*, University Press of Kansas (Kindle Edition), 2012

Maochun Yu, *The Dragon's War: Allied Operations and the Fate of China, 1937–1947*, Naval Institute Press, New York, 2013

Minoru, Kitamura, and Lin Si-Yun, *The Reluctant Combatant: Japan and the Second Sino-Japanese War*, University Press of America, 2014

Mitter, Rana, *China's Good War: How World War II Is Shaping a New Nationalism*, Harvard University Press, London, 2020

Mitter, Rana, *China's War with Japan, 1937–1945: The Struggle for Survival*, Penguin Books (Kindle Edition), 2013

Moore, Aaron William, *Writing War: Soldiers Record the Japanese Empire*, Harvard University Press, London, 2013

Moran, James, *Staging the Easter Rising: 1916 as Theatre*, Cork University Press, Cork, 2006

Mulready-Stone, Kristin, *Mobilizing Shanghai Youth: CCP Internationalism, GMD Nationalism and Japanese Collaboration*, Routledge, 2015

Peattie, Mark, Drea, Edward and Van de Ven, Hans, eds., *The Battle for China: Essays on the Military History of the Sino-Japanese War of 1937–1949*, Stanford University Press, Stanford, 2011

Rand, Peter, *China Hands: The Adventures and Ordeals of the American Journalists Who Joined Forces with the Great Chinese Revolution*, Simon and Schuster, USA, 1995

Roberts, Randy. *A Line in the Sand: The Alamo in Blood and Memory*, Free Press (Kindle Edition), New York, 2001

Schultz-Naumann, Joachim, *under the Kaiser's Flag, Germany's Protectorates in the Pacific and in China then and today*, Universitas Verlag, Munich, 1985

Sih, Paul K.T., ed., 'Introduction: Reflections on the Conference', in *Nationalist China During the Sino-Japanese War 1937–1945*, Exposition Press, New York, 1977

Shuge, Wei, *News under Fire: China's Propaganda against Japan in the English-Language Press, 1928–1941*, Hong Kong University Press, 2017

Snow, Edgar, *The Battle For Asia*, Random House, New York, 1941

Sun Yat-sen, *The International Development of China*, The Knickerbocker Press, New York, 1929

Sun Yat-sen, *The Three Principles of the People*, China Publishing Co., Taipei, 1970

Unger, Jonathan, ed. *Chinese Nationalism*, M.E. Sharpe, New York, 1996

Van de Ven, Hans. *China at War: Triumph and Tragedy in the Emergence of the New China 1937–1952*, Profile Books (Kindle Edition), London, 2017

Van de Ven, Hans, *War and Nationalism in China: 1925–1945*, Routledge, New York, 2003

Wakeman, Frederic, *The Shanghai Badlands: Wartime Terrorism and Urban Crime, 1937–1941*, Cambridge University Press, 1996

Wang Gungwu, *Home is Not Here*, National University of Singapore Press (Kindle Edition), Singapore, 2018

Wasserstein, Bernard, *Secret War in Shanghai: Treachery, Subversion and Collaboration in the Second World War*, I.B. Tauris (Kindle Edition), London, 2017

Weatherley, Robert and Qiang Zhang, *History and Nationalist Legitimacy in Contemporary China: A Double-Edged Sword*, Palgrave Macmillan (Kindle Edition), United Kingdom, 2017

Wicks, James, *Transnational Representations: The State of Taiwan Film in the 1960s and 1970s*, Hong Kong University Press, Hong Kong, 2014

Yeh, Wen-hsin, ed., *Wartime Shanghai*, Routledge (Kindle Edition), London, 1998

Zhang, Yingjin, *Chinese National Cinema*, Routledge, New York, 2004

WEBSITES

Ambassador Li Ruiyou held a Rally in East New Britain Province to Commemorate the War Veterans and the 70th Anniversary of the Victory of the Chinese People's War of Resistance Against Japanese Aggression and the World Anti-Fascist War, Chinese Embassy in Papua New Guinea, in *Ministry of Foreign Affair of the People's Republic of China*, 6 April 2015, https://www.fmprc.gov.cn/mfa_eng/wjb_663304/zwjg_665342/zwbd_665378/t1252267.shtml

'Archive Review: Eight Hundred Heroes (1976)', Review Section Originally Published in UK Monthly Films and Filming, February 1978, *Sino-Cinema*, 25 August 2020, https://sino-cinema.com/2020/08/25/archive-review-eight-hundred-heroes-1976/

'Eight Hundred Heroes', *Film Programme Office Leisure & Cultural Services Department (Hong Kong)*, 25 July 2016, https://www.lcsd.gov.hk/fp/en_US/web/fpo/programmes/2016cm/film01.html

'Gen. Xie Jinyuan Honored as National Martyr', *Kuomintang Official Website*, 2 September 2014, http://www1.kmt.org.tw/english/page.aspx?type=article&mnum=112&anum=15072

Guan Hu, 'Film Review: The Eight Hundred (2020)', in *Asian Movie Pulse*, 29 August 2020, https://asianmoviepulse.com/2020/08/film-review-the-eight-hundred-2020-by-guan-hu/

Harmsen, Peter, 'China's War as History: A Paradox', in *China in WW2*, 9 April 2016, http://www.chinaww2.com/2016/04/09/paradox/

Harmsen, Peter, 'Media War Over Shanghai', in *Asia Dialogue*, 22 July 2013, https://theasiadialogue.com/2013/07/22/media-war-over-shanghai/

MacNamara, Brian, 'The Eight Hundred — Movie Review', in *TL; DR Reviews*, 1 September 2020, https://tldrmoviereviews.com/2020/09/01/the-eight-hundred-the-800-babai-%e5%85%ab%e4%bd%b0-movie-review/

'Review: The Eight Hundred (2020)', in *Sino-Cinema*, 25 August 2020, https://sino-cinema.com/2020/08/25/review-the-eight-hundred-2020/

'Sihang Warehouse in Shanghai to Be Memorial of War of Resistance Against Japanese Aggression', in *National Policy Foundation*, 15 July 2014, http://www.taiwannpfnews.org.tw/english/page.aspx?type=article&mnum=112&anum=14754

'Special Program: Grand Symphonic Chorus Eight Hundred Heroes by Shanghai Opera House', in *China Shanghai International Arts Festival*, 15 September 2015, http://www.artsbird.com/NEWCMS/artsbird//en/en_17/enwtyc_17/enmusic_17/20150915/21411.html

Tay, Sue Anne, 'Conversations: Peter Harmsen on the Battle of Shanghai in 1937', in *Shanghai Street Stories*, 14 March 2015, http://shanghaistreetstories.com/?p=7383

Tay, Sue Anne, 'Footage of the Lost Battalion in 1937 Battle of Shanghai', in *Shanghai Street Stories*, 27 July 2015, http://shanghaistreetstories.com/?p=8956

'Wartime Valor Commemorated by Photography Exhibition', 3 July 2015, https://www.moc.gov.tw/en/information_196_75478.html

Xi Jinping, 'Speech at a Medal Presentation Ceremony Marking the 70th Anniversary of the Chinese People's Victory in the War of Resistance Against Japanese Aggression', 2 September 2025, http://english.qstheory.cn/2016-03/08/c_1118034573.htm

NOTES

Introduction

1   Kubacki, *On The Precipice Of Change*, 70

2   'Remnant of 88th Division'

3   Chen and Chin, 'Veterans Protest Pension Reform Plans'

4   'China Ends 6th Year of War With Victories in Field on Home Front'

5   Lu, 'The Invisible Turn to the Future', 134

6   Yeh, Wen-hsin, 'Prologue: Shanghai Besieged, 1937-45, in *Wartime Shanghai*, 213/6097

7   Harmsen, *Shanghai 1937*, 44/6628

8   Niderost, 'Chinese Alamo'

9   Fu, *Passivity, Resistance, and Collaboration*, 17-18

10 'All Chapei in Flames! Shanghai Captured!'

11 Blackburn and Ern, 'Dalforce at the Fall of Singapore in 1942', 234

12 Xie, *My Father, General Xie Jinyuan*, 68-9

13 'Sihang Warehouse in Shanghai to Be Memorial of War of Resistance Against Japanese Aggression'

14 Harmsen, 'Media War Over Shanghai'

15 Zhang, 'Tribute to comrade Shangguan Zhibiao', 60-1

16 Zhang, 'Tribute to comrade Shangguan Zhibiao', 61-2

17 Mulready-Stone, *Mobilizing Shanghai Youth*, 125

18 Tillman, 'Engendering Children of the Resistance', 153

19 Murray, '"Christ, Our Leonidas"', 113

20 Cartledge, 'What Have the Spartans Done For Us?, 171

21 Murray, '"Christ, Our Leonidas"', 107

22 Trundle, 'Greek Historical Influence on Early Roman History', 26

23 Murray, '"Christ, Our Leonidas"', 108

24 Laplander, *Finding the Lost Battalion*, 384/20234

25 Guttman, 'Other Lost Battalions', 65

26 Laplander, *Finding the Lost Battalion*, 392/20234

27 Laplander, *Finding the Lost Battalion*, 500/20234

28 Laplander, *Finding the Lost Battalion*, 570/20234

29 Laplander, *Finding the Lost Battalion*, 17533/20234

30 William Terpeluk, 'Foreword', in Laplander, *Finding the Lost Battalion*, 213/20234

31 'Doomed Chinese Refuse U.S. Aid'

32 'War in China: Never Anything Greater!'

33 Thompson, 'Reprinting the Legend', 20

34 Roberts, *A Line in the Sand*, 5413/7195

35 Brear, *Inherit the Alamo*, 95/4016

36 Roberts, *A Line in the Sand*, 35/7195

37 Roberts, *A Line in the Sand*, 42/7195

38 Roberts, *A Line in the Sand*, 56/7195

39 Hogan, 'The Sacrificial Emplotment of National Identity', 28

40 Hogan, 'The Sacrificial Emplotment of National Identity', 28

41 Hogan, 'The Sacrificial Emplotment of National Identity', 28-9

42 Hogan, 'The Sacrificial Emplotment of National Identity', 31-2

43 Hogan, 'The Sacrificial Emplotment of National Identity', 29

44 Moran, *Staging the Easter Rising*, 5-6

45 Moran, *Staging the Easter Rising*, 15

46 Moran, *Staging the Easter Rising*, 15

47 Moran, *Staging the Easter Rising*, 18

48 Moran, *Staging the Easter Rising*, 18

Chapter One: Revolution and the Republic

1 Xie Jinyuan's son Xie Jimin questioned the generally agreed date of his father's birth: 'Some maintain that my father was born on 29 April 1904, a date deduced from the fact that he deceased in April 1941 at the age of 37, which, nonetheless, proves an alleged nominal age based on contemporary convention rather than his actual age of 36. It was recorders' and revisers' mistake for actual age of the nominal age exclusively used in my mother's initial recollections that accounted for the inaccuracy of one-year period pertaining to my father's date of birth and marriage among many other events in some articles. Additionally, the corresponding date of the lunar calendar annually differs from that of the solar calendar within the range of a couple of days. (When incarcerated in the "Lost Battalion Barracks" in 1940, his birthday was 29 April in the lunar calendar.) He was posthumously interred in the "Lost Battalion Barracks" along Jiaozhou Road. His tombstone and epitaph read "General Xie was born on 26 April seven years before the initiation of the Republic of China", "deceased on 24 April in the 30th year of the Republic of China", and "barely reached 37 when assassinated". It follows from the aforesaid that accurately speaking my father was born on 26 April 1905 and died at his nominal age of 37.' Xie, *My Father, General Xie Jinyuan*, 50-1

2 Xie, *My Father, General Xie Jinyuan*, 50

3 Sun, *The Three Principles*, 2

4 Sun, *The Three Principles*, 2

5 Praenjit Duara, 'De-Constructing the Chinese Nation', 45

6 Sun, *The Three Principles*, 237

7 Bergere, *Sun Yat-sen*, 89

8 Sun, *The International Development of China*, 11

9 Carradice, *The Shanghai Massacre*, 51

10 Rodriguez, *Journey to the East*, 11-12

11 Fenby, *The Penguin History of Modern China*, 160

12 Sun Yat-sen, 'Adoption of the Russian Party System, 1923', in *China's Response to the West*, 265 and 266

13 Fenby, *The Penguin History of Modern China*, 160

14 Worthing, 'The Road Through Whampoa', 972

15 Sacca, 'Like Strangers in a Foreign Land', 705

16 Fenby, *Generalissimo*, 1391/12320

17 Sacca, 'Like Strangers in a Foreign Land', 720

18 Worthing, 'The Road Through Whampoa', 973

19 Worthing, 'The Road Through Whampoa', 973

20 Sacca, 'Like Strangers in a Foreign Land', 720

21 Russell, *From Imperial Soldier to Communist General*, 394

22 Fenby, *Generalissimo*, 1391/12320

23 Xie, *My Father, General Xie Jinyuan*, 50

24 Xie, *My Father, General Xie Jinyuan*, 50

25 Fenby, *Generalissimo*, 1412/12320

26 Worthing, 'The Road Through Whampoa', 274

27 Worthing, 'The Road Through Whampoa', 274

28 Worthing, 'The Road Through Whampoa', 274-5

29 Blackburn and Ern, 'Dalforce at the Fall of Singapore in 1942', 233-4

30 Worthing, 'The Road Through Whampoa', 972-3

31 Sacca, 'Like Strangers in a Foreign Land', 722

32 Fenby, *The Penguin History of Modern China*, 163

33 Fenby, *Generalissimo*, 1540/12320

34 Worthing, 'The Road Through Whampoa', 982

35 Worthing, 'The Road Through Whampoa', 983

36 Fenby, *The Penguin History of Modern China*, 165

37 Carlson, 'Marines as an Aid to Diplomacy in China', 49

38 Fenby, *Generalissimo*, 1391/12320

39 Fenby, *The Penguin History of Modern China*, 170

40 Worthing, 'The Road Through Whampoa', 278-9

41 Carradice, *The Shanghai Massacre*, 70

42 Fenby, *Generalissimo*, 2351/12320

43 Sacca, 'Like Strangers in a Foreign Land', 722

44 Smith, 'Military Lessons from the Chinese-Japanese War', 25

45 Jowett, *Soldiers of the White Sun*, 13

46 Rodriguez, *Journey to the East*, 17

47 Leitz, *Nazi Foreign Policy, 1933-1941*, 129

48 Bergere, *Sun Yat-sen*, 389

49 Schultz-Naumann, *Under the Kaiser's Flag*, 184

50 Showalter, 'Bring In the Germans', 60

51 Showalter, 'Bring In the Germans', 60

52 Rodriguez, *Journey to the East*, 34

53 Rodriguez, *Journey to the East*, 38-9

54 Rodriguez, *Journey to the East*, 80

55 Yu, *The Dragon's War*, 2

56 Carlson, 'Marines as an Aid to Diplomacy in China', 47

57 Gordon, 'The China-Japan War, 1931-1945', 137-8

58 Carlson, 'Marines as an Aid to Diplomacy in China', 51-2

59 Gordon, 'The China-Japan War, 1931-1945', 140

60 Carlson, 'Marines as an Aid to Diplomacy in China', 52

61 Rodriguez, *Journey to the East*, 133

62 Showalter, 'Bring In the Germans', 61

63 Grescoe, *Shanghai Grand*, 923/8920

64 Rodriguez, *Journey to the East*, 133-4

65 Jowett, *China and Japan at War 1937–1945*, 113

66 Crozier, *The Man Who Lost China*, 236

67 Rodriguez, *Journey to the East*, 149

68 Showalter, 'Bring In the Germans', 61-2

69 Rodriguez, *Journey to the East*, 158

70 Smith, 'Military Lessons from the Chinese-Japanese War, 27

71 Smith, 'Military Lessons from the Chinese-Japanese War, 27

72 Crouch, 'The Shanghai Gambit', 52-3

73 Harmsen, *Shanghai 1937*, 239/6628

74 Ven, *China at War*, 1569/9583

75 Xie, *My Father, General Xie Jinyuan*, 51

76 Rodriguez, *Journey to the East*, 253-4

77 Fenby, *The Penguin History of Modern China*, 275

78 Harmsen, *Shanghai 1937*, 260/6628

79 Crouch, 'The Shanghai Gambit', 53-4

80 Harmsen, *Shanghai 1937*, 316/6628

81 Fenby, *The Penguin History of Modern China*, 275

Chapter Two: The Battle of Shanghai

1 Lai, *Shanghai and Nanjing 1937*, 18

2 Harmsen, *Shanghai 1937*, 339/66280

3 A variety of different aircraft, such as Italian Fiat CR.32 and American Curtiss Hawks, generated logistics and spare parts issues. In late 1937, Madame Chiang recruited Claire Lee Chennault as an aviation adviser who founded a volunteer air force combat wing which became the American Volunteer Group.

4 Lai, *Shanghai and Nanjing 1937*, 8

5 The Republic of China Navy had two fleets near Shanghai — the class light cruisers *Ninghai* and *Pinghai*, the light cruiser *Yatsen*, the training cruiser *Jingswei*, the gunboats *Jiankang* and *Chuyu* and eight torpedo boats.

6 Zhang, 'Summary of the Songhu Battle', 106

7 Rodriguez, *Journey to the East*, 256

8 Harmsen, *Shanghai 1937*, 712/6628

9 Lai, *Shanghai and Nanjing 1937*, 27

10 Ven, *War and Nationalism in China*, 212-13

11 Wasserstein, *Secret War in Shanghai*, 196/6699

12 Foreign ratepayers elected the council board members to the oligarchic Shanghai Municipal Council, dominated by British and Americans interests, which represented around 5 per cent of the foreign population.

13 Rothwell, 'Shanghai Emergency', 47

14 Earnshaw, *Tales of Old Shanghai*, 5

15 Rayns, 'Labyrinth of Chances', 30-3

16 Wasserstein, *Secret War in Shanghai*, 176/6699

17 Rayns, 'Labyrinth of Chances', 30-3

18 Wasserstein, *Secret War in Shanghai*, 183/6699

19 Ven, *China at War*, 1528/9583

20 Ven, *War and Nationalism in China*, 213-14

21 Rothwell, 'Shanghai Emergency', 48

22 In light of this mystery, Peter Harmsen concluded: '. . . nearly eight decades later,

the balance of the available evidence suggests that the two Japanese soldiers were lured into a Chinese ambush. Zhang Fakui, the commander of the Chinese right wing, attributed the act to members of the 88th Division, led by General Sun Yuanliang. "A small group of Sun Yuanliang's men disguised themselves as members of the Peace Preservation Corps," Zhang Fakui said years later, when he was an old man. "On August 9, 1937 they caught two Japanese servicemen on the road near the Hongqiao military aerodrome. They accused the two of forcing their way into the aerodrome. A clash took place. The Japanese were killed." This left their superiors with a delicate problem. Two dead Japanese were hard to explain away. Mayor Yu, who must have been informed about the predicament by members of the military, consulted with Tong Yuan-liang, who was chief of staff of the Songhu Garrison Command, a unit set up after the 1932 fighting. They agreed on a quick and cynical measure to make it look as if the Chinese guards had fired in self-defense. On their orders, soldiers marched a Chinese death convict to the gate of the airport, dressed him in the uniform of the paramilitary guards, and shot him dead.' Harmsen, *Shanghai 1937*, 492/6628

23 Harmsen, *Shanghai 1937*, 6628

24 Zhang, 'Summary of the Songhu Battle', 104

25 Zhang, 'Summary of the Songhu Battle', 105

26 Lai, *Shanghai and Nanjing 1937*, 31

27 Kubacki, *On The Precipice Of Change*, 21

28 Zhang, 'Summary of the Songhu Battle', 103

29 'General Sun Yun-liang'

30 Crouch, 'The Shanghai Gambit', 55

31 Clark, *Treading Softly*, 108

32 Niderost, 'Chinese Alamo'

33 Froeschle, 'Shanghai 50 Years Ago', 35

34 Harmsen, *Shanghai 1937*, 592/6628

35 'Rollman Observer of Conflict in China Describes Horrors'

36 Ven, *War and Nationalism in China*, 197

37 Dera, Edward J. and Hans Van de Ven, 'An Overview of Major Military Campaigns During the Sino-Japanese War, 1937-1945', *The Battle for China*, 30

38 'War in China: Never Anything Greater!'

39 Harmsen, *Fighting the Last War*

40 Harmsen, *Shanghai 1937*, 1232/6628

41 Showalter, 'Bring In the Germans', 65

42 Zhang, 'Summary of the Songhu Battle', 106

43 Harmsen, *Shanghai 1937*, 734/6628

44 Lai, *Shanghai and Nanjing 1937*, 33

45 French, *Bloody Saturday*, 894/1228

46 Harmsen, *Shanghai 1937*, 1142/6628

47 Zhang, 'Summary of the Songhu Battle', 1050

48 Zhang, 'Summary of the Songhu Battle', 109-10

49 Ven, *China at War*, 1650/9583

50 Zhang, 'Summary of the Songhu Battle', 108

51 Harmsen, *Shanghai 1937*, 1217/6628

52 Moore, *Writing War*, 73

53 Harmsen, *Shanghai 1937*, 1202/6628

54 Zhang, 'Summary of the Songhu Battle', 106-7

55 Crouch, 'The Shanghai Gambit', 56

56 Zhang, 'Summary of the Songhu Battle', 108-9

57 Zhang, 'Summary of the Songhu Battle', 107

58 Moore, *Writing War*, 74

59 Crouch, 'The Shanghai Gambit', 56-7

60 Hattori, Satoshi, with Dera, Edward J., 'Japanese Operations from July to December 1937', *The Battle for China*, 169

61 Moore, *Writing War*, 98

62 Moore, *Writing War*, 99

63 Harmsen, *Shanghai 1937*, 2043/6628

64 Harmsen, *Shanghai 1937*, 2303/6628

65 Hattori, Satoshi, with Dera, Edward J., 'Japanese Operations from July to December 1937', *The Battle for China*, 170

66 Hattori, Satoshi, with Dera, Edward J., 'Japanese Operations from July to December 1937', *The Battle for China*, 171

67 Hattori, Satoshi, with Dera, Edward J., 'Japanese Operations from July to December 1937', *The Battle for China*, 172

68 Hattori, Satoshi, with Dera, Edward J., 'Japanese Operations from July to December 1937', *The Battle for China*, 172

69 The powers of the Nine-Power Pact were America, Britain, Japan, China, France, Italy, the Netherlands, Portugal and Belgium. Minoru, and Lin, *The Reluctant Combatant*, 52

70 Zhang, 'Summary of the Songhu Battle', 107

71 Harmsen, *Shanghai 1937*, 3056/6628

72 Crouch, 'The Shanghai Gambit', 58

73 Ven, *China at War*, 1535/9583

74 Hattori, Satoshi, with Dera, Edward J., 'Japanese Operations from July to December 1937', *The Battle for China*, 172-3

75 Hattori, Satoshi, with Dera, Edward J., 'Japanese Operations from July to December 1937', *The Battle for China*, 173

Chapter Three: Last Stand at Sihang Warehouse

1 Sun, 'Xie Jinyuan and the 800 Heroes', 89

2 Sun, 'Xie Jinyuan and the 800 Heroes', 89

3 Gu, 'The Chinese Nation's Spirit of "Allowing no Affront"', 2-3

4 Zhang, 'Summary of the Songhu Battle', 111-12

5 Zhang, 'Summary of the Songhu Battle', 111-12

6 Zhang, 'Summary of the Songhu Battle', 111-12

7 Zhang, 'Summary of the Songhu Battle', 111-12

8 Zhang, 'Summary of the Songhu Battle', 111-12

9 Zhang, 'Summary of the Songhu Battle', 112-13

10 Zhang, 'Summary of the Songhu Battle', 113

11 Lai, *Shanghai and Nanjing 1937*, 53

12 Chen, 'The Isolated Soldiers Desperately Fighting for the Country in Sihang Warehouse', 133

13 Xie, *My Father, General Xie Jinyuan*, 138

14 Harmsen, *Shanghai 1937*, 3513/6628

15 Zhang, 'Tribute to Comrade Shangguan Zhibiao', 59

16 Zhang, 'Summary of the Songhu Battle', 113

17 Zhang, 'Summary of the Songhu Battle', 113

18 Yang, 'Account of the Lone Unit's Four Days of Battle', 119

19 Yang, 'Account of the Lone Unit's Four Days of Battle', 119

20 Kubacki, *On The Precipice Of Change*, 2

21 Kubacki, *On The Precipice Of Change*, 47

22 Shangguan, 'Records of Defence of Sihang Warehouse', 31-2

23 Yang, 'Account of the Lone Unit's Four Days of Battle', 120

24 Chen, 'The Isolated Soldiers Desperately Fighting for the Country in Sihang Warehouse', 133

25 Harmsen, *Shanghai 1937*, 3459/6628

26 Mitter, *China's War with Japan*, 1730/8492

27 '"Doomed Battalion" Nearby'

28 Harmsen, *Shanghai 1937*, 3490/6628

29 Lai, *Shanghai and Nanjing 1937*, 51

30 Yang, 'Account of the Lone Unit's Four Days of Battle', 121

31 Yang, 'Account of the Lone Unit's Four Days of Battle', 121

32 Yang, 'Account of the Lone Unit's Four Days of Battle', 121

33 Yang, 'Account of the Lone Unit's Four Days of Battle', 121

34 Lai, *Shanghai and Nanjing 1937*, 21

35 Xie, *My Father, General Xie Jinyuan*, 69

36 Shangguan, 'Records of Defence of Sihang Warehouse', 33

37 Yang, 'Account of the Lone Unit's Four Days of Battle', 122

38 Chen, 'The Isolated Soldiers Desperately Fighting for the Country in Sihang Warehouse', 134

39 Harmsen, *Shanghai 1937*, 3528/6628

40 Yang, 'Account of the Lone Unit's Four Days of Battle', 122

41 Xie, *My Father, General Xie Jinyuan*, 69

42 Yang, 'Account of the Lone Unit's Four Days of Battle', 123

43 Yang, 'Account of the Lone Unit's Four Days of Battle', 124

44 Yang, 'Account of the Lone Unit's Four Days of Battle', 124

45 Yang, 'Account of the Lone Unit's Four Days of Battle', 124

46 Yang, 'Account of the Lone Unit's Four Days of Battle', 124

47 Niderost, 'Chinese Alamo'

48 Chen, 'The Isolated Soldiers Desperately Fighting for the Country in Sihang Warehouse', 135

49 'Lone Battalion Still Hold on To Their Posts'

50 'Doomed Chinese Refuse U.S. Aid'

51 Yang, 'Account of the Lone Unit's Four Days of Battle', 125

52 Fu, *Passivity, Resistance, and Collaboration*, 18

53 'Japanese Cross Soochow Creek'

54 'War in China: Never Anything Greater!'

55 Kubacki, *On The Precipice Of Change*, 54

56 Niderost, 'Chinese Alamo'

57 Yang, 'Account of the Lone Unit's Four Days of Battle', 126

58 Fu, *Passivity, Resistance, and Collaboration*, 18

59 Xie, *My Father, General Xie Jinyuan*, 68

60 'Chinese Fight to Finish'

61 'Humane Conduct of British Troops'

62 'Japanese Brutality in Shanghai'

63 Mulready-Stone, *Mobilizing Shanghai Youth*, 123

64 Mulready-Stone, *Mobilizing Shanghai Youth*, 123

65 'Lone Battalion Still Hold on To Their Posts'

66 'Chinese Fight to Finish'

67 Xie, *My Father, General Xie Jinyuan*, 69

68 Yang, 'Account of the Lone Unit's Four Days of Battle', 127

Chapter Four: Arrival of the Flag

1 Tillman, 'Engendering Children of the Resistance', 137

2 Tillman, 'Engendering Children of the Resistance', 144

3 Tillman, 'Engendering Children of the Resistance', 151

4 Xie, *My Father, General Xie Jinyuan*, 82

5 'Chinese Girl Tells of Daring Trips'

6 Sun, 'Xie Jinyuan and the 800 Heroes', 92

7 Xie, *My Father, General Xie Jinyuan*, 82-3

8 Kubacki, *On The Precipice Of Change*, 54

9 'China Heroine Toast of LA'

10 Sun, 'Xie Jinyuan and the 800 Heroes', 92

11 Tillman, 'Engendering Children of the Resistance', 152

12 Sun, 'Xie Jinyuan and the 800 Heroes', 93

13 Tillman, 'Engendering Children of the Resistance', 155

14 Yang, 'Account of the Lone Unit's Four Days of Battle', 127

15 Chen, 'The Isolated Soldiers Desperately Fighting for the Country in Sihang Warehouse', 135

16 Sun, 'Xie Jinyuan and the 800 Heroes', 93

17 Sun, 'Xie Jinyuan and the 800 Heroes', 93

18 Shangguan, 'Records of Defence of Sihang Warehouse', 30

19 Sun, 'Xie Jinyuan and the 800 Heroes', 93

20 'Battalion in Chapei Flies Chinese Flag'

21 Shangguan, 'Records of Defence of Sihang Warehouse', 30

22 Arundel, '200 in Chinese Alamo Hold off 40,000 Japs'

23 Sun, 'A Moment in a Billion Years', 6-7

24 Sun, 'A Moment in a Billion Years', 6-7

25 Yang, 'Account of the Lone Unit's Four Days of Battle', 128

26 Yang, 'Account of the Lone Unit's Four Days of Battle'

27 Niderost, 'Chinese Alamo'

28 Yang, 'Account of the Lone Unit's Four Days of Battle', 128

29 Yang, 'Account of the Lone Unit's Four Days of Battle', 128

30 Yang, 'Account of the Lone Unit's Four Days of Battle', 128

31 Niderost, 'Chinese Alamo'

32 Niderost, 'Chinese Alamo'

33 Arundel, '200 in Chinese Alamo Hold off 40,000 Japs'

34 'Battalion in Chapei Flies Chinese Flag'

35 '"Lost Battalion" Fights on. International Settlement Watches Gallant Defence'

36 Kubacki, *On The Precipice Of Change*, 54 and Qi, 'War of the Warehouse'

37 Harmsen, *Shanghai 1937*, 1907/6628

38 Yang, 'Account of the Lone Unit's Four Days of Battle', 129

39 'Epic Chinese Heroism. "Suicide Legion" Will Not Surrender'

40 *Japan's War in China*, 92

41 'Battalion in Chapei Flies Chinese Flag'

42 'Epic Chinese Heroism. "Suicide Legion" Will Not Surrender'

43 Yang, 'Account of the Lone Unit's Four Days of Battle', 129

44 Yang, 'Account of the Lone Unit's Four Days of Battle', 129

45 'Epic Stand by Chinese'

46 Arundel, '200 in Chinese Alamo Hold off 40,000 Japs'

47 Arundel, '200 in Chinese Alamo Hold off 40,000 Japs'

48 'Chinese Still Hold Death Post'

49 'Lone Battalion Still Hold on To Their Posts'

50 'Battalion in Chapei Flies Chinese Flag'

51 Grescoe, *Shanghai Grand*, 3438/8920

52 Arundel, '200 in Chinese Alamo Hold off 40,000 Japs'

53 'Fierce Fight for Capture of Bank Godowns'

54 'Fierce Fight for Capture of Bank Godowns'

55 'China Suicide Squad Leaves Post of Peril'

56 Yang, 'Account of the Lone Unit's Four Days of Battle', 130

57 'Fierce Fight for Capture of Bank Godowns'

58 'Fierce Fight for Capture of Bank Godowns'

59 'China Suicide Squad Leaves Post of Peril'

60 'Lost Battalion to Take Refuge in Foreign Area'

61 'Hostility Shown By Japanese'

62 'Lost Battalion Doomed'

63 'War in China: Never Anything Greater!'

64 Madame Chiang Kai-shek, 'Heroes Thank British'

65 Madame Chiang Kai-shek, 'Stand of the "Death Brigade" Seen Inspiring to China'

66 Mulready-Stone, *Mobilizing Shanghai Youth*, 128

67 Zhang, 'Summary of the Songhu Battle', 114-15

68 'Lost Battalion to Take Refuge in Foreign Area'

69 'Lost Battalion to Take Refuge in Foreign Area'

70 Niderost, 'Chinese Alamo'

71 Zhang, 'Summary of the Songhu Battle', 114-15

72 Zhang, 'Summary of the Songhu Battle', 114-15

73 'Japanese Mop Up in Chapei'

74 Zhang, 'Summary of the Songhu Battle', 114-15

75 '"Lost Battalion" Men Promoted'

76 Shangguan, 'Records of Defence of Sihang Warehouse', 33

77 '"Lost Battalion" Runs Gauntlet to Withdraw to International Zone'

78 Yang, 'Account of the Lone Unit's Four Days of Battle', 131

79 'Fierce Fight for Capture of Bank Godowns'

Chapter Five: Breakout and Aftermath

1 'Artillery's Blast Precede Battalion's Withdrawal'

2 *Four Months of War*, 14

3 'Artillery's Blast Precede Battalion's Withdrawal'

4 Yang, 'Account of the Lone Unit's Four Days of Battle', 132

5 'Artillery's Blast Precede Battalion's Withdrawal'

6 'Artillery's Blast Precede Battalion's Withdrawal'

7 'Artillery's Blast Precede Battalion's Withdrawal'

8 Lloyd Lehrbas, 'Runs Gauntlet of Jap Gunfire'

9 'Dash To British Post'

10 Harmsen, *Shanghai 1937*, 3688/6628

11 'Japanese Mop Up in Chapei'

12 Yang, 'Account of the Lone Unit's Four Days of Battle', 132

13 'Life of Adventure Readies Kansas City "Ranger" for Job'

14 Auden and Isherwood, *Journey to a War*, 243

15 Shangguan, 'Records of Defence of Sihang Warehouse', 33

16 'Dash To British Post'

17 'Japan and China'

18 'Suicide Troops Retreat; Marines Escape Death'

19 'Artillery's Blast Precede Battalion's Withdrawal'

20 Yang, 'Account of the Lone Unit's Four Days of Battle', 132

21 'Dash To British Post'

22 '"Lost Battalion" Runs Gauntlet to Withdraw to International Zone'

23 'Japanese Mop Up in Chapei'

24 Shangguan, 'Records of Defence of Sihang Warehouse', 33

25 Zhang, 'Summary of the Songhu Battle', 117

26 Shangguan, 'Records of Defence of Sihang Warehouse', 33

27 '"Lost Battalion" Saved in Shanghai: Will Be Interned'

28 Lehrbas, 'Runs Gauntlet of Jap Gunfire'

29 'The evacuation occupied three hours in which 377 Chinese dashed over, with the loss of six killed and 10 wounded.' in 'Fortress Abandoned. Doomed Battalion Ordered to Withdraw'. 'It is officially reported that two soldiers were killed and 24 wounded when the "doomed battalion" dashed for safety from the warehouse to the settlement, and that 377 of the original 500 escaped alive.' in 'The "Doomed Battalion". 377 Escaped Alive'

30 'Artillery's Blast Precede Battalion's Withdrawal'

31 '"Lost Battalion" Men Promoted'

32 Xie, My Father, General Xie Jinyuan, 138

33 Sun, 'A Moment in a Billion Years', 8-9

34 Xie, My Father, General Xie Jinyuan, 138

35 Hattori, Satoshi with Dera, Edward J., 'Japanese Operations from July to December 1937', The Battle for China, 172

36 'Artillery's Blast Precede Battalion's Withdrawal'

37 'Japanese Send Wreaths. British Soldiers Buried'

38 '"Lost Battalion" Men Promoted'

39 'Japanese Mop Up in Chapei'

40 '"Lost Battalion" Men Promoted'

41 '"Lost Battalion" Men Promoted'

42 '"Lone Battalion" Remembered'

43 Xie, Xie Jinyuan's Anti-Japanese Diary, 133

44 Xie, My Father, General Xie Jinyuan, 136

45 Kubacki, On The Precipice Of Change, 57

46 'Missionary to China Writes of Experiences'

47 Ven, War and Nationalism in China, 216

48 Harmsen, Shanghai 1937, 4193/6628

49 Crouch, 'The Shanghai Gambit', 59

50 Ven, China at War, 1695/9583

51 Rodriguez, Journey to the East, 260

52 'Famous Chinese Division Wiped Out'

53 Zhang, 'Summary of the Songhu Battle', 117

54 Fenby, Generalissimo, 5460/12320

55 Wasserstein, Secret War in Shanghai, 446/6699

56 Ven, China at War, 1695/9583

57 Ven, China at War, 1812/9583

58 Tay, 'Conversations: Peter Harmsen on the Battle of Shanghai in 1937'

59 Ven, China at War, 1812/9583

60 'Brussels Conference in New Peace Move'

61 Yeh, 'Prologue: Shanghai besieged, 1937-45, in Wartime Shanghai, 197/6097

62 Macri, Clash of Empires in South China, 46

63 Macri, Clash of Empires in South China, 47

64 Macri, Clash of Empires in South China, 45

65 Yu, The Dragon's War, 5

66 Yu, The Dragon's War, 4

67 Lary, 'Drowned Earth', 194

68 Rodriguez, Journey to the East, 266

69 Yu, The Dragon's War, 4-5

70 Rodriguez, Journey to the East, 274

71 Polk, 'Belgium's Benevolent Occupier', 63

72 Polk, 'Belgium's Benevolent Occupier', 63

73 Geller, 'The Role of Military Administration in German-Occupied Belgium, 1940-1944', 125

74 Rodriguez, Journey to the East, 219

75 Polk, 'Belgium's Benevolent Occupier', 63

76 Gordon, 'The China-Japan War, 1931-1945', 153

77 Ven, China at War, 2428/9583

78 Gordon, 'The China-Japan War, 1931-1945', 157

79 'Away From the Settlement'

80 Wakeman, The Shanghai Badlands, 2

81 Lai, Shanghai and Nanjing 1937, 61

82 Harmsen, Shanghai 1937, 4357/6628

83 Snow, The Battle For Asia, 51-2

84 '"I'm Still Mayor". Chinese Version of Old Job'

85 'Doomed Remnants. Chinese Still Holding Sections of Kiangyin Forts'

86 'A Second "Doomed Battalion"'

87 'Not Ended, Say Chinese'

Chapter Six: Betrayal and the Last Days of Old Shanghai

1   Mulready-Stone, *Mobilizing Shanghai Youth*, 128
2   Shangguan, 'Records of Defence of Sihang Warehouse'
3   Shangguan, 'Records of Defence of Sihang Warehouse'
4   Zhang, 'Summary of the Songhu Battle'
5   'Lost Battalion Escapes. 200 of its Members Die'
6   'British Soldiers' Funeral'
7   'Japan's Grip'
8   'Heroic Chapei Defenders Sold to Invaders'
9   Xie, *Xie Jinyuan's Anti-Japanese Diary*, 18-19
10 Xie, *Xie Jinyuan's Anti-Japanese Diary*, 161
11 Chen, 'The Isolated Soldiers Desperately Fighting for the Country in Sihang Warehouse', 136
12 Shangguan, 'Records of Defence of Sihang Warehouse', 34
13 Sun, 'Xie Jinyuan and the 800 Heroes', 95
14 Shangguan, 'Records of Defence of Sihang Warehouse', 34
15 Shangguan, 'Records of Defence of Sihang Warehouse', 35
16 Shangguan, 'Records of Defence of Sihang Warehouse', 35
17 'Settlement Looms in Camp Dispute'
18 Chen, 'The Isolated Soldiers Desperately Fighting for the Country in Sihang Warehouse', 136
19 '"Doomed Battalion" Riot'
20 Shangguan, 'Records of Defence of Sihang Warehouse', 35
21 Auden and Isherwood, *Journey to a War*, 248-9
22 '"Doomed Battalion" Riot'
23 'Lone Battalion Incident'
24 'No Camp in Wuhan Area'
25 'Evening Post on "Lost Battalion"'
26 Mulready-Stone, *Mobilizing Shanghai Youth*, 129
27 '"Doomed Battalion" Now Athletic'
28 Grescoe, *Shanghai Grand*, 3696/8920
29 'Inmate Disappears from Lone Battalion Camp'
30 'Lone Battalion Men Escape in Fog'
31 Zhang, 'Preface', 1-2
32 Xie, *Xie Jinyuan's Anti-Japanese Diary*, 48
33 Xie, *Xie Jinyuan's Anti-Japanese Diary*, 48
34 '"Lone Battalion" Support'
35 '"Lone Battalion" Angers Japanese'
36 'Chungking and "Lone Battalion"'
37 '"Lone Battalion" Head Claims Privileges'
38 Xie, *Xie Jinyuan's Anti-Japanese Diary*, 49
39 Xie, *Xie Jinyuan's Anti-Japanese Diary*, 50
40 Xie, *Xie Jinyuan's Anti-Japanese Diary*, 85
41 'Anniversary Observed in Internment Camp'
42 'Generalissimo Observes 53rd Birthday Quietly'
43 'Untitled', in *North China Daily News*, 14 January 1940
44 '"Lone Battalion" to Start Factory'
45 'Mob Trouble Near Internment Camp'
46 Xie, *Xie Jinyuan's Anti-Japanese Diary*, 85
47 Xie, *Xie Jinyuan's Anti-Japanese Diary*, 132
48 'Riot of Internees Averted by Guards'
49 'Untitled', in *Japan Chronicle*, 22 September 1940
50 'Internment Camp Inquiry Ordered by Chungking'
51 'Chungking Protest Against Internment Camp Fray'
52 'Chungking Protest Against Internment Camp Fray'
53 'Chungking Protest Against Internment Camp Fray'
54 'A Letter From Shanghai — By a Shanghai Englishman'
55 'Conditions in Camp Revert to Normal'
56 'Internment Camp Settlement'
57 'A New Spirit'
58 'Internment Camp Situation Calm'
59 'Internee Wounded While Escaping'
60 'Internment Camp Situation Calm'
61 'Untitled', in *North China Daily News*, 13 October 1940
62 'Untitled', in *North China Daily News*, 4 November 1940
63 'Lone Battalion of China Holds Fete'
64 'Untitled', in *North China Daily News*, 4 January 1941
65 Mulready-Stone, *Mobilizing Shanghai Youth*, 129

66　Lai, *Shanghai and Nanjing 1937*, 87

67　'Mr. Wang Ching-wei is Denounced'

68　'Anniversary Precautions Show Results as Day Passes Calmly'

69　'70th Anniversary of Songhu Battle Against Japan in Shanghai'

70　Shangguan, 'Records of Defence of Sihang Warehouse', 36

71　Chen, 'The Isolated Soldiers Desperately Fighting for the Country in Sihang Warehouse', 137

72　Sun, 'A Moment in a Billion Years', 7-8

73　Xie, *Xie Jinyuan's Anti-Japanese Diary*, 307

74　Mulready-Stone, *Mobilizing Shanghai Youth*, 122

75　Mulready-Stone, *Mobilizing Shanghai Youth*, 138

76　Mulready-Stone, *Mobilizing Shanghai Youth*, 130

77　Mulready-Stone, *Mobilizing Shanghai Youth*, 122

78　Mulready-Stone, *Mobilizing Shanghai Youth*, 131

79　Mulready-Stone, *Mobilizing Shanghai Youth*, 130

80　'Chungking Deplores Murder'

81　Mulready-Stone, *Mobilizing Shanghai Youth*, 132

82　Mulready-Stone, *Mobilizing Shanghai Youth*, 131

83　'Lone Battalion's Leader Encoffined'

84　'Mass Tribute Paid to Col. Hsieh'

85　'Untitled', in *North China Daily News*, 28 April 1941

86　Sun, 'A Moment in a Billion Years', 7-8

87　Mulready-Stone, *Mobilizing Shanghai Youth*, 132

88　'Memorial Meeting for Late Col. Hsieh'

89　'Last Rites for "Lone Commander"'

90　'Lone Battalion Murder Trial'

91　'Lone Battalion Murder Trial'

92　'One Mutineer Saved'

93　Shangguan, 'Records of Defence of Sihang Warehouse', 36

94　Xie, *Xie Jinyuan's Anti-Japanese Diary*, 308

Chapter Seven: Captivity and Victory

1　Wasserstein, 'Collaborators and Renegades in Occupied Shanghai', 24

2　Wasserstein, 'Collaborators and Renegades in Occupied Shanghai', 24

3　Grescoe, *Shanghai Grand*, 4342/8920

4　Sun, 'Xie Jinyuan and the 800 Heroes', 100

5　Chen, 'The Isolated Soldiers Desperately Fighting for the Country in Sihang Warehouse', 137

6　The approximate number of Eight Hundred prisoners in each camp are: 50 in Guanghua Gate, 50 in Yuxikou, 100 in Hangzhou, 60 in Xiaolingwei and 50 in New Guinea. Sun, 'Xie Jinyuan and the 800 Heroes', 100

7　Shangguan, 'Records of Defence of Sihang Warehouse', 36

8　Grescoe, *Shanghai Grand*, 4377/8920

9　The nine soldiers were Shi Biao, Chen Yusong, Duan Haiqing, Chen Zumo, Xu Wenqing, Wan Guoqing, Zhang Yongxiang, Li Shide and Xiao Yisheng. Yao, *The Patron Saint of Shanghai*

10　'17 Chinese Flee Prison Camp'

11　'17 Chinese Flee Nanking. Sole Survivors of "Lone Battalion" Escape Jap Camp'

12　Chen, 'The Isolated Soldiers Desperately Fighting for the Country in Sihang Warehouse', 137

13　'"Doomed" Battalion Kept Fighting Japs'

14　Shangguan, 'Records of Defence of Sihang Warehouse', 36

15　Wasserstein, *Secret War in Shanghai*, 4396/6699

16　'Survivors of 1937 Battle Reach China'

17　Lan, '"Crime" of Interpreting Taiwanese Interpreters as War Criminals of World War II', in *New Insights in the History of Interpreting*, 211

18　Lan, '"Crime" of Interpreting Taiwanese Interpreters as War Criminals of World War II', in *New Insights in the History of Interpreting*, 211

19　Long, *The Final Campaigns*, 556-7

20　Long, *The Final Campaigns*, 557

21　'Chinese Troops Among Japs on Gazelle Peninsula'

22　'Forgotten Army of Chinese Located in Camp on Rabaul'

23　Vu, 'Bones of Contention', 59

24　'Chinese "Lost Army" Found'

25 'Happy Chinese in Rabaul Did Not Want Swing Music'

26 'Happy Chinese in Rabaul Did Not Want Swing Music'

27 'Japs Go Home But Chinese Must Wait'

28 'Chinese Shed Inscrutability as They Identify Rabaul Japs'

29 'Murder of Chinese Evidence of Survivor'

30 'Death Penalties For Execution of War Prisoners'

31 'Jap Commander Faces Atrocity Trial Against Chinese at Rabaul'

32 'Evidence Against Japs for Cruelty Towards Chinese in Rabaul'

33 'Jap General Sentenced Gaol For Seven Years'

34 'Japs Go Home But Chinese Must Wait'

35 'Japs Go Home But Chinese Must Wait'

36 'Japs Go Home But Chinese Must Wait'

37 These 36 survivors were Tang Yan, Chen Risheng, Leng Guangqian, Wang Changlin, Wu Cuiqi, Tong Zibiao, Zou Mo, Tang Pinshen, Liu Yiling, Yan Zhanbiao, Tao Xingchun, Wu Jie, Yang Deyu, Liu Huikun, Xu Guiqing, Zhao Qingquan, Li Zifei, Zhao Chunshan, Fu Meishan, Fu Guanzhi, Shi Honghua, Xie Xuemei, Xu Yufang, Zhou Zhengming, Zou Bin, Chen Hanqin, Yang Bozhang, Zhao Xianliang, Zhang Yongshan, Xu Yukai, Wei Cheng, He Yingshu, Yang Zhenxing, Ren Quanfu, Lei Xinhai and Qian Shuisheng. Sun, 'Xie Jinyuan and the 800 Heroes', 101

38 Gordon, 'The China-Japan War, 1931-1945', 149

39 Rodriguez, *Journey to the East*, 282-3

40 'It is universally acknowledged that the Japanese invasion transformed the Chinese Communist movement by gravely weakening Chiang Kai-shek's efforts to destroy the Communist organization of the countryside. The CCP was able, as a result, to extend its control over large parts of the country. This contributed greatly to the Communist victory in 1949.' Gordon, 'The China-Japan War, 1931-1945', 166

41 Gordon, 'The China-Japan War, 1931-1945', 160

42 Mitter, *China's Good War*, 50

43 Mitter, *China's Good War*, 54

44 Shangguan, 'Records of Defence of Sihang Warehouse', 36

45 Zhang, 'Tribute to Comrade Shangguan Zhibiao', 60-1

Chapter Eight: Inspiration and Glorification

1 Shuge, *News Under Fire*, 11

2 Grescoe, *Shanghai Grand*, 1825/8920

3 Crozier, *The Man Who Lost China*, 10

4 Rand, *China Hands*, 102

5 Lary, *The Chinese People at War*, 51

6 Lary, *The Chinese People at War*, 51

7 Fu, *Passivity, Resistance, and Collaboration*, 7

8 Fu, *Passivity, Resistance, and Collaboration*, 17

9 Fu, *Passivity, Resistance, and Collaboration*, 17

10 Fu, *Passivity, Resistance, and Collaboration*, 18

11 Fu, *Passivity, Resistance, and Collaboration*, 18

12 Fu, *Passivity, Resistance, and Collaboration*, 19

13 Howard, 'Music for a National Defense', 34

14 Xie, *My Father, General Xie Jinyuan*, 242

15 Peacock, 'Chinese Art in War-Time'

16 Blackburn and Ern, 'Dalforce at the Fall of Singapore in 1942', 234

17 Ven, *China at War*, 1804/9583

18 Lary, *The Chinese People at War*, 52

19 Fu, Poshek, 'Projecting Ambivalence Chinese Cinema in Semi-occupied Shanghai, 1937-41', in *Wartime Shanghai*, 2381/6097

20 Guo, *China's Nationalism and its Quest for Soft Power through Cinema*, 15-16

21 Johnson, *International and Wartime Origins of the Propaganda State*, 163

22 Hu, *Projecting a Nation*, 141

23 Bao, *Fiery Cinema*, 287

24 Guo, *China's Nationalism and its Quest for Soft Power through Cinema*, 16

25 'Hankow Hit by Bombs. Attack Marks Anniversary of Japanese Shanghai Offensive'

26 Johnson, *International and Wartime Origins of the Propaganda State*, 353. Lai, *Shanghai and Nanjing 1937*, 215

27 Stein, *The Chinese Combat Film Since 1949*, 47

28 Xie, *My Father, General Xie Jinyuan*, 242

29 Johnson, *International and Wartime Origins of the Propaganda State*, 258

30 Johnson, *International and Wartime Origins of the Propaganda State*, 353

31 *Film Programme Office Leisure & Cultural Services Department (Hong Kong)*

32 Tillman, 'Engendering Children of the Resistance', 155-6

33 Tillman, 'Engendering Children of the Resistance', 156

34 Bao, *Fiery Cinema*, 356-7

35 Auden and Isherwood, *Journey to a War*, 166-7

36 Kua, *Scouting in Hong Kong*, 201

37 Kwan, *The Dragon and the Crown*, 25

38 Blackburn and Ern, 'Dalforce at the Fall of Singapore in 1942', 234

39 Gungwu, *Home is Not Here*, 651/3671

40 Gungwu, *Home is Not Here*, 556/3671

41 Shuge, *News Under Fire*, 12

42 Li, *The Military Versus the Press*, 13

43 Li, *The Military Versus the Press*, 30

44 Shuge, *News Under Fire*, 186

45 Shuge, *News Under Fire*, 209

46 Shuge, *News Under Fire*, 210

47 Shuge, *News Under Fire*, 194

48 Harmsen, *Shanghai 1937*, 2384/6628

49 Shuge, *News Under Fire*, 7

50 Shuge, *News Under Fire*, 9

51 Zhang, 'Summary of the Songhu Battle', 116

52 Li, *The Military Versus the Press*, 30-1

53 Harmsen, 'Media War Over Shanghai'

54 Li, *The Military Versus the Press*, 31

55 Li, *The Military Versus the Press*, 31

56 'The Enemy We Face'

57 Johnson, *International and Wartime Origins of the Propaganda State*, 166-7

58 Tillman, 'Engendering Children of the Resistance', 156

59 'Program Set for China Week'

60 Zhang Baijia, 'China's Quest for Foreign Military Aid', *The Battle for China*, 294

61 Carradice, *The Shanghai Massacre*, 92

62 Brinkley, *The Publisher*, 188

63 Jespersen, 'Western Influences and Images of China', 13-4

64 Jespersen, 'Western Influences and Images of China', 14-5

65 Brinkley, *The Publisher*, 188

66 Zhang, 'China's Quest for Foreign Military Aid', *The Battle for China*, 294-5

67 Shuge, *News Under Fire*, 249

68 Shuge, *News Under Fire*, 1

69 Tillman, 'Engendering Children of the Resistance', 152

70 'Untitled', in *North China Daily News*, 20 July 1938

71 Jobs, *Transnational Histories of Youth in the Twentieth Century*, 105

72 'A Chinese Girl Guide'

73 'A Chinese Girl Guide'

74 Tillman, 'Engendering Children of the Resistance', 154

75 McCarthy, 'Chinese Girl Hero Scorns Dress, Love'

76 McCarthy, 'Chinese Girl Hero Scorns Dress, Love'

77 *Life*, 28 August 1938

78 'Chinese Girl Tells of Daring Trips'

79 'Dialling Data'

80 'Chinese Plead for Help'

81 'Financial Ruin of Japan is Predicted by Chinese Speaker Delegates to Youth Conference'

82 'China Youth Here Condemn Jap Acts'

83 'War's Victims Tell of China'

84 'Forecasts Final Defeat of Japan in Guerrilla War'

85 'Chinese Ill; Substitute to Speak Here'

86 'Chinese Student Asks Aid for China'

87 'Young Chinese Here Tonight'

88 'Sobs, "China is Not Lost"'

89 'Chinese Delegates Say Cause Strong'

90 'Girls to Greet Chinese Visitor'

91 'Chinese Youth Leaders Will Receive a Cordial Welcome'

92 'Young Chinese War Workers Describe Horrors of Battle'

93 'China Heroine Toast of LA'

94 'A Chinese Heroine'

95 'China's Joan of Arc £50,000 On Her Head'

96 'Price on Head But She Return to China'

97 'China's Mata Hari Has No Fear of $250,000 Reward'

98 'Generalissimo Observes 53rd Birthday Quietly'

99 'Advertisement', in *The Guardian* (London), 16 October 1942

100 Tillman, 'Engendering Children of the Resistance', 159

Chapter Nine: Legacy in Exile

1 Mackinnon, *China Reporting*, 4

2 Kallgren, 'Nationalist China's Armed Forces', 35

3 Dickson, 'The Lessons of Defeat', 56

4 Glass, 'Some aspects of Formosa's Economic Growth', 18

5 'Since then [1947] there have been occasional riots, charges of torture, and "disappearances" of political opponents, but nothing remotely akin to the mass murders and expulsions that have figured so prominently in the post-revolutionary history of Marxist regimes.' Gregor and Chang, 'The Republic of China and U.S. Policy: A Study in Human Rights', 95

6 Lu, 'The Invisible Turn to the Future', 134

7 Wakeman, *The Shanghai Badlands*, 151

8 'Wartime Valor Commemorated by Photography Exhibition'

9 Moore, 'The Problem of Changing Language Communities', 404

10 'Patriotism Prompts Girl Guide to Bravery in 1937 Shanghai Battle'

11 Mulready-Stone, *Mobilizing Shanghai Youth*, 146

12 Mulready-Stone, *Mobilizing Shanghai Youth*, 146

13 Shangguan, 'Records of Defence of Sihang Warehouse', 36

14 Zhang, 'Tribute to Comrade Shangguan Zhibiao', 59

15 Zhang, 'Preface', 1-2

16 Zhang, 'Preface', 1-2

17 Zhang, 'Preface', 1-2

18 Shangguan, 'Records of Defence of Sihang Warehouse', 30

19 Shangguan, *The Eight Hundred Heroes and the Diary of Xie Jinyuan*, 1

20 'Chinese Men Honored'

21 Wicks, *Transnational Representations*, 18-19

22 Wicks, *Transnational Representations*, 18-19

23 Yu, 'Standing Against the Tide'

24 Yu, 'Standing Against the Tide'

25 Zhang, *Chinese National Cinema*, 143

26 Wicks, *Transnational Representations*, 19

27 Zhang, *Chinese National Cinema*, 143

28 Chiu, *Taiwanese Cinema and National Identity Before and After 1989*, 59

29 Chiu, *Taiwanese Cinema and National Identity Before and After 1989*, 59

30 Lu, 'The Invisible Turn to the Future', 134

31 Zhang, 'Preface', 1-2

32 Gu, 'The Chinese Nation's Spirit of "Allowing no Affront"', 2-3

33 'Archive Review: Eight Hundred Heroes (1976)'

34 'Archive Review: Eight Hundred Heroes (1976)'

35 'Taiwan President Wants To Make Coming Years "Golden Decade"'

36 'The Liberty Times Editorial: Stop Fabricating Taiwan's History'

37 'Kaohsiung Lady Makes Name for Self Selling Flags'

38 'Sihang Warehouse in Shanghai to Be Memorial of War of Resistance Against Japanese Aggression'

39 'Patriotism Prompts Girl Guide to Bravery in 1937 Shanghai Battle'

40 Chen and Chin, 'Veterans Protest Pension Reform Plans'

41 Chen and Chin, 'Veterans Protest Pension Reform Plans'

42 'Veterans Begin Month Long Pension Protest'

43 'Veterans Begin Month Long Pension Protest'

44 'Veterans Begin Month Long Pension Protest'

45 Chen and Chin, 'Veterans Protest Pension Reform Plans'

46 Peng, 'The Decline of Taiwan's Military'

47 Chi, 'Protesters Have No Ground to Stand On'

48 Chi, 'Protesters Have No Ground to Stand On'

49 Chen, 'Films and TV Must Tell Taiwanese War Stories'

50 'Tsai vs Taiwan's Veterans: The Cage Fight That Wasn't'

51 'Tsai vs Taiwan's Veterans: The Cage Fight That Wasn't'

52 'Tsai vs Taiwan's Veterans: The Cage Fight That Wasn't'

53 Lin, 'Military Retirees Demand Pension Talks'

54 Lin, 'Military Retirees Demand Pension Talks'

55 Maxon, 'Police Thwart Legislature Break-in by Protesters'

56 Maxon, 'Veteran Injured in Legislative Protest Last Week Dies'

57 Maxon, 'Veteran Injured in Legislative Protest Last Week Dies'

58 Lin, 'Amendments to Set Lower Limit on Military Pensions'

59 'Unprecedented Violence, Possible China Link as Anti-Pension Reform Protesters Storm Taiwan's Legislature'

60 'Editorial: Meaningful Protest and Futile Rage'

61 Maxon, 'Returning Pensions Tops Gou's List'

Chapter Ten: Memory After Revolution

1 Mitter and Moore, 'China in World War II, 1937-1945', 226-7

2 Mitter and Moore, 'China in World War II, 1937-1945', 238-9

3 Diamant, 'Conspicuous Silence', 458-9

4 Mitter, *China's Good War*, 75

5 Cole, 'China's "New Remembering" of the Anti-Japanese War of Resistance, 1937-1945', 395

6 Reilly, 'Remember History, Not Hatred', 467

7 Ven, *War and Nationalism in China*, 209

8 Cole, 'China's "New Remembering" of the Anti-Japanese War of Resistance, 1937-1945', 395-6

9 Reilly, 'Remember History, Not Hatred', 469-70

10 Reilly, 'Remember History, Not Hatred', 469-70

11 Reilly, 'Remember History, Not Hatred', 470

12 Moore, 'The Problem of Changing Language Communities', 412

13 Cole, 'China's "New Remembering" of the Anti-Japanese War of Resistance, 1937-1945', 400

14 Moore, 'The Problem of Changing Language Communities', 411

15 Mitter, *China's Good War*, 81

16 Cole, 'China's "New Remembering" of the Anti-Japanese War of Resistance, 1937-1945', 398-9

17 Xie, *Xie Jinyuan's Anti-Japanese Diary*, 1-2

18 Reilly, 'Remember History, Not Hatred', 470-1

19 Lu, 'The Invisible Turn to the Future', 135

20 Lin and Wu, 'Chinese National Identity Under Reconstruction', 81

21 Reilly, 'Remember History, Not Hatred', 481-2

22 Hamada, 'Constructing a National Memory', 128-9

23 'Gen. Xie Jinyuan Honored as National Martyr'

24 Kor, 'China Shines Spotlight on WWII Heroes'

25 Weatherley and Zhang, *History and Nationalist Legitimacy in Contemporary China*, 141

26 'Chinese President's Speech on War Victory Commemoration'

27 Xi, 'Speech at a Medal Presentation Ceremony Marking the 70th Anniversary of the Chinese People's Victory in the War of Resistance Against Japanese Aggression'

28 Diamant, 'Conspicuous Silence', 444-5

29 Diamant, 'Conspicuous Silence', 445-6

30 Weatherley and Zhang, *History and Nationalist Legitimacy in Contemporary China*, 152

31 '76 years Ago Today, April 24, 1941'

32 Ng, 'I Let Fate Determine My Future'

33 Reilly, 'Remember History, Not Hatred', 482

34 Jacobs, *When the River of History Disappears*, 103

35 Yao, *The Patron Saint of Shanghai*

36 Xie, *Xie Jinyuan's Anti-Japanese Diary*, 1

37 'Special Program: Grand Symphonic Chorus Eight Hundred Heroes by Shanghai Opera House'

38 Li, 'Cartoon Industry More Than Mere Child's Play'

39 Li and Wang, *Eight Hundred Heroes*, 1

40 Li and Wang, *Eight Hundred Heroes*, 61-2

41 Li and Wang, *Eight Hundred Heroes*, 86

42 Li and Wang, *Eight Hundred Heroes*, 129

43 Guo, *Anti-Japanese Heroes Story Series*, 111

44 Guo, *Anti-Japanese Heroes Story Series*, 111

45 Wang, 'Pioneer of Modernity'

46 Li, 'Historical Monuments to Nation-Building'

47 'Sihang Warehouse in Shanghai to Be Memorial of War of Resistance Against Japanese Aggression'

48 'War Memorabilia Donated to Warehouse Museum'

49 Lu, 'The Invisible Turn to the Future', 135

50 Kubacki, *On The Precipice Of Change*, v

51 Kubacki, *On The Precipice Of Change*, 23

52 'Sihang Warehouse in Shanghai to Be Memorial of War of Resistance Against Japanese Aggression'

53 'Former Country Club Hides Dark Past'

54 'Son's Pride in Tribute to Leader of the "800 heroes"'

55 Kor, 'China Shines Spotlight on WWII Heroes'

56 'An Exhibition of Legends'

57 'Technology Enhances Other Museum Sites in the District'

58 '6 More City Sites Put on List of Landmarks'

59 Xu, 'Chinese Netizens Urge Govt to Criminalize Japanese Military Uniform Cosplay'

60 Xu, 'Chinese Netizens Urge Govt to Criminalize Japanese Military Uniform Cosplay'

61 Li, 'Symbols of Fascism Have No Place in Our Society'

62 'Photos of "Japanese Soldiers" Posing at Chinese War Memorial Site Spark Anger Online'

63 Zhou, '4 Men Criticized For "Insulting" War Heroes'

64 Zhou, '4 Men Criticized For "Insulting" War Heroes'

65 'Photos of "Japanese Soldiers" Posing at Chinese War Memorial Site Spark Anger Online'

66 'Photos of "Japanese Soldiers" Posing at Chinese War Memorial Site Spark Anger Online'

67 Li, 'Symbols of Fascism Have No Place in Our Society'

68 'China, Taiwan Press'

69 Zhou, '4 Men Criticized For "Insulting" War Heroes'

70 Xu, 'Chinese Netizens Urge Govt to Criminalize Japanese Military Uniform Cosplay'

71 '5 Punished Over Japanese Uniforms Outrage'

72 Cang, 'Historic Battlefield Disrespect Slammed'

73 Cang, 'Historic Battlefield Disrespect Slammed'

74 'China Watchlist for 22 February'

75 Cang, 'Historic Battlefield Disrespect Slammed'

76 Cao, 'Outrage Grows Over Nanjing Selfies'

77 Cao, 'Outrage Grows Over Nanjing Selfies'

78 Cao, 'Outrage Grows Over Nanjing Selfies'

79 Cao, 'Outrage Grows Over Nanjing Selfies'

80 Cao, 'Outrage Grows Over Nanjing Selfies'

81 Wang, 'Proposed Law Aims to Curb Insulting of Heroes, War Victims'

82 Yau, 'Why the First Chinese Imax War Film The Eight Hundred was Pulled from Shanghai Film Festival'

83 Xu, 'Heroes Coming'

84 Xu, 'Heroes Coming'

85 'Review: The Eight Hundred (2020)'

86 Rose, 'The Eight Hundred: How China's Blockbusters Became a New Political Battleground'

87 'Roll up! Roll up! A Festival of the Classic and New'

88 Frater and Davis, 'Shanghai Film Festival Abruptly Pulls Opening Film "The Eight Hundred"'

89 Yau, 'Why the First Chinese Imax War Film The Eight Hundred was Pulled from Shanghai Film Festival'

90 Yau, 'Why the First Chinese Imax War Film The Eight Hundred was Pulled from Shanghai Film Festival'

91 Rose, 'The Eight Hundred: How China's Blockbusters Became a New Political Battleground'

92 Myers, 'Patriotic Movie Apparently Falls Afoul of China's Censors'

93 Yau, 'Why the First Chinese Imax War Film The Eight Hundred was Pulled from Shanghai Film Festival'

94 Yau, 'Why the First Chinese Imax War Film The Eight Hundred was Pulled from Shanghai Film Festival'

95 Mitter, China's Good War, 166

96 Myers, 'Patriotic Movie Apparently Falls Afoul of China's Censors'

97 Myers, 'Patriotic Movie Apparently Falls Afoul of China's Censors'

98 'Double Ten Day Fervor Humiliates History'

99 Rose, 'The Eight Hundred: How China's Blockbusters Became a New Political Battleground'

100 'Review: The Eight Hundred (2020)'

101 Freer, 'The Eight Hundred Review'

102 Guan, 'Film Review: The Eight Hundred (2020)'

103 Chen, 'Trending in China'

104 Pang, 'Director Guan Hu's War Epic an Ode to Patriotic Soldiers and the Great Chinese People'

105 Yau, 'Chinese War Movie The Eight Hundred a Hit with Film-Goers, but Critics Say it is Sensationalist and Distorts History'

106 'The Sihang Warehouse Turns into Hot Tourist Spot Following Success of War Epic "The Eight Hundred"'

107 'Lest We Forget the Sacrifice of Battle Heroes'

108 Gong, 'Never Forget the Great Achievement of Our Heroes During WWII'

109 'Lest We Forget the Sacrifice of Battle Heroes'

110 'Lest We Forget the Sacrifice of Battle Heroes'

111 Cao, 'War Epic "The Eight Hundred" Prompts Spike in Visits to Site'

112 Cao, 'War Epic "The Eight Hundred" Prompts Spike in Visits to Site'

113 Ordoña, 'Review: Chinese Soldiers Face Overwhelming Odds in Historical War Blockbuster "Eight Hundred"'

114 Lee, '"The Eight Hundred" Review: Blockbuster Chinese War Epic Delivers Imax-Scale Spectacle'

115 'One-Armed Fighter'

116 MacNamara, 'The Eight Hundred — Movie Review'

117 Pang, 'Director Guan Hu's War Epic an Ode to Patriotic Soldiers and the Great Chinese People'

118 Cao, 'War Epic "The Eight Hundred" Prompts Spike in Visits to Site'

119 'The Eight Hundred', in The Times (London), 18 September 2020

120 Lo, 'Opinion — The Soft Politics of a Mainland Film'

121 Lo, 'Opinion — The Soft Politics of a Mainland Film'

Epilogue

1 Vu, The Sovereignty of the War Dead, 328

2 Vu, 'Bones of Contention', 90

3 Vu, 'Bones of Contention', 91

4 Vu, 'Bones of Contention', 91

5 Vu, 'Bones of Contention', 92

6 'Australia Refuses to Mark Chinese Graves'

7 Weatherley and Zhang, History and Nationalist Legitimacy in Contemporary China, 153

8 Tan, 'Footage of the Lost Battalion in 1937 Battle of Shanghai'

9 'WWII Graves Located'

10 Lan, '"Crime" of Interpreting Taiwanese Interpreters as War Criminals of World War II', in New Insights in the History of Interpreting, 210-11

11 'China To Bring Back Remains of its Soldiers from Papua New Guinea'

12 Orere, 'War Cemetery to be Revived'

13 Lowa, 'Chinese Remember War Dead in East New Britain'

14 'Ambassador Li Ruiyou held a Rally in East New Britain Province to Commemorate the War Veterans and the 70th Anniversary of the Victory of the Chinese People's War of Resistance Against Japanese Aggression and the World Anti-Fascist War'

15 'China Holds Memorial Ceremony in PNG for Martyrs in Anti-Japanese War'

16 'General Sun Yun-liang'

17 Ven, China at War, 2340/9583

18 Fan, 'Soldier Recalls Resistance to Japan'

19 Fan, 'Soldier Recalls Resistance to Japan'

20 Fan, 'Soldier Recalls Resistance to Japan'

21 'War Hero Returns to Shanghai'

22 'War Hero Returns to Shanghai'

23 'War Hero Returns to Shanghai'

24 Harmsen, 'China's War as History: A Paradox'

25 'War Hero Returns to Shanghai'

26 Weatherley and Zhang, *History and Nationalist Legitimacy in Contemporary China*, 151

27 Weatherley and Zhang, *History and Nationalist Legitimacy in Contemporary China*, 151

28 Weatherley and Zhang, *History and Nationalist Legitimacy in Contemporary China*, 151

29 Weatherley and Zhang, *History and Nationalist Legitimacy in Contemporary China*, 173

30 Harmsen, 'China's War as History: A Paradox'

31 'China Suicide Squad Leaves Post of Peril'

32 'The War in China'

33 Mulready-Stone, *Mobilizing Shanghai Youth*, 127

34 Zhang, 'Preface', 1-2

35 Zhang, 'Preface', 1-2

INDEX